The Ultimate Guide To
IELTS
WRITING

The ONLY book with IELTS Writing Band Descriptors

Contents

- ☛ 7 Step Improvement Course in IELTS Writing
- ☛ Structures of High Band Score Answers
- ☛ 50+ Letters for General Training Task 1
- ☛ 50 Graphs for Academic Task 1
- ☛ 200+ Essays for IELTS and TOEFL

PARTHESH THAKKAR

The Ultimate Guide to IELTS Writing

Parthesh Thakkar

ISBN - 978-81-925676-0-0

First Edition   : January, 2013

Revised Edition : 24th Reprint : June, 2019

Published by   : **Mr. Parthesh Thakkar**
Angel Edunext
304, Third Floor, The Grand Mall,
Opp. SBI, Nehrunagar to C. N. School Road,
Ambvadi, Ahmedabad-380015, Gujarat, India
Phone No. 079-26305110, 079-30177464
Email:parthesh@angeledunext.com
Website : www.angeledunext.com

Distributed by   : M. K. Book Distributors
1, Tulsi Complex, 2 Azad Society,
Ambawadi, Ahmedabad-380015.
Phone : +91-79-26763012, +91-79-26763022
Email : mkbooksd@gmail.com
Website : www.mkbooksd.com

Acknowledgements

I take this opportunity to express a deep sense of gratitude towards my wife, Vaishali Thakkar for her invaluable contribution to the creation of this book. I am also thankful to my daughter, 'Sakshi' who has always energized me by her innocent and playful nature.

I convey sincere thanks to my parents, Mr. Mohan Kirpalani and Mr. Indru Kirpalani of M K Book Distributors. I am extremely thankful to Dr. Sneh Desai (www.snehworld.com) who was kind enough to grace the launching ceremony of this book and gave the book his blessings.

Finally, I am thankful to you for reading this book. I am sure this book will make a creative and constructive contribution to your preparation for IELTS Writing.

Parthesh Thakkar

Author's Note

I am feeling extremely happy that I am presenting my Second Book to all of you. This book is not just another book for me. This book is a compendium of my last 11 years of work. Painstakingly, I have slowly but surely evolved the structure of this book keeping in mind the learning abilities of students and specific requirements of the IELTS exams.

This book is for students at all levels of English language. It can be used as a self-study book and as classroom study material. All the essay and letter topics covered in this book are actually those which appeared in IELTS exams in the past. All the graphs used in this book are created after a careful study of various samples from past question papers of IELTS.

This book is also useful for TOEFL iBT candidates in their Essay Writing Section.

The book is divided into four sections :-

The first three sections contain 7 step improvement course, possible high band answer structures, 5 points to follow when you are writing the task, dos and don'ts in IELTS writing and sample answers of writing tasks

The fourth section contains a list of linking words, a list of some useful books for IELTS preparation and IELTS Writing Band Descriptors.

I suggest to the readers to go through the introduction and assessment part before they start reading the sections given in the book. I also suggest you to go through the band descriptors and study them thoroughly, so that you can understand what the IELTS Writing examiner is expecting from you.

Finally, I suggest to the readers to use the sample answers expressed in this book as a reference only. Please do not try to memorise any of the answers given in the book.

I take this opportunity to wish you all the very best for your IELTS exam. I wish this book helps you to clear your IELTS exam and fulfils your dreams of studying or settling in a foreign country.

Parthesh Thakkar

INDEX

* Reproduced with the kind permission of Cambridge ESOL.

Introduction to IELTS

What is IELTS ?

IELTS stands for INTERNATIONAL ENGLISH LANGUAGE TESTING SYSTEM. This exam is designed to judge the English proficiency of candidates.

IELTS is jointly managed worldwide by Cambridge ESOL, British Council and IDP Education Australia.

Who can appear for IELTS?

Candidates who want to study in countries like the UK, the USA, Canada, Australia, New Zealand and Singapore and some European Union Countries.

Individuals who want to migrate to Canada, Australia, the UK and New Zealand are required to take IELTS as a proof of their English language proficiency.

Person who is more than 16 years and has a valid passport can appear for IELTS.

What is the format of IELTS?

IELTS is available in two formats;

Academic and General Training.

Academic IELTS is for students who want to study abroad and professionals like Doctors, Pharmacists and Nurses who want to migrate to the U.K., the USA and Australia.

General Training IELTS is for candidates who want to migrate to countries like Canada, Australia, UK and New Zealand.

What is the format of the exam?

There are four modules in this exam; Listening, Reading, Writing and Speaking.

LISTENING

Approximately 30 minutes + 10 minutes transfer time.

The test is divided into four sections. It has 40 items in total.

Students get a question booklet on which the questions are printed. The tape is then played and students write answers simultaneously while the tape is going on.

Students get time to look at the questions before the listening starts and check their work at the end of each section.

	No of speakers	No of items (questions)
Section 1	2	10
Section 2	1	10
Section 3	2-4	10
Section 4	1	10

The Ultimate Guide To IELTS Writing

Discourse Types

Section 1: Usually a conversation between two people on general, everyday topic. In two parts, first you are given some time to look at the questions for section 1. Then you will hear an example where you will listen to the correct answer. Then the listening is played (including the example). Approx 4 minutes. You will get around 45 seconds (in two parts) to look at the questions.

Section 2: Usually a monologue (only one speaker) of a social functional nature, informational talk. Can be social or academic setting. In two parts, you get around 50 seconds (in two parts) to look at the questions. There will be no spoken example; you can see a written example. Approx 3-4 minutes.

Section 3: Usually a conversation between two to four people. Academic setting. Education / training based context. In two parts, there is no example on the tape in this section. Approx 4 minutes. You will get around 50 seconds (in two parts) to look at the questions.

Section 4: Usually a lecture or speech given as a monologue. Academic setting. Education / training based context. No breaks in between. There might be a written example. You may get note or summary completion or multiple choice or a mixture of question types. You get approx 45 seconds to look at all the questions in the beginning of section 4. Approx 4-5 minutes. Here, the question types are divided in two parts. For example, question no 31 to 35 are multiple choice and question no 36 to 40 are summary or table completion. Now, when the speaker moves from question 35 to 36 i.e. when the question type changes, there will be a pause of 2-3 seconds. This pause is a hint for you that now the question type is changed.

NOTE: As the Listening test progresses, the recording becomes more difficult. It does not mean that it becomes faster as it progresses; it becomes complex progressively and tests all the Listening skills of the candidate.

READING

Two Formats ACADEMIC and GENERAL TRAINING.

60 minutes and no extra time 40 items.

ACADEMIC READING

	No of items
Reading Passage 1	13-14
Reading Passage 2	13-14
Reading Passage 3	13-14
Total	**40**

Reading passages are based on research, case studies, and biography, and they are argumentative. They are taken from journals, textbooks or web sites.

It becomes progressively difficult.

The Ultimate Guide To IELTS Writing

GENERAL TRAINING READING

	No of items
Section 1	13-14
Section 2	13-14
Section 3	13-14
Total	**40**

Passages are taken from newspapers, magazines, and catalogs and from web sites. A
least one section contains detailed argumentative text.

WRITING

Two Formats ACADEMIC and GENERAL TRAINING.

60 minutes and no extra time.

Two tasks in writing

Minimum 150 words are required for Task 1 and 250 words are required for Task 2.

ACADEMIC WRITING

Task 1- a Bar chart, Pie chart, line graph, table, flow chart or a process or a
combination of more than one charts containing figures and details.

Task 2 – an essay topic is a specific topic about specific research areas i.e.
environment, pollution, education, science and research, technology etc.

GENERAL TRAINING

Task 1 - a short letter – formal, informal or semiformal style

Task 2 - an essay topic about day to day life i.e. society, children, family, education,
lifestyle etc.

SPEAKING

Organized on a day other than the day of the main exam (i. e. Listening, Reading and
Writing are arranged on one day).

11-14 minutes time

Three parts.

Part 1

4-5 minutes

Introduction and interview.

Examiner first introduces himself/herself and asks questions about familiar topics to the candidate.

Part 2

3-4 minutes

Individual long turn

Candidate gets a Cue card with a topic on which he / she has to speak for 1-2 minutes and he /she gets one-minute time to prepare for the topic before he / she starts to speak. Examiner also asks one or two follow-up questions when the candidate stops speaking

Part 3

4-5 minutes

Extended discourse

Examiner asks questions that are thematically linked to the topic in part 2 and the questions are more of abstract nature.

For Reading and Listening, the following table can be used for the candidates as a reference.

Listening		Academic Reading		General Training Reading	
Band score	Raw score out of 40	Band score	Raw score out of 40	Band score	Raw score out of 40
5	16	5	15	4	15
6	23	6	23	5	23
7	30	7	30	6	30
8	35	8	35	7	34

◆ ◆ ◆

IELTS Writing Assessment Criteria

IELTS writing is assessed on four criteria. Each of them is described below.

Task 1 (Both Academic and General Training)

Task Achievement

This criterion evaluates how appropriately, accurately and relevantly the response fulfils the requirements given in the task, using a minimum of 150 words.

For Academic Writing Task 1, Task Achievement means that the candidates have a defined data given in the form of a diagram. They have to describe the data as accurately as possible. Here, they should cover the most important features of the diagram. However, they must avoid any explanation or prediction or speculation which is not a part of the diagram or the data given in the diagram.

General Training writing task 1 is also a writing task with a largely predictable output. In the letter, the task comes with a set context and purpose of the letter. The candidate should write the letter in such a way that all the functions demanded by the topic question and the context of the letter are achieved.

I would like to explain the same in a different manner mentioned below:

In Task Achievement criterion (for both Academic and General Training), the writing is assessed in terms of two aspects, content and organisation.

'content' refers to :-

Are the main points of the task covered in the response by the candidate?

Are those points clearly described?

'organisation' refers to :-

Is the structure of the writing appropriate to the task and to the content of the topic question ?

Is it logical ?

Coherence and Cohesion

This criterion is concerned with the overall clarity and fluency of the message: how the response organises and links information, ideas and language. Coherence refers to the linking of ideas through logical sequencing. Cohesion refers to the varied and appropriate use of cohesive devices (for example, logical connectors, linking words, pronouns and conjunctions) used to create the conceptual and referential relationships or to make links between and within sentences clear.

Lexical Resource

This criterion refers to the range of vocabulary the candidate has used and the accuracy and appropriateness of those words in connection with the specific task. For example, when a line graph shows trend, the vocabulary used in the description of graph should also be of the same. But, if the candidate writes vocabulary of comparison, he will not get good bands even if his vocabulary is very good in terms of quality of words. This is so because he has not used appropriate language which can satisfy the demand of the graph. In the same manner, if a given letter topic demands the language of a request, the candidate use the vocabulary accordingly. Now, in such a letter, if the candidate uses aggressive language, even if it is good in quality and variety of words, he cannot expect a better band score.

In addition, some variety is always expected from the candidates. For example, if the answer contains a word that comes repeatedly in the text, the candidate should try to use a synonym of that word and avoid using the same word again to show the level of vocabulary to the examiner.

Grammatical Range and Accuracy

This criterion refers to the range and accurate use of the candidate's grammatical resource as manifested in the candidate's writing at the sentence level.

These are two aspects combined in one criterion. The first is Grammatical Range. It refers to the type of and the variety of sentences the candidate has used in his writing. Some candidates have a tendency to write short and simple sentences. This tendency can help them to reach a band 5 easily, but if you want 6 or more bands, at least one complex sentence in each paragraph of your response is almost compulsory. You can write different types of sentences for example, sentences joined with a conjunction, conditional sentences (if or whether sentences), sentences that start with although or even though, and so on.

Task 2

Task Response

In both Academic and General Training modules Task 2 requires the candidates to formulate and develop a position in relation to a given prompt in the form of a question or statement. Ideas should be supported by evidence, and examples may be drawn from the candidate's own experience. Responses must be at least 250 words in length. In simple words, this criterion means that the answer must be completely relevant to the topic of the task. If the candidate has written an off-topic answer, no matter how good it is in terms of language and vocabulary, the answer cannot get a high band score.

The Ultimate Guide To IELTS Writing   **11**

I would like to explain the same in a different manner mentioned below:

In Task Response Criterion (for all candidates), the writing is assessed in terms of three aspects, content, position and organisation

'content' refers to :-

Are the main ideas relevant, and are they well elaborated and supported?

'position' refers to :-

Is the writer's point of view clear?

Is it effectively presented?

'organisation' refers to :-

Is the structure of the writing appropriate to the task and to the writer's purpose ?

Is it logical ?

Remaining three criteria and their explanation are the same as mentioned above.

I strongly insist that the candidates should refer the IELTS Writing Band Descriptors given at the end of this book before moving to the next page.

♦ ♦ ♦

Process of assessment by IELTS examiners

Based on my understanding, research, training and interaction with various IELTS authorities during seminars and workshops, IELTS examiners follow a 9 step process when they mark the IELTS writing scripts of candidates.

Step 1

They work through all the four criteria of assessment in their order given in the IELTS Writing Band Descriptors. As per the descriptors, they start their assessment with Task Achievement (Task 1) or Task Response (Task 2). They also keep the length of the script in mind i.e. whether the script is short or it is too long.

Step 2

For each criterion, they start with the over-arching statement that is given in the IELTS Writing band score descriptors that most closely matches the writing features of the script. In other words, they read the response and they try to match the response to the statement that is given in the IELTS Writing band descriptors. (Please note that IELTS Writing Band Descriptors Public Version is printed in section 4 of this book).

For example, an examiner reads the script and then feels that the script matches with the statement that is given at band score 7 in Task Achievement (or Task Response depending on the type of task). Accordingly, the examiner repeats the process for the other three assessment criteria.

Step 3

Examiners read through more detailed features of performance at that band score and match those detailed descriptors to the response of the candidate. This process is done for all four criteria of assessment.

Step 4

Examiners confirm that all positive features of language that are described in that specific band descriptors are present in the response of the candidate or not.

Step 5

After that, the examiners also check the band descriptors below the band score that they have earlier assessed and check that the response of the candidate falls in that range or not.

Step 6

Examiners also check the band descriptors above the band score that they have earlier assessed and confirm that the response of the candidate happens to be in that range or not.

Step 7

If required, they count the number of words and if the word count is less, they also note the required penalty for under length writing.

Step 8

Write the band for all the four criteria in the appropriate boxes on the answer sheet. They also ensure that other boxes are also completed.

Other boxes in the writing answer sheet are, 'under length', if yes, how many words, and the decided penalty for that word count. For example if 0.5 bands are deducted for the word range of 140 to 131, 0.5 will be written in the penalty box. If 1 band is deducted for the range of 130 to 121, 1.0 will be written in the penalty box.

'Off-topic', tick the box appropriately, which demonstrates whether the candidate's response is off-topic or not.

'Memorised', some candidates have a tendency to memorize readymade writing answers and they simply write the text that they prepared. If that is the case, the box is marked accordingly.

Step 9

Give a band score to both the tasks and give an overall band score to the candidate.

For giving an overall band score, the following table is one of the sources that I have found on internet that may be followed by the examiners.

For example, if a candidate gets a band 6.5 in Task 2 and 5.5 in Task 1, he will get an overall band score of 6.5 in writing. Likewise, if a student scores 7 bands in task 1 and 6 bands in task 2, he will get an overall band score of 6.0 in writing.

The Ultimate Guide To IELTS Writing

Writing Test Score Sheet

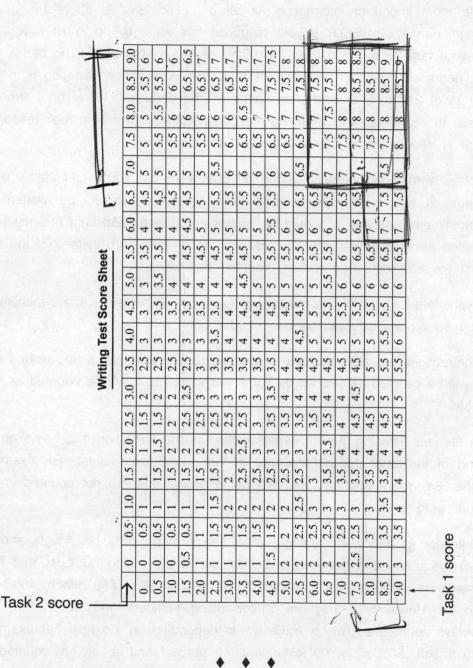

Task 2 score ↑ \ Task 1 score →	0	0.5	1.0	1.5	2.0	2.5	3.0	3.5	4.0	4.5	5.0	5.5	6.0	6.5	7.0	7.5	8.0	8.5	9.0
9.0	6	6	6.5	6.5	6.5	7	7	7	7.5	7.5	7.5	8	8	8	8.5	8.5	8.5	9	9
8.5	5.5	6	6	6	6.5	6.5	6.5	7	7	7	7.5	7.5	7.5	8	8	8	8.5	8.5	8.5
8.0	5.5	5.5	5.5	6	6	6	6.5	6.5	6.5	7	7	7	7.5	7.5	7.5	8	8	8	8.5
7.5	5	5	5.5	5.5	5.5	6	6	6	6.5	6.5	6.5	7	7	7	7.5	7.5	7.5	8	8
7.0	4.5	5	5	5	5.5	5.5	5.5	6	6	6	6.5	6.5	6.5	7	7	7	7.5	7.5	7.5
6.5	4.5	4.5	4.5	5	5	5	5.5	5.5	5.5	6	6	6	6.5	6.5	6.5	7	7	7	7.5
6.0	4	4	4.5	4.5	4.5	5	5	5	5.5	5.5	5.5	6	6	6	6.5	6.5	6.5	7	7
5.5	3.5	4	4	4	4.5	4.5	4.5	5	5	5	5.5	5.5	5.5	6	6	6	6.5	6.5	6.5
5.0	3.5	3.5	3.5	4	4	4	4.5	4.5	4.5	5	5	5	5.5	5.5	5.5	6	6	6	6.5
4.5	3	3	3.5	3.5	3.5	4	4	4	4.5	4.5	4.5	5	5	5	5.5	5.5	5.5	6	6
4.0	2.5	3	3	3	3.5	3.5	3.5	4	4	4	4.5	4.5	4.5	5	5	5	5.5	5.5	5.5
3.5	2.5	2.5	2.5	3	3	3	3.5	3.5	3.5	4	4	4	4.5	4.5	4.5	5	5	5	5.5
3.0	2	2	2.5	2.5	2.5	3	3	3	3.5	3.5	3.5	4	4	4	4.5	4.5	4.5	5	5
2.5	1.5	2	2	2	2.5	2.5	2.5	3	3	3	3.5	3.5	3.5	4	4	4	4.5	4.5	4.5
2.0	1.5	1.5	1.5	2	2	2	2.5	2.5	2.5	3	3	3	3.5	3.5	3.5	4	4	4	4.5
1.5	1	1	1.5	1.5	1.5	2	2	2	2.5	2.5	2.5	3	3	3	3.5	3.5	3.5	4	4
1.0	0.5	1	1	1	1.5	1.5	1.5	2	2	2	2.5	2.5	2.5	3	3	3	3.5	3.5	3.5
0.5	0.5	0.5	0.5	1	1	1	1.5	1.5	1.5	2	2	2	2.5	2.5	2.5	3	3	3	3.5

Task 2 score ← (vertical axis)

Task 1 score → (horizontal axis)

♦ ♦ ♦

Important information for the word count in IELTS Writing

❖ The most important information for all the candidates is about the under length penalty. In IELTS, if your response falls short by up to 10 words i.e. of your task 1 response is in the range of 141 to 149 words, no bands will be deducted. The same is true for Task 2, if your essay response is in the range of 241 to 249 words, no bands will be deducted. However, I strongly insist the candidates to write the required number of words in their response that is 150 words in task 1 and 250 words in task 2.

❖ Some words are normally written as one word but some candidates write them as two words for example some times (it should be written as sometimes), can not (it should be written as cannot) flash light (it should be written as flashlight) and so on are counted as one word instead of the fact that the candidate has written them as two words.

❖ Hyphenated words like ex-student, anti-religion, all-inclusive, above-mentioned and so on are counted as one word.

❖ Contractions are also counted as one word. For example, if you write I am, it will be counted as two words but if you write I'm, it will be counted as one word.

❖ In General Training Task 1, words written in the salutation and name at the end of the letter are not counted in the overall word count. For example, Dear Sir, Yours Faithfully and the name at the end are not counted in the final word count.

❖ Numbers (currency, percentage, area, temperature, distance, weight and so on) are counted as one word if they are written using numbers and their respective symbols. For example, 20,000,000 or 20m, $50, 90km, 40% and so on. However, if they are written using numbers and words, they are always counted as two or more words depending on the text. For example, 20 million, 50 dollars, 90 kilometres, 40 percent and so on are counted as two words.

- ❖ Symbols and abbreviations are always counted as one word, for example, i.e., BC, AD and so on.

- ❖ All the dates are always counted in the following manner, one word (31-01-2013) two words (31st January) and three words (31st January, 2013)

- ❖ Any title or heading that you write are not counted in the overall word count. However, I strongly suggest that there is no need to write any title or heading in IELTS writing.

- ❖ Some students think that articles like 'a', 'an' and 'the' are not counted in IELTS writing, but they ARE counted.

◆ ◆ ◆

Frequently Asked Questions in IELTS Writing

Q. **I have heard that if I write in cursive writing, I will get more bands.**

No. There is no need for you to learn cursive writing. If you simply learn it to get more bands, it will be a waste of your time.

Q. **Are the articles like 'a', 'an' and 'the' counted in the word count in IELTS writing?**

Yes. They are counted.

Q. **Is there any higher word limit in IELTS writing like 280 words or 290 words in Task 2 and 180 or 190 words in Task 1? Will my bands be reduced if I write more words than that?**

No. There is no upper world limit in IELTS writing. I have seen many 9 band answers of essays that are of 300 or 310 words. The students who believe in such upper word limit are always under pressure of exceeding the word count. They always count the words at the end in writing test, which is nothing but a waste of time.

Q. **Can I make some points above my response in Task 1 or Task 2 ?**

You can, but it will not help you in getting more bands. Whatever words are written in the title or bullet points above the response are not counted in the total word count. And, examiners will give you bands based on the words that are included in the response and not on the words that are not a part of the response. Such practice is time consuming and it will waste your valuable time.

Q. **Someone told me that I should draw an arrow sign or a bullet sign in the beginning of each paragraph. How useful is it?**

It is completely useless. It rather looks as if a school going child has written an essay and tried to make it visually attractive by such signs.

Q. **What is the proportion of task 1 and task 2 in the final band score?**

The task 2 carries almost double weight than the task 1 in the final band score.

♦ ♦ ♦

Section 1

Academic Task 1

This section contains:

- 7 step improvement course to get a high band score in Academic Writing Task 1

- Structure of a high band answer

- 5 points to follow when you write Academic Writing Task 1

- What you should do and what you should avoid in Academic Writing Task 1

- 50 sample answers of IELTS Academic Writing Task 1

7 Step improvement course to get a high band score in Academic Writing Task 1

Step 1 ➤ Introduction to Academic Writing or Report Writing

Task 1 of the Academic Module asks you to describe some information presented in a visual format (graph, chart, table or diagram) in about 20 minutes. Candidates must write at least 150 words.

The graphs can be of the following types :-

Line Graph (generally used to show trend)

Bar Chart (generally used to show comparison)

Pie Chart (generally used to show contribution or sharing)

Table (can be used to show any of the above mentioned function)

Process Diagram or Flow Chart or Picture or Map

Step 2 ➤ Structure of a high band answer

First, we will look at the structure of a high band score answer for all the types of graphs and then, I will separately explain you about how to write a process or flow chart or a picture.

I personally feel that the first paragraph of the answer in Academic Task 1 should not be called introduction and the last paragraph should not be called conclusion. This is because Academic writing is report writing. It means, the candidate has to write only what is given in the task and the candidate must not add his or her personal opinion or explanation in it and so, I will call it an opening paragraph and not introduction and I will call closing paragraph and not conclusion. However, I have seen many students using the word introduction for Academic Writing Task 1, and so, I will use those words also, but in a bracket to ease the common understanding.

1. Opening Paragraph (Introduction)	1 paragraph of 1 to 2 sentences. These sentences explain what you are going to describe.
2. Body	2-4 paragraphs depending upon the type of graph and the number of graphs given in the question.
	Describe the most important feature of the graph, generally the first paragraph of the body should begin with that. However, if you have to describe two graphs or even more, you may allocate one paragraph to each of the graphs and describe them accordingly.
	You may divide the paragraphs like this (if there is only one graph) 1-the most important change 2-the other changes.
	You may divide paragraphs like this (if there are two or more graphs) 1- the first graph (start with the most important change in the first graph) 2- the second graph 3- the third graph.However, when there are two graphs given of the same kind,
	you should go for the first method described above.
3. Closing Paragraph (Conclusion)	1 paragraph of 1 to 2 sentences. The closing paragraph should sum up the overall change or trend shown in the graph(s)

Step 3 ➜ How to write opening paragraph?

Most students are often confused about how should they write the first paragraph and this is the reason why they often copy the information printed with the graph in the question paper. However, such tendency is harmful because if you copy words literally from the topic questions (rubrics), examiners will underline those words and will write a note 'copied from topic question' and there are chances that these words will not be counted in your final word count and you may fall short of 150 words.

The most effective technique is, ask two questions to yourself.

Q.1   'What do the graphs show?' or 'What does the graph show?'

Q.2   'What are the graphs about? Or 'What is the graph about?'

Your answer to the above-mentioned questions will help you in writing the opening paragraph.

You should study the table given below to begin the opening paragraph.

Type of chart (Subject)		Main verb	Object Noun Clause
The (given)	chart	shows	
	graph	indicates	the number of...
	table	illustrates	the proportion of...
	diagram	describes	information on...
	table	gives	information about...
		presents	
	figures	show	data on...
	data	indicate	that...
	statistics	illustrate	
	maps	depict	
	pictures	express	
		Give	

Step 4 ➔ How to write body paragraphs?

It is advisable to start with the most important point. However, it is not a thumb rule and so some of my answers will not begin like this, but they will certainly highlight the most important point of the graph.

The first line of the first body paragraph should begin with the expressions shown in the table below...

According to the	table/chart		
As (is) shown in the	diagram		
As can be seen from the	graph		
	figures		
It can be seen		table/chart	
We can see	from the	diagram	
It is clear/apparent/evident	graph		that...
		figures	

Please understand that you must use words/verbs according to the function of the graph.

For example, if the graph given is a line graph, the words/verbs you should use are of trends like increase, decrease, rising sharply, reaching the peak, hitting the bottom, falling gradually and so on.

Likewise, if you are asked to describe a pie chart, you should not use the language that is used in the description of a bar chart.

Step 5 ➔ More practice on appropriate language for Line Graphs, Bar Charts and Pie Charts

For Line Graphs, you may use following types of sentences:

When you describe a graph, you should first identify the obvious trend in the graph because it is important to mention the same in your answer. You must also mention the highest and the lowest points in the graph. You should also cover the changes in the initial, middle and the last part of the line graph.

Trends can be described using different types of sentences.

I strongly insist you to practice the types of examples given below as they can help you in scoring high in Grammatical Range and Lexical Resource criteria of IELTS Writing.

One such type of sentence is mentioned below:

Subject + verb + adverb + time

i.e.

The sales of something or the number of something + verb + adverb + from.. to or between... and ....or in the ....

Subject	Verb that indicates changes	Adverb	Period of time (if applicable)
The sales of (laptops)	increased	suddenly	
	rose	dramatically	
	swelled	significantly	
	shot up	steeply	in the last quarterorfrom
	climbed up	sharply	
	went up	rapidly	Or
	jumped up	quickly	
		promptly	(2005) to (2007)
		smoothly	
Or			Or
		decreased	consistently
	dropped	continually	
	fell	gradually	between (January) to (June)
	reduced	suddenly	
The number of (international visitors)	went down	slowly	
		slightly	
		steadily	
	fluctuated		
	varied		

The same sentence can be written with the following style:

Period of time + subject + verb + adverb

Period of time	Subject	Verb that indicates changes	Adverb
In the last quarter, or From (2005) to (2007), or Between (January) to (June),	the sales of (laptops) or the number of (international visitors)	increased	Sharply
		went up	Slightly
		shot up	Slowly
		grew	Dramatically
		swelled	Significantly
		rose	Greatly
		dropped	
		tumbled	Drastically
		declined	Moderately
		fell	Gradually
		reduced	
		went down	

One more variety in the type of sentence you may use

There + be + a (very) + adjective + noun + in the number of something (subject) + from... to... / between... and.....

There + be	Adjective that indicates changes	Noun that indicates changes	In the scale or subject	Period of time
There was a (very)	sudden	increase	in the sales of (laptops) or the number of (international visitors)	in the last quarterorfrom (2005) to (2007) or between (January) to (June)
	rapid	jump		
	dramatic	rise		
	significant	growth		
	sharp	steep		
	large	decrease		
	marked	drop		
		fall		
	steady	decline		
	gradual	reduction		
	slow			
	small	fluctuation		
	slight	variation		

Now, as I said earlier, it is also important for you to cover the highest and the lowest point in the description of a line graph. Some possible sentence structures given below can be of help in that case.

The Ultimate Guide To IELTS Writing

Subject + verb that indicates top or bottom + expression of time or point of time

Subject	Verb that indicates top or bottom	Expression of time or point of time
The sales of (laptops)	topped	in the last quarteror in
	peaked	Or
		in January
Or	bottomed out	or
The number of (international visitors)		at 1000 (number)
		or
		at 22% (percentage)

Subject + verb that indicates a transition + a noun that indicates top or bottom + expression of time or point of time

Subject	Verb	A noun that indicates top or bottom	Expression of time or point of time
The sales of (laptops)	reached	a peak	in the last quarteror
	hit	a high point	or
Or	touched	a low point	in January
	kissed	the bottom	at 1000 (number)
The number of (international visitors)			or
			at 22% (percentage)

Now, let us see some possible ways to describe Bar chart. Bar charts are generally used to show comparison and the following types of sentences help you in describing comparison

One possible structure for the same is:

Subject + main verb + adverb of degree of comparison + fraction + the scale of comparison

Subject + main verb	Adverb of degree of comparison	Fraction	The scale of comparison
Company A has	nearly a/one third almost	a/one quarter half three quarters	of the (total) number of (workers)
	approximately about just over	a quarter three quarters twice three quarters twice three times	as many (workers) as company B
		half	as much (profit) as company B

Subject + main verb + adverb of degree of comparison + comparison word or noun+ the scale of comparison

Subject + main verb	Adverb of degree of comparison	Comparison word or noun			The scale of comparison
Company A has	almost nearly about	as many workers as			Company B
	approximately	as much profit as	number as	of workers	Company B
	exactly precisely	the same	proportion amount		

Now, let me show you some ways to describe Pie Charts. Pie charts are generally used to show proportion/percentage/sharing and if you get more than one pie charts, you are expected to compare proportion/percentage/sharing.

The Ultimate Guide To IELTS Writing

I am giving you some example sentences that can be useful in describing Pie charts. Some of them may be useful to you in describing Bar chart and Line graph as well.

Country X and Country Y both had 40% each.

The sales remained steady at 20%.

The sales rose to 40%

The sales peaked at just about 80%.

The quarterly profit increased/fell (by 15%) or (from 15% to 25%) or (from 25% to 15%)

University A had 15% of the male students.

15% of the male students studied/enrolled in University A.

University A accounted for 15% of the total students.

They made twice/three times/half of the profit percentage/percentage of profit in June than in April.

The profit percentage/the percentage of the profit doubled/sliced to half/rose threefold from 2001 to 2005.

Company A's profit contribution rose steadily, whereas that of Company B fell slightly/sharply.

There were more boys than girls (25% and 18% respectively)

Finally, I also suggest the students to go through the sample answers of different types of graphs given in the book to learn some more ways of describing information so that they can get higher bands in their IELTS writing.

Step 6 ➡ How to describe a process or a picture or a map?

There are two possible types of diagrams that may be asked in IELTS. I would like to explain each of them separately.

The first type is a picture or a map or an object. We should look for the following points when we are given to describe such a task.

❖ Look at the object in the picture and observe its shape, size, colour, location of various parts, condition of past and present (if applicable), texture, direction, contents. Also, see if the functions of any parts are given in the picture or not.

❖ If you have two pictures, you have to compare their features. Thus, identify the features which are different. You will have to describe the most striking change or difference and you will also have to cover the areas where there is no change. The only difference in this covering is that you can group all the features that are similar or less important and describe them in one or two sentences also. But you should describe the major and noticeable changes in detail.

❖ Provide details of the key changes and describe them accordingly.

The second type is a process or a flow chart. We should look for the following point when we are given to describe such a task.

❖ The most important point is that you must try to understand the defining stages of the process or the flow chart or the diagram. You should also make a note of their sequence so that you can write them in proper order in your response.

You can use the same technique that I have mentioned earlier to write the opening paragraph of process or flow chart. However, in process, you may not need to write the closing paragraph. In some cases, if you cannot reach the 150 word mark, I suggest that you should add a closing paragraph. Please note that some of my responses do have a closing paragraph. I have included them as an example for the students.

Step 7 → How to write a closing paragraph (conclusion)?

Three different examples are given below for your reference.

Linking word + Content

Therefore,		can		interpreted	
Thus,				deduced	
On this basis,	it	may	be	derived	that...
Given this,				inferred	

From		table,			seen	
		figures,			shown	
		data,		Can	estimated	
	the	results,	it	Be	calculated	that...
		information,		May	inferred	
		graphs,			derived	
		charts,			deduced	

Finally,	we can see/we may say	
All in all,	it can be seen/it can be observed	that...
In the closing,	it is clearly seen/it is evident	

The Ultimate Guide To IELTS Writing

5 points to follow when you are writing Academic Writing Task 1

Point 1 ➔ **Preparation (3-4 minutes)**

Look at the graph or graphs given. Note what kinds of graphs are given. Try to understand the pattern of movement or shift of data for example, trend or comparison or contribution or a combination of them.

Look at the instructions and the graph, if they contain time or date or year; write your response in past tense. If no time is given, your response should be in present tense.

Prepare the opening paragraph using the tip given in the previous section and write it in your answer sheet.

Point 2 ➔

Look at the most important or striking feature of the graph and you can write some points or a sentence regarding that feature of the graph.

Certain graphs contain too much information. It is not possible and not advisable for you to mechanically describe all the fields of data given in the graph. Thus, you should learn to group the information. You may refer to some of the sample answers of graphs in this book where the data is grouped and described together in a range

Point 3 ➔

You should write some verbs that can be used in the description of the graphs. It is very important for you to create such a list so that you do not need to stop and think of a synonym or a new word while you are writing the response.

Point 4 ➔ **Start writing the response (14 - 15 minutes)**

When you have already invested a few minutes and worked on the graph, you should not find any difficulty in writing the response. As per my experience, 15 minutes are more than sufficient.

While writing, you should also keep the word count in mind. You should count the number of words that you write for the first 2-3 lines and then take an average of the words written per line. For example, if you have written 25 words in 3 lines, it means your average word per line is 8 and you should write 20-22 lines in total in the response. I suggest you to download a sample of IELTS Writing answer sheet from [http://www.ielts.org/PDF/114184_IELTS_Writing_Answer_Sheet.pdf]

---

and use that to write your responses so that you will never have to waste your time in counting words per line in your actual exam.

Point 5 ➤ Editing (2 – 3 minutes)

Check your response for any errors in spelling or grammar. Also, whether you have described the data accurately or you have misread or wrongly represented the data given in the graph. Sometimes, students may commit mistakes even in expressing proper units given in the graph. For example, they may write meters instead of kilometres or millions instead of billions.

◆ ◆ ◆

The Ultimate Guide To IELTS Writing

What you should do and what you must avoid in Academic Writing Task 1

You should do the following:

❖ Use the appropriate words for the function expressed in the graph i.e. for a graph that shows trend, use the words that describe the trend.

❖ You should write complex sentences and try to write a variety of sentences.

❖ Do not describe all the data when there are more graphs or more fields of data given in the question. Group the information properly and combine them in proper sentences.

❖ In Line Graph, cover the highest and the lowest point. For example, "The sales touched a high of 200 in the month of June". "In the month of December, the sales fell sharply to the lowest point at 115."

❖ In Bar Chart, cover the most significant and the least significant change. For example, "The maximum difference in the sales was seen in year 2000 where Company A was ahead of company B by 4000 units. However, the margin narrowed to as little as 500 in the following year."

❖ In Pie Chart, cover the field that contributes the most and the field that contributes the least. For example,"80% of the visitors who travelled to Japan in 2012 were from Europe whereas the same year, the share of Chinese tourists was only 2%."

❖ In case of picture or map, you should include all important features and compare them with each other.

❖ You should use linking words and connectors to link your information logically. (A list of such words is given in section 4 of the book)

You must avoid the following:

❖ You may avoid minor details in process or pictures.

❖ Please do not copy the printed introduction that is given with the task in the question paper.

❖ Avoid repetition of words or verbs when you describe the graphs. You should use synonyms of the words or verbs that you have used already in your response.

❖ IELTS Academic Writing task 1 is actually report writing and thus, you must not try to explain the information given. Predict the possible outcome for the future or give any suggestions in the response.

For example, a task contains following information:

The table provides information about market share of various digital data storage devices.

Year	Floppy Discs	CD	DVD	USB Drives
1995	90%	08%	02%	00%
2000	50%	40%	08%	02%
2005	05%	50%	25%	20%
2010	00%	10%	20%	70%

Now, your description must not contain three features : Explaination, prediction and suggestion. I will give an example of each of them for your understanding.

Explanation:

It is clear from the table that floppy discs have lost their market share because they offer a limited data storage capacity. You cannot store more than 1.44MB of data in a floppy disc whereas you can easily store 700MB in CD and 4.7 GB in DVD.

Now, the information presented in the lines above is correct, but it is not expected from you by your examiner. They do not want you to explain why something is happening. They want you to describe what is happening or what has happened in the data given to you.

Prediction:

The table illustrates that the market share of USB drives is increasing with time. If the same trend continues, I think the CDs and DVDs will also be outdated from the market and only USB drives will be used for digital data storage.

Again, the prediction given here cannot be ruled out, but the examiners want you to write whatever is given in the chart. They do not want you to predict what will happen in the future or what may happen in the future. They want you to describe what is happening or what has happened in the data given to you.

Suggestion:

The table reveals weakness of CD and DVD as a device of data storage. I suggest that the manufacturers of CDs and DVDs should try to add some more attractive features and try to reduce the prices of their products to survive against USB drives. Or, they should stop producing CDs and DVDs and they should start manufacturing USB drives to keep their profits in line.

The examiners do not want you to tell what should be done to change the possible outcome or future of the trend shown in the graph. They want you to describe what is happening or what has happened in the data given to you.

♦ ♦ ♦

50 sample answers of IELTS Academic Writing Task 1

1.   **The diagram below shows information about member attendance at various clubs in a metro city.**

     Summarize the information by selecting and reporting the main features, and make comparisons where relevant.

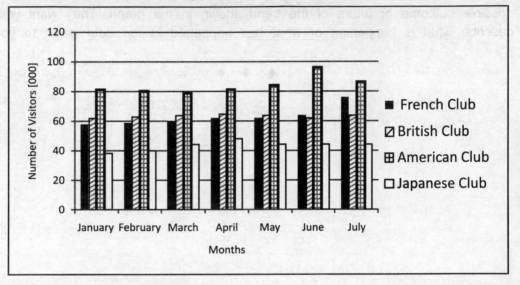

The given bar chart reveals information on visits of members to four clubs in a metro city for a seven month period.

It is clearly seen from the graph that the number of visits to French Club had been almost constant in the first six months, amounting to around 60000. However, in the month of July, they increased to almost 78000. The most regularity in number of visits was also seen in the case of British Club where, members' visits again remained in the range of around 60000.

Japanese Club observed nearly 39000 visitors in January and that increased to about 47000 in April, but after that, the visits decreased and remained steady at about 43000. Finally, the clear winner in terms of number of visitors was the American Club, with nearly 80000 visitors for the first four months, and then the numbers soared to nearly 97000 in June and settled at about 85000 in July.

In conclusion, the bar chart shows that the entry to all the clubs remained almost steady with an exception of the American Club, which saw a handsome rise in visits in the last two months.

◆ ◆ ◆

2. **The charts below show the amount of area used for growing grains between 1990 and 2010 in a state in Canada.**

   Summarise the information by selecting and reporting the main features, and make comparisons where relevant.

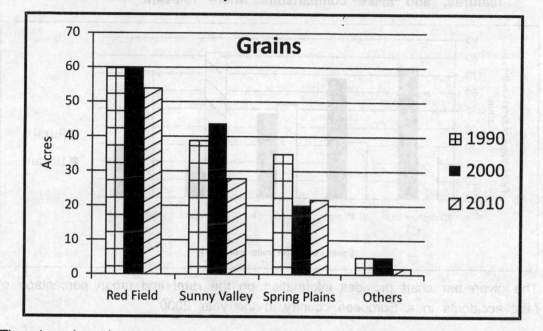

The given bar charts compare the changes in the amount of land used to grow grains in different regions in a state of Canada for a period of 20 years.

Grains were grown to the maximum with respect to area in the region of Red Field. Grains were grown here on 60 acres in 1990 and ended up at a slightly lower figure of around 55 acres of cultivation in 2010. A different pattern was followed in Sunny Valley where the area to grow was almost 40 acres, which grew to 45 acres and then declined to 28 acres in 2010.

Spring Planes also witnessed a reduction in land used for farming where 35 acres of land was used in 1990. However it reduced to 22 acres in 2010. Lastly other ares were also used less compared to what they were in 2010.

Finally, it is clearly depicted in the graph that the area utilized to grow grains reduced substantially.

♦ ♦ ♦

3.   The charts below show the percentage of fatal accidents by locations in a European country. The survey was conducted in 2000.

Summarise the information by selecting and reporting the main features, and make comparisons where relevant.

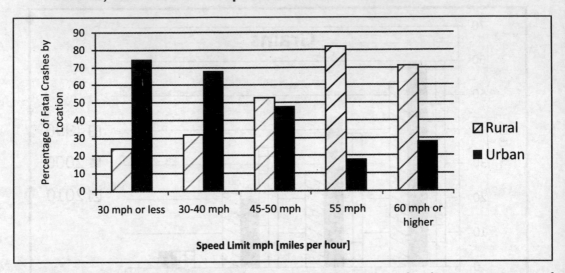

The given bar chart provides information on the rural and urban percentage of fatal accidents in a European country in the year 2000.

The chart showed that in rural areas, with higher speed limits, the intensity of life taking crashes was very high. Speed limit of 30 mph or less caused around 24% fatal accidents, which was the least, followed by 35-40 mph limit where the mortality caused was about 31%. In case of 45-50 mph, the percentage of death causing accidents was nearly 50%. However, it soared to 81% when the speed limit was 55 mph but surprisingly, in the case of 60 mph or more the fatal crash proportion was lesser and at nearly 70%.

The scene in urban areas is almost the opposite, at 30 mph or less speed, death causing accidents stood at 75%, whereas at 35-40 mph it was at 68%. In case of 45-50 mph, it was at 52% and it shrunk to 18% at 55 mph and then it increased to almost 28% at 60 mph or more.

The bar chart reveals that chances of mortality were higher at high speed in countryside, contrary to city areas where more chances of casualty were noted at lesser speeds.

◆ ◆ ◆

4. The diagram below shows time spent watching TV by age and gender in the UK in 1995 and 1999.

Summarise the information by selecting and reporting the main features, and make comparisons where relevant.

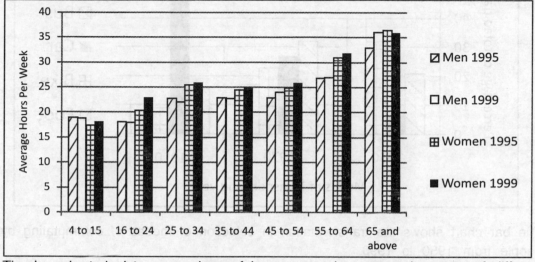

The bar chart depicts comparison of hours spent by men and women of different age groups watching TV in 1995 and 1999 in the United Kingdom.

It is seen from the chart that both males and females between 4 to 15 yrs watched the television for around 17 hours in 1995 and in 1999. In the case of 16 to 24 year olds, no significant change was seen in males, as they stood around 17 hours but females showed a rise from 21 hours to 23 hours.

In addition, the age groups of 25-34 and 35-44 also showed a similar pattern where only women viewers spent more hours watching television. However, noticeable changes were seen in 55-64 age groups. Men spent 27 hours but women spent 31 and 32 hours in 1995 and 1999 respectively. Lastly, men above 65 watched television for 3 hours more in 1999 i.e. from 33 the figure went to 36. However, women watched television for around 36 hours in both years.

Overall, the graph depicts that the time spent watching television was higher as the age progresses. It also reveals that women spent more time watching television in 1999.

◆ ◆ ◆

5. The diagram below shows changes in modes of transport chosen by travellers in a European country from 1950 to 1990.

Summarise the information by selecting and reporting the main features, and make comparisons where relevant.

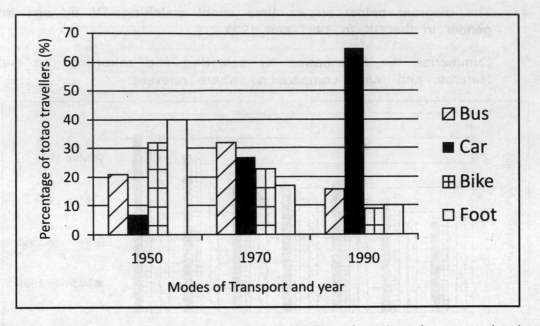

The bar chart shows the transformation in selection of modes of commutating by people from 1950 to 1990.

The graph reveals that 40% people chose to commute on foot in 1950 followed by 32% who opted for bikes. Almost 20% selected to travel by bus and about 7% people travelled by car.

This scenario changed and showed a clear shift towards public transport in 1970 where maximum number of people - 32% travelled by bus, followed by 27% who used cars and were in turn followed by 23% who chose bikes. The least proportion of people and at that only 17% preferred to walk.

However, 1990 showed a complete dominance of cars which were the choice of nearly 65% people. Next in line, the mode chosen by approximately 16% was the bus; bikes and walking were opted for, by around 10% of travellers each.

Finally, the graph depicts that cars indeed became the prime choice over this period of four decades for people to travel in this European country.

♦ ♦ ♦

6.   **The diagram below shows information about the amount of money spent on alcohol and drugs.**

     Summarize the information by selecting and reporting the main features, and make comparisons where relevant.

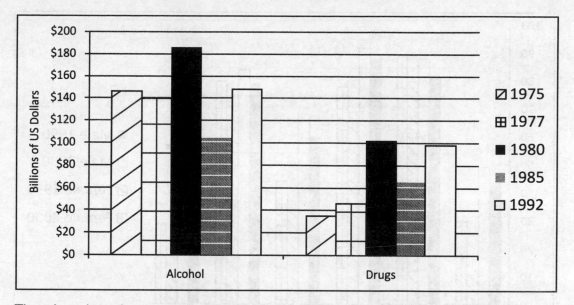

The given bar chart reveals information on billions of dollars spent on alcohol and drugs over a period of 17 years.

It is shown in the chart that around US$ 140 billion were spent in 1975 and 1977, and then in 1980, it shot up to nearly $185 billion. However, a steep reduction to $ 100 billion occurred in 1985 followed by a rise of nearly $45 billion in 1992.

On the other hand, spending on drugs also showed a similar pattern. In 1975 and 1977, it remained around US$ 40 billion and then it swelled to US$ 100 in 1980. But, it came down to nearly US$ 60 billion in 1985 only to shoot up again to almost US$ 100 billion in 1992.

Finally, it is seen from the graph that the spending on alcohol and drugs did not decrease over the period of 17 years. It was almost at the same levels in 1992 as it was in 1975.

♦ ♦ ♦

7. **The diagram below shows comparison of literacy rates of males and females in 1990 and in 2000 in six states of a country.**

    Summarize the information by selecting and reporting the main features, and make comparisons where relevant.

The bar chart provides changes in literacy rates of both genders in six states of a country in 1990 and 2000.

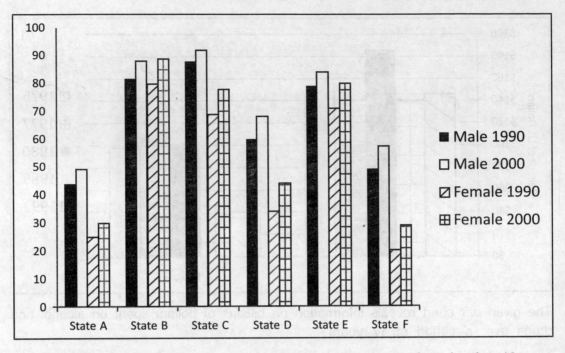

It is evident that literacy has increased among both genders in the 10 year period. State A showed nearly 5% rise in both genders i.e. from 43% t0 48% in males and 25% to 30% in females. Next is state B, which had higher rate of literacy, where nearly 9 out of 10 males were literate in 2000 compared to 8 out of 10 in 1990 and an almost similar rise was observed for females.

State C showed hardly 3% growth in male literacy ratio (88% to 91%) but it showed considerable growth in female literacy ratio i.e. from 79% to 88%. After that, state D's growth figures were 60% to 68% for males and 34% to 42% for females for the year 1990 and 2000 respectively. Next is State E where female literacy growth is higher (70% to 80%) over male literacy growth, which stood at 83% in 2000 compared to 79% in 1990. Finally, State F also showed nearly 9% gain in both genders. Its figures stood at 58% for males and 39% for females in 2000.

◆   ◆   ◆

8.   **The diagram below shows the percentage of deaths from heart disease and cancer, and calories consumed from processed foods in different countries**

Summarize the information by selecting and reporting the main features, and make comparisons where relevant.

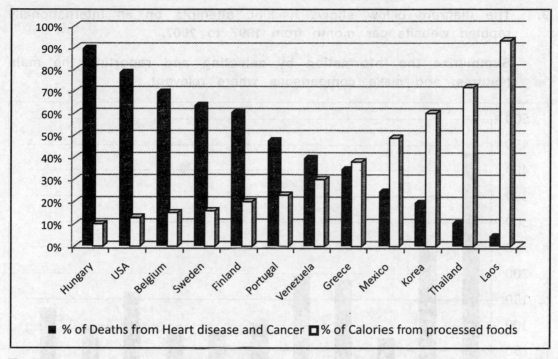

■ % of Deaths from Heart disease and Cancer □ % of Calories from processed foods

The given bar chart provides information on proportion of deaths from heart disease and cancer and it also depicts percentage of calories consumed from processed foods in 12 countries.

A paradoxical pattern is observed in the graph. The percentage of heart and cancer diseases is the highest in Hungary at 90% whereas percentage calorie consumption is the least at 9%. Every 8 in 10 Americans are suffering from heart or cancer disease followed by Belgium, Sweden and Finland where the proportion remains between 60 to 70%. Moreover, cancer and heart patients remain in the range of 45% and 55% in Portugal, Venezuela and Greece. Lastly, less than 20% people suffer from such diseases in Mexico, Korea, Thailand and Laos.

On the other hand, calorie consumption from processed foods is the highest in Laos (90%), followed by Thailand (70%), Korea (59%), Mexico (48%) and Greece (37%). Moreover, intake of calories from processed foods in countries like Hungary, USA, Belgium, Sweden, Finland, Portugal and Venezuela is in the range of 10% to 30%.

Ironically, the countries where less calories are consumed show a higher proportion of cancer and cardiac diseases.

◆ ◆ ◆

9. **The diagram below shows hacking attempts on an internationally reputed website per month from 1997 to 2007.**

   Summarize the information by selecting and reporting the main features, and make comparisons where relevant.

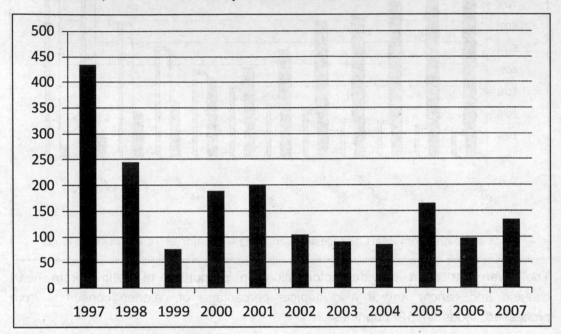

The bar chart reveals average number of attempts per month to hack a website acclaimed worldwide, over a period of eleven years.

It can be clearly observed that average number of hacking attempts per month was nearly 440 in the year 1997. However, after that, it declined to almost 245 the following year and it hit the lowest number of 75 in 1999. After that, the website again attracted more hacking attempts and that remained around 200 average endeavours per month for the following two years.

Average monthly efforts to hack the website then, stayed in the range of 90 between 2002 and 2004. Then, it shot up to more than in 2005, followed by nearly 100 and 140 in year 2006 and 2007 respectively.

All in all, the graph shows that number of hacking attempts per month declined to one third compared to what it was ten years before.

♦   ♦   ♦

10. **The diagram below shows incidents of theft in two states of a South American country from 1990 to 2000.**

   Summarize the information by selecting and reporting the main features, and make comparisons where relevant.

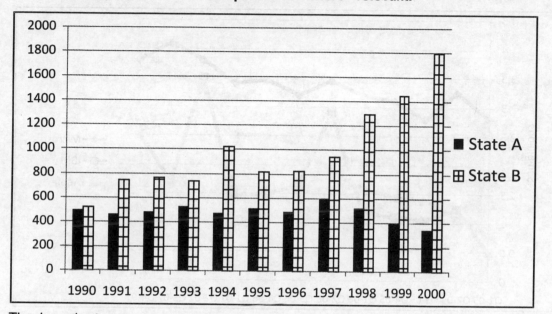

The bar chart expresses number of thefts that occurred in two states of a South American country over a period of 11 years.

The chart reveals that both states witnessed nearly 500 incidents of theft in 1990. After that, theft incidents remained in the range of 500 till 1996 for state A but they kept steadily rising for state B. However, it rose to 600 in 1996 followed by a down fall in the coming years and in year 2000, state A observed least number of theft cases, which stood at around 370.

On the other hand, theft incidents rose to the range of 780 in state B and remained in the same range for following three years. Later, in 1994, they rose drastically to over 1000. After going down to almost 800 for 1995 and 1996, theft events constantly kept rising at an alarming rate for the following years and touched a high of almost 1800 in the year 2000.

Finally, the bar chart depicts that theft incidents had been controlled well in state A whereas state B showed poor control over theft events and therefore witnessed unusually high numbers of theft in the year 2000.

◆ ◆ ◆

11. The diagram below shows information about quarterly profit for three companies of United States from 2005 to 2007.

Summarize the information by selecting and reporting the main features, and make comparisons where relevant.

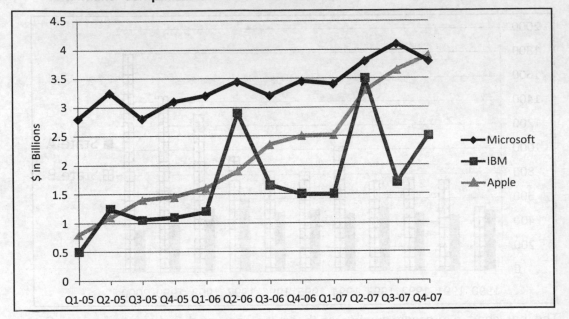

The given line graph provides information on billions of dollars earned per quarter by Microsoft, IBM and Apple from 2005 to 2007.

Firstly, Microsoft earned nearly USD 2.8 Billion in Q1 2005 followed by a steady rise till second quarter of 2006 and the income reached to 3.5 billion. It fluctuated for the next four quarters and then rose sharply to reach the high of 4.2 billion in Q3 07 followed by a slight dip to 3.8 billion in Q4 07.

Secondly, IBM's revenues stood lowest at 0.5 billion. However, it increased and remained range bound around 1 billion for the next four quarters. Then, it showed phenomenal jump to 3 billion in Q2 06 followed by a sharp fall to 1.8 billion. After staying in the same range for the next three quarters, it again shot up to the peak of 3.5 billion in Q2 07. In the end, it fluctuated and closed at 2.5 in Q4 07.

Thirdly, Apple started at 0.7 billion and grew steadily to reach 2.5 billion in Q1 07 and then showed smart jumps in the following quarters and reached to the highest at 3.9 billion.

Finally, all the companies witnessed rise in their profits, however, Apple was an obvious outperformer over its peers in the graph.

♦ ♦ ♦

The Ultimate Guide To IELTS Writing

12. The diagram below shows information about performance of sector wise indexes in India from 2000 to 2010.

Summarize the information by selecting and reporting the main features, and make comparisons where relevant.

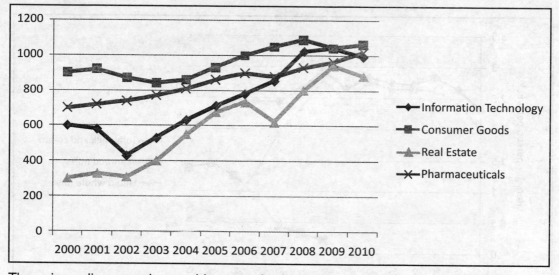

The given line graph provides trends in various sector specific indices over eleven years in India.

Sectors like real estate and information technology have done really well in the last eleven years. Real estate index was at 300 in 2000, stayed there for nearly three years and then rose dramatically by 2.5 times in mid 2006. However, it corrected to a low of 610 by the end of 2007 and then it rallied smartly to the top of 950 in early 2009 and settled at around 880 in 2010. IT on the other hand began at 600 and then it dipped drastically to a bottom of 420 in mid 2002. However, it expressed a consistent growth and touched a peak of 1050 in mid 2009 and closed at around 980 in 2010.

Consumer goods and Pharmaceuticals sectors have shown a defensive movement. Pharmaceuticals sector has shown the most consistent performance. It was at 700 in 2000 and excepting a small volatility in 2006-07, it grew steadily to a high of 1020 at the end. Lastly, Consumer Goods sector witnessed a slight gain followed by gradual slow down till mid 2004 and then it saw a strong and consistent rise to 1100 in mid 2008 and consolidated at the same level till 2010.

Finally, it is clearly observed that all sectors showed gains over the past eleven years on the charts, however, real estate and information technology were outperformers over other sectors.

♦ ♦ ♦

13. The charts below show the consumption of various food groups by people in Germany from 1945 to 2010

Summarize the information by selecting and reporting the main features, and make comparisons where relevant.

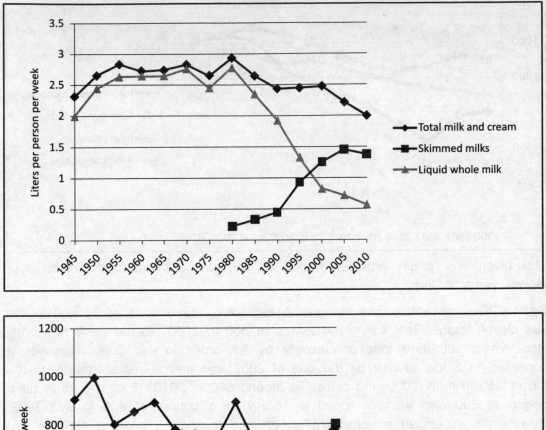

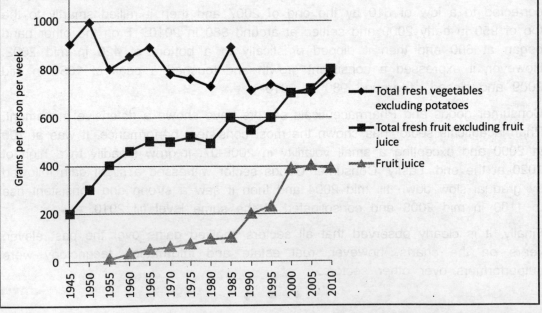

The Ultimate Guide To IELTS Writing

The line graphs offer information on utilization of milk, vegetable fruits and related products in Germany over a period of 65 years.

The first line graph shows that the consumption of total milk and liquid whole milk rose steadily to nearly 2.7 litres per week per person till 1967. However, after that with some deviation, in 1977, when skimmed milks were introduced, it started gaining popularity over its peers. In 2010, weekly consumption of total milk and cream was 2 litres; liquid milk, which showed huge reduction in popularity stood at hardly 0.5 litre and skimmed milks gained ground and reached to almost 1.5 litre.

The other graph reveals that Germans are inclining towards fruits and fruit juices. It shows that in 1945, consumption of fresh vegetables excluding potatoes was at 900 grams per week, which fluctuated in the range of 1000 in 1950 to 700 in 1990 and stayed at 780 in 2010. Compared to that, utilization of total fresh fruits was at 200 in 1945, which rose to almost 800 in 2010. Fruit juices also did well to reach 400 grams per week at the end.

The graph shows that Germans are choosing more fruit and juices and total milk and skimmed milk in their food intake and avoiding liquid whole milk and vegetables.

♦ ♦ ♦

14. **The graph shows the consumption of meat products in a country from 1985 to 2010.**

   Summarize the information by selecting and reporting the main features, and make comparisons where relevant.

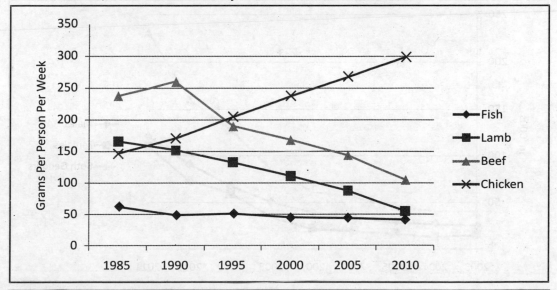

The given line graph shows the pattern of meat products consumption in a country over a period of 25 years. The consumption figures are given in grams per person per week.

It is seen from the chart that beef was consumed the highest at around 250 grams in 1985. Lamb and chicken were in the range of 150 grams and fish was the least popular and stood at 70 grams. Next, in 1990, consumption of beef peaked at 260 grams and then constantly dipped and reached the bottom to 110 grams in 2010. Following the same pattern, consumption of lamb meat also constantly declined to reach to a low of 60 grams in 2010. Fish consumption also lost ground in first five years but after that, it steadied and remained in the range of 50 grams till 2010.

On the other hand, the clear winner in this case is chicken. It was consumed at almost 150 grams in 1985 and then, its intake rose steadily and it reached to the highest level of 300 grams in 2010.

Finally, except chicken, that showed a smart rise in its consumption, intake of all other meat products declined in this country from the year 1985 to 2010.

♦ ♦ ♦

15. **The line graph shows subscription of 3-G (Third Generation) mobile services among males and females in a city in USA from 2003 to 2011.**

Summarize the information by selecting and reporting the main features, and make comparisons where relevant.

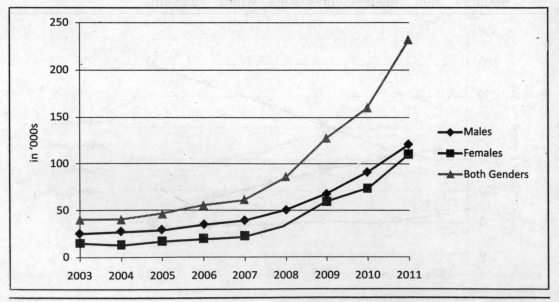

The given line graph provides information on overall and gender specific subscribers of third generation mobile services from 2003 to 2011 in a city in USA.

It is clearly visible that male subscribers outnumbered female subscribers right from the beginning till the end. In 2003, the number of male subscribers was at 25000 and female subscribers were 20000. The figures stagnated till 2006 and then a gradual rise was observed in both groups but in 2008, they reached nearly 50000 and 40000 for males and females respectively. However, after that, the popularity of 3-G services took a boost and subscriptions swelled manifolds to nearly 120000 for yang and 110000 for yin. This boost also increased the overall subscription number in that city to an all time high of 230000 in 2011.

Finally, it is seen that popularity of 3-G services increased by almost five times in eight years. In addition, it is also been seen that males showed more interest in third generation mobile services than their counterparts.

◆ ◆ ◆

16. The Graph below shows data of CFC (Chloro Fluoro Carbon, a gas that is harmful to the environment and also responsible for Ozone Depletion in the atmosphere) emissions in four countries between 1994 and 2006.

Summarize the information by selecting and reporting the main features, and make comparisons where relevant.

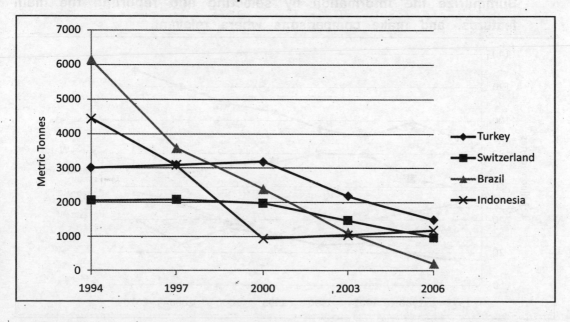

The given line graph depicts decline in emission of CFC gas over a period of 12 years in four countries.

It is evident from the graph that CFC emissions in Brazil were at the highest at nearly 6000 metric tonnes. However, the levels declined dramatically and reached nearly zero in 2006. Turkey and Switzerland also had CFC emission levels at 3000 and 2000 metric tonnes respectively. It appears from the graph that their CFC emission levels remained the same till the end of millennia, but, after that, both countries succeeded in bringing CFC emission levels down to half in 2006.

Indonesia on the other hand showed a rapid decline from 4500 metric tonnes in 1994 to almost 1000 metric tonnes in 2000. However, after that, the levels stagnated and surprisingly, they increased and settled at around 1200 metric tonnes at the end.

Finally, all countries have shown reduction in CFC emission amongst which, Brazil was the outperformer. On the other hand, Indonesia seems to have stopped working on CFC reduction since 2000.

◆ ◆ ◆

17. **The graph below shows the quantities of goods exported from Russia to several countries between 1975 and 2010 by different modes of transport.**

Summarize the information by selecting and reporting the main features, and make comparisons where relevant.

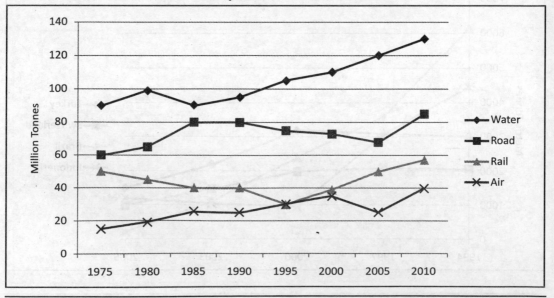

The Ultimate Guide To IELTS Writing

The line graph depicts tonnes of goods exported from Russia via different transport channels over a period of 35 years.

It is visible from the graph that waterways were the mode of choice in 1975 with 90 million tonnes transported through their channels. There was some fluctuation in the following 10 years and then tonnage of goods sent via water increased steadily and reached the peak of 130 million tonnes in 2010. The second most preferred method was road, which showed smart rise in first 10 years and rose from 60 million tonnes to 80 million tonnes. However, it then stagnated and declined to less than 70 in 2005, followed by a steep rise to 85 million tonnes in 2010.

50 million tonnes of goods were transported through railways in 1975, which declined gradually and reached 30 m tonnes in 1995 and then picked up to nearly 60 m tonnes in 2010. With the smallest figure of 18 million tonnes in 1975, the least preferred mode was air that almost doubled in 2000, followed by a sharp dip in 2005; then it further rose to a peak of 40 million tonnes in 2010.

Finally, the graph reveals that overall export of Russia has increased in the given period. However, their preferences of modes of exporting goods remained the same with waterways as the first choice and air as the last one.

♦ ♦ ♦

18. The line graph shows changes in two wheeler ownership between 1980 and 2010 in Singapore. The table shows the main method of travel to work in Singapore in 2010.

Summarize the information by selecting and reporting the main features, and make comparisons where relevant.

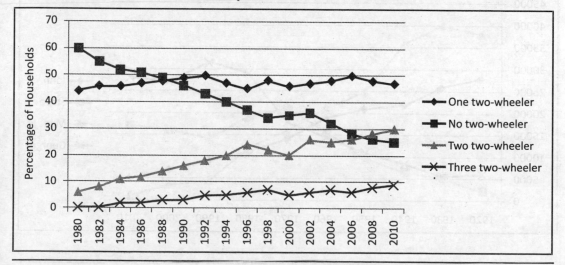

The line graph shows trends of two wheeler ownership in Singapore over a period of 30 years.

It is evident from the graph that usage of two wheelers has increased over this timeframe. If we look at single two wheeler ownership, it remained in the range of 40 to 50 percent and at the end little less than half of households had one two wheeler. Compared to that, around 60% households did not own a two wheeler in 1980 and hardly 5% had two in the decade.

An upswing is observed in houses with two and three two wheelers with time and at the end, in 2010, one in three households had two two-wheelers and one in ten had three two- wheelers. However, only 25% households were left with no two-wheelers in 2010.

Finally, the graph shows that usage of two wheelers increased so much that nearly 40% of households owned at least a two-wheeler in Singapore in 2010.

♦ ♦ ♦

19. **The chart shows popularity of four names that were given to newborn babies in United States from 1920 to 2010.**

Summarize the information by selecting and reporting the main features, and make comparisons where relevant.

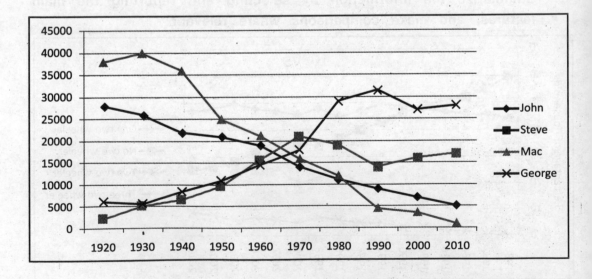

The given line graph offers ranking of four names that parents gave to their babies

Nearly 38000 babies were named Mac in 1920, making Mac the most popular in that era, followed by John with 28000, George with 6000 and Steve with only 2000 takers. However, the scenario changed and an interesting pattern was seen that all the names were given to baby numbers in the range of 15000 to 20000 in mid 1960s.

The trend then remained the same on the chart and in the end, nearly 25000 babies were named as George followed by 15000 newborns named Steve. Moreover, the usage of the name John declined steadily and reached to the bottom of 10000 in 2010. However, the word Mac lost its popularity and touched the lowest point of 2000 only at the end.

Finally, the chart reveals that George and Steve names gained popularity whereas John and Mac lost their appeal over the period of 90 years.

◆ ◆ ◆

20. **The graphs below show results of a survey of college going boys and girls activities other than academic studies.**

Summarize the information by selecting and reporting the main features, and make comparisons where relevant.

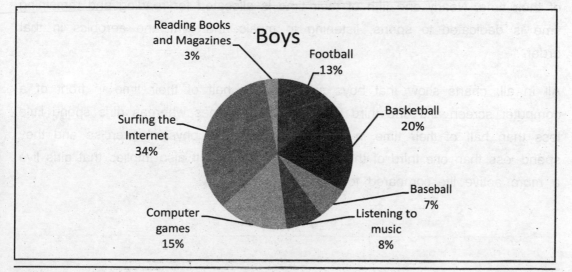

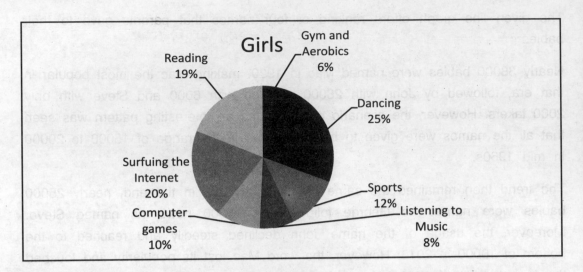

The pie charts compare non-academic activities of college going boys and girls.

It is clearly visible from the chart that boys spend almost one third of their surfing the internet and 15% of their time in playing games on computers. Nearly 40% time is invested in outdoor games like basketball (20%), football (13%) and baseball (7%). Lastly, they spend 8% of their time listening to music and devote only 3% to reading.

On the other hand, girls show a good variety in their non-academic activities. Their most popular activity is dancing that accounts for one fourth of their time. This is followed by internet and computer gaming that cumulatively occupy 30% of their time. Nearly one fifth of their time is allocated for reading and remaining time is dedicated to sports, listening to music and gym and aerobics in that order.

All in all, charts show that boys spend nearly half of their time in front of a computer screen and one third behind outdoor games whereas girls spend little less than half of their time in activities that require physical exercise and they spend less than one third of their time on computers. It also implies that girls live a more active life compared to boys.

◆ ◆ ◆

21. **The given charts show the pattern of expenditure on music in three different years in England.**

Summarize the information by selecting and reporting the main features, and make comparisons where relevant.

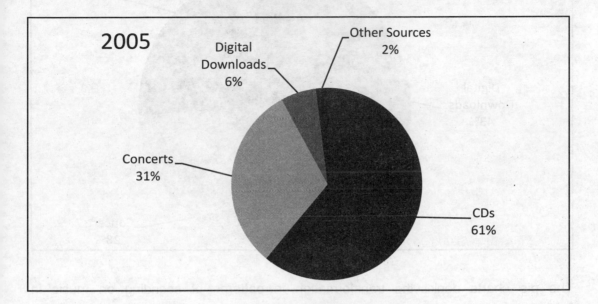

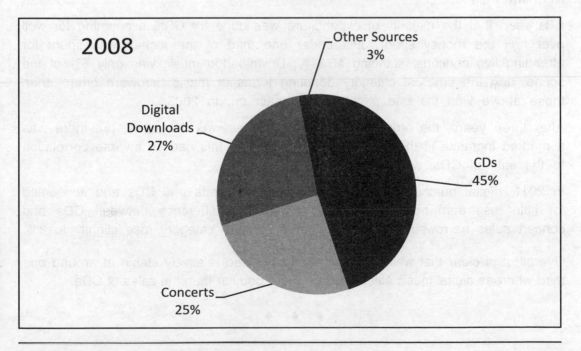

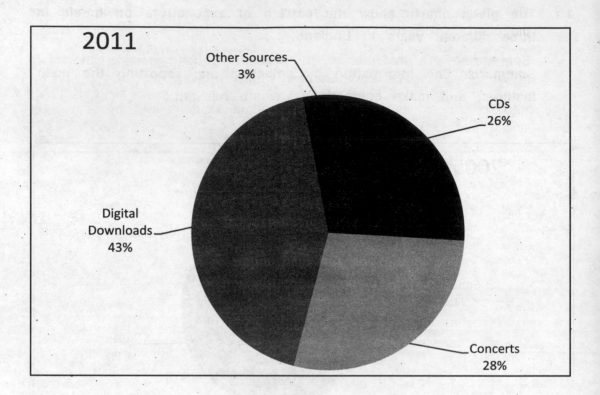

2011

Other Sources 3%

CDs 26%

Digital Downloads 43%

Concerts 28%

The pie charts depict the transformation in patterns of spending on music in Northern Ireland.

It is seen that the majority of expenditure was done for CDs, accounting for well over half the money spent. Just under one third of the money was spent for attending live concerts, standing at 31%. Downloaded music was only 6% of the scene, and the smallest category denoting forms of music hardware other than those above was the one people spent least on, in 2003.

After three years, the order of the four categories was the same, but there was a marked increase in the sale of digital music and this had an inverse correlation to the sale of CDs, which fell to 41%.

In 2011, digital purchases had overtaken both concerts and CDs and accounted for little less than half of all sales (43%). The difference between CDs and concert sales narrowed to only 2%, and the 'other' category rose slightly to 3%.

Overall, it is clear that while concert sales remained relatively stable at around one third whereas digital music sales became more popular than the sales of CDs.

◆ ◆ ◆

22. **The charts illustrate how recycling is carried out in Greece, and the pie charts show the percentage of recycled and non-recycled waste.**

Summarize the information by selecting and reporting the main features, and make comparisons where relevant.

The charts provide comparative information about recycling in Greece in 1980, 1990 and 2000.

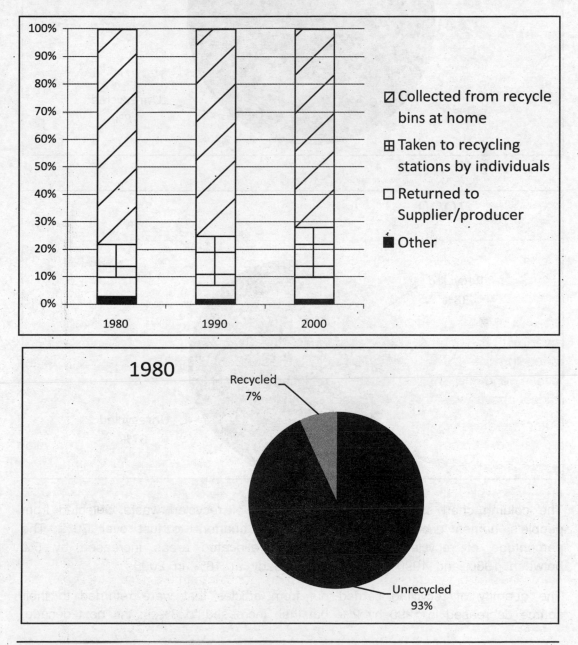

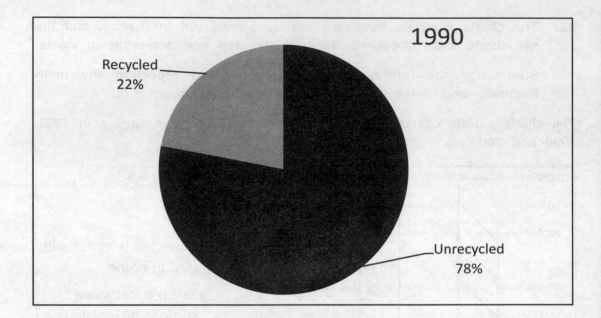

1990

Recycled
22%

Unrecycled
78%

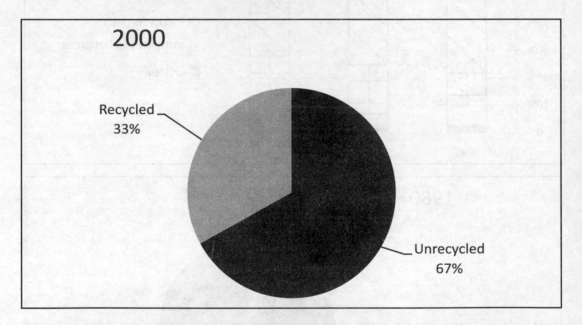

2000

Recycled
33%

Unrecycled
67%

The column chart shows that the percentage of recycled waste collected from people's homes decreased from over three quarters to just over 70%. The percentage of recycled material taken to allocated areas increased by 5% between 1980 and 1990 but remained steady at 18% in 2000.

The quantity of recycling carried out from articles that were returned to their source decreased in 1990 by 2%, but then increased to 8% in the next decade.

Categories other than above decreased by 1% then remained stable at 2% for the final two given years.

The pie charts indicate a threefold jump in the amount of waste recycled between 1980 and 1990 from 7% up to 22%. These numbers rose in 2000 at a less dramatic rate though. Finally, they ended at one third of waste being recycled.

Overall, it can be seen that recycling increased over the time given, while the proportion collected from each house gradually decreased.

◆ ◆ ◆

23. **The graphs show the cost for watching movies and change in market share of three different ways of watching movies.**

   Summarize the information by selecting and reporting the main features, and make comparisons where relevant.

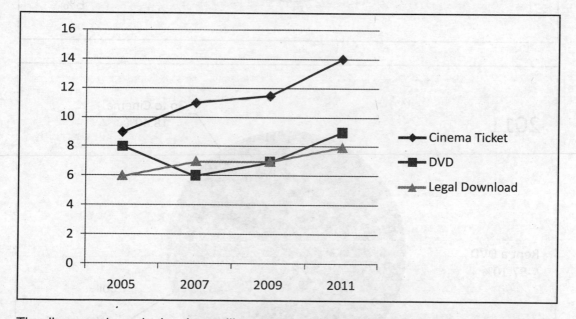

The line graph and pie charts illustrate the cost for watching movies in different formats, as well as the percentage split between the types.

The most notable trend with regard to cost is that cinema tickets remained the most expensive way to watch a movie from 2005 to 2011, rising to a peak of slightly over £14 a ticket. Over the same period, DVD prices also increased to

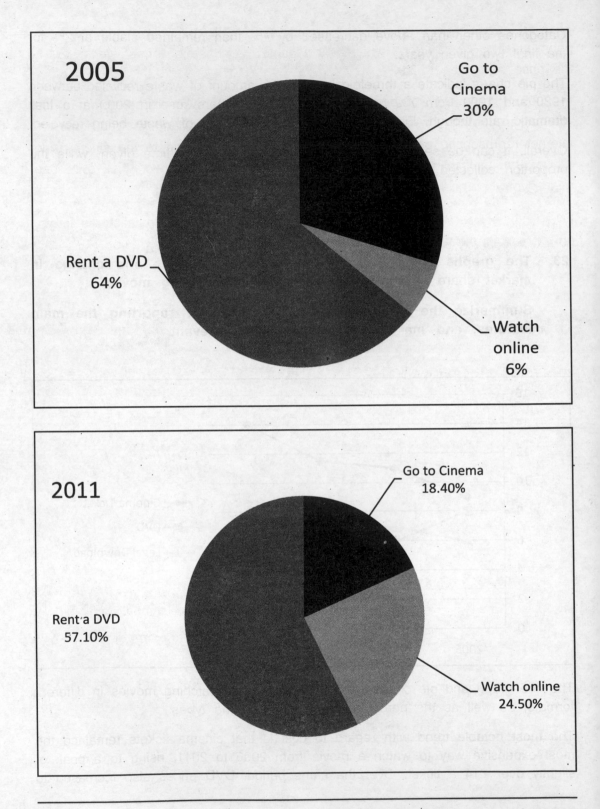

2005

Go to Cinema
30%

Rent a DVD
64%

Watch online
6%

2011

Go to Cinema
18.40%

Rent a DVD
57.10%

Watch online
24.50%

£8 from £6. Moreover, downloaded movies were more expensive than DVDs in 2005; this changed in 2007 when they became the cheapest format, yet by 2011, the price had risen to £9.

In 2005, the majority of people opted to hire DVDs, with those going to the cinema accounting for less than one third of the total, and movies from the internet representing only 6%. By 2011, however, both going to the cinema and renting had fallen as downloaded movies increased to cover just over one quarter of the market.

Overall, it is clear that although prices increased on average for all three forms, an increasing percentage of people chose to download movies.

◆ ◆ ◆

24. **The charts show information about the number of kilometres travelled in an average month and the distribution of vehicle types in Britain.**

Summarise the information by selecting and reporting the main features, and make comparisons where relevant.

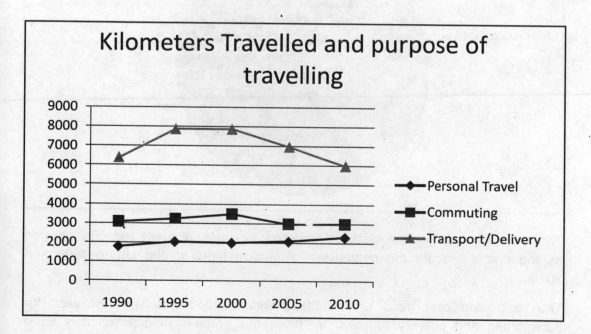

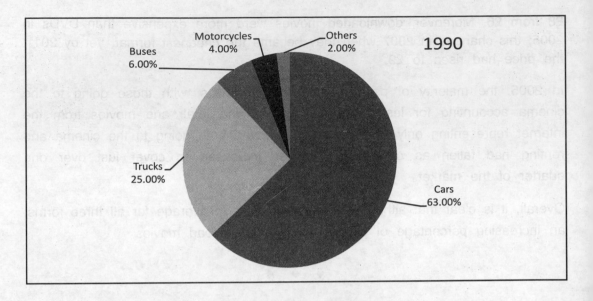

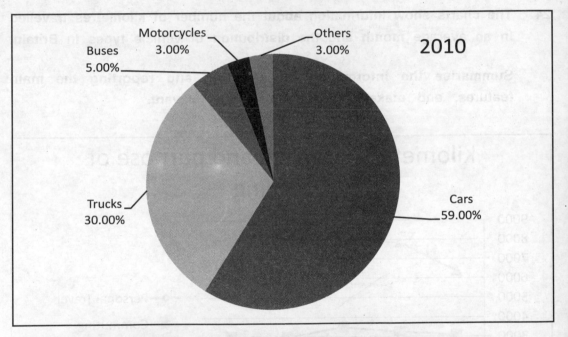

The table is given for the distance travelled for three different reasons, as well as the charts indicate the percentage of vehicle types in the UK in 1990 and 2010.

The most significant trend is that the maximum kilometres were travelled for transporting and delivery reasons. In 1990, this figure was approximately 6500 kilometres, rising to almost 8000 kilometres by 1995 and 2000 but falling to 6,000 by 2010.

Personal travel was at 1800 km in 1990 and showed marginal growth of 500 km and settled as the highest point of 2300 in the end. On the other hand, kms used for commuting were at 3000 km gained to 3500 km in 2000 and then bounced back to 3000 in 2010.

The pie charts indicate that in the twenty year difference, the percentage of cars fell by ,4% while the number of trucks increased by 5%. Over the same period, buses and motorcycles both fell by 1% while the category labelled 'other' increased by 1%.

Overall, it is clear that there were number of changes in the distance travelled and type of vehicles from 1990 to 2010.

◆ ◆ ◆

25. **The charts show the distribution of employed and unemployed people in Philippines in 1932 and in 1992.**

    Summarize the information by selecting and reporting the main features, and make comparisons where relevant.

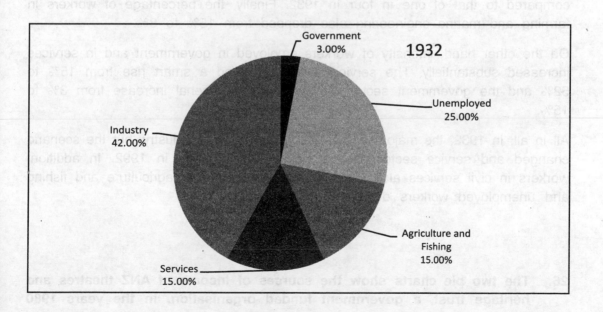

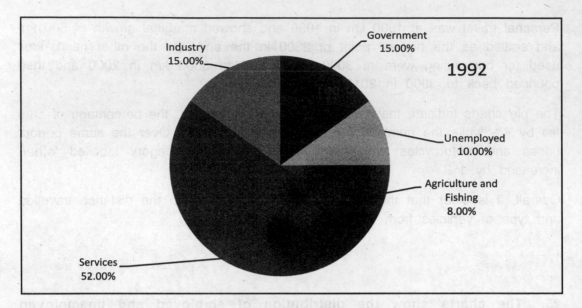

Pie chart labels:
Government 15.00%
1992
Industry 15.00%
Unemployed 10.00%
Agriculture and Fishing 8.00%
Services 52.00%

The given pie charts display comparative data on how the Philippines workforce was engaged among different sectors between 1932 and 1992.

The amount of workforce employed in industry has reduced from 42% to 15% in 1992. On !the same note, there was only one in ten unemployed workers in 1992 compared to that of one in four in 1932. Finally, the percentage of workers in farming and marine engineering also dropped from 15% to 8%.

On the other hand, intensity of workers employed in government and in services increased substantially. The service sector observed a smart rise from 15% to 52% and the government sector witnessed a phenomenal increase from 3% to 15%.

All in all, in 1932, the major source of employment was industry, but the scenario changed and service sector offered majority of the jobs in 1992. In addition, workers in civil services also increased whereas those in agriculture and fishing and unemployed workers decreased considerably.

◆ ◆ ◆

26. The two pie charts show the sources of income of ANZ theatres and heritage trust, a government funded organisation, in the years 1980 and 2000.

   Summarize the information by selecting and reporting the main features, and make comparisons where relevant.

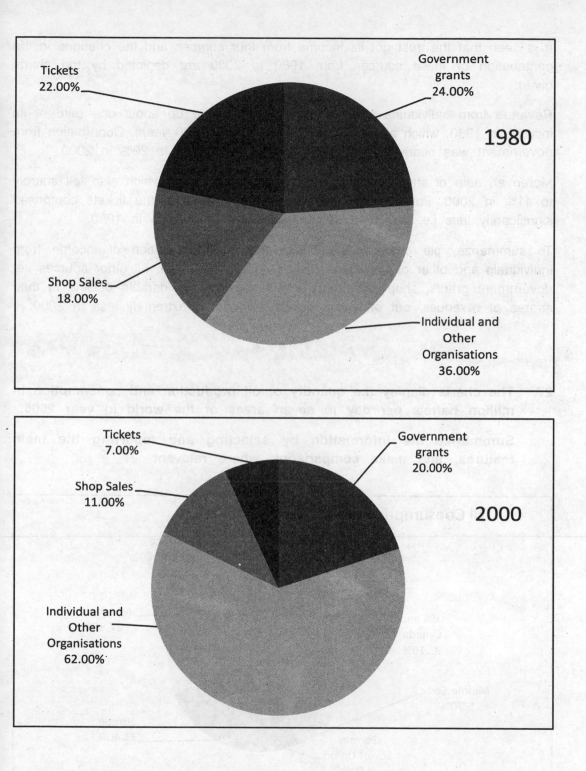

1980

Tickets
22.00%

Government
grants
24.00%

Shop Sales
18.00%

Individual and
Other
Organisations
36.00%

2000

Tickets
7.00%

Shop Sales
11.00%

Government
grants
20.00%

Individual and
Other
Organisations
62.00%

It is seen that the trust got its income from four sources and the changes in the contribution of these sources from 1980 to 2000 are depicted by the charts given.

Revenue from individuals and other companies made up about one third of its income in 1980, which almost doubled in the span of 20 years. Contribution from government was nearly 25% in 1980, which fell slightly to 20% in 2000.

Moreover, sale of shops contributed to one fifth in 1980, which also fell sharply to 11% in 2000. Furthermore, the last source of income, the tickets comprised significantly less i.e. 7% in 2000 compared to that of 22% in 1980.

To summarize, pie charts given depict that the contribution of income from individuals and other organisations gained smartly. However, all other sources i.e. government grants, shop sales and tickets showed considerable decline in their shares of revenues, out of which, tickets contributed extremely less in 2000.

◆ ◆ ◆

27. **The charts display the quantity of oil production and consumption in million barrels per day in seven areas of the world in year 2005.**

Summarize the information by selecting and reporting the main features, and make comparisons where relevant.

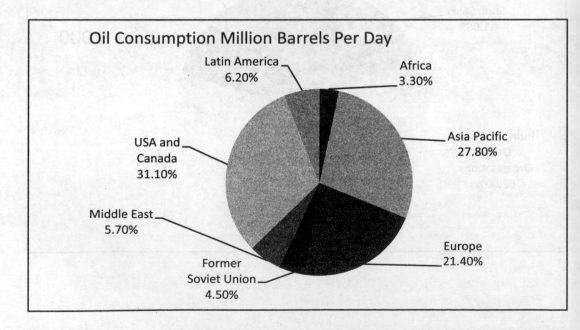

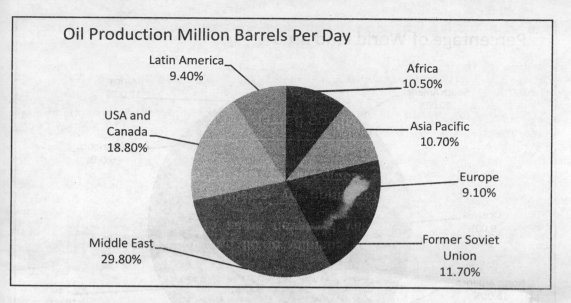

Oil Production Million Barrels Per Day

- Latin America 9.40%
- Africa 10.50%
- USA and Canada 18.80%
- Asia Pacific 10.70%
- Europe 9.10%
- Middle East 29.80%
- Former Soviet Union 11.70%

The given pie charts depict the seven regions of the Earth and the amount of oil produced and utilized in these areas.

One of the pie charts shows that nearly 30% of world's oil is produced in the Middle East region. USA and Canada contribute 18.8% of the oil produced globally. Remaining areas- Former USSR, Latin America, Europe, Africa and Asia Pacific contribute nearly 10% each of the total oil that is produced on this Earth.

The other chart displays that USA and Canada consume more than 31% of oil produced globally. Thus, they consume more than they produce. The same pattern is also observed in Asia Pacific and Europe as they consume 27% and 21% oil respectively. Finally, regions like Middle East, Former Soviet Union, Africa and Latin America consume nearly half of the oil that they produce.

Thus, it is clearly visible from the pie charts that USA, Canada, Europe and Asia Pacific utilize most of the oil produced in the world whereas other regions actually consume less oil than they produce.

◆ ◆ ◆

28. **The charts below display the percentage of the area and the current population of the seven continents of the Earth. Summarise the information and make comparisons where relevant.**

Summarize the information by selecting and reporting the main features, and make comparisons where relevant.

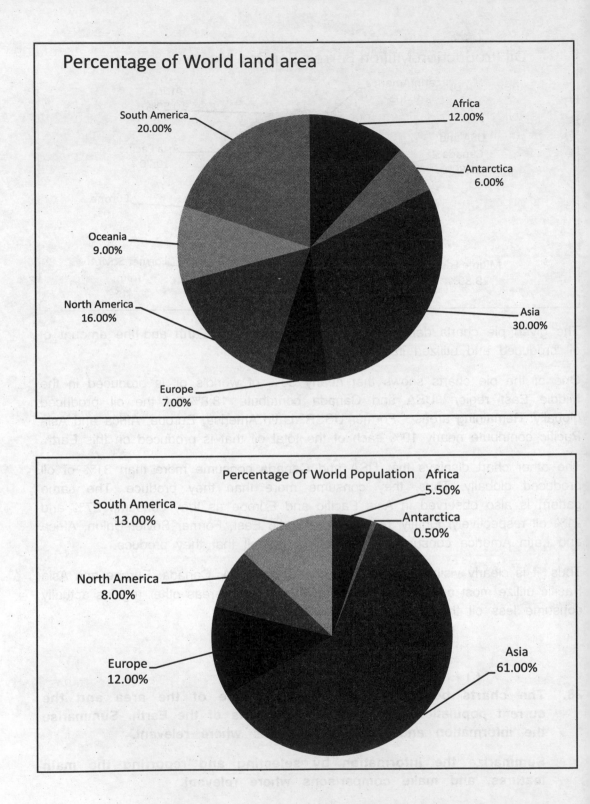

Percentage of World land area

- Africa 12.00%
- Antarctica 6.00%
- Asia 30.00%
- Europe 7.00%
- North America 16.00%
- Oceania 9.00%
- South America 20.00%

Percentage Of World Population

- Africa 5.50%
- Antarctica 0.50%
- Asia 61.00%
- Europe 12.00%
- North America 8.00%
- South America 13.00%

The pie charts given depict the percentage of total land area of the Earth covered by all the seven continents and the proportion of population of the world that they comprise of.

It is evident that maximum population density is observed in Asia which contains 30% of the landmass and accommodates every 6 of 10 human beings who live on this earth. Rest all other continents have higher landmass over the proportion of population.

The second largest continent is Europe (20% area and 12% population), followed by North America (16% land and 8% population). Next is Africa that possess a land mass of 12% land and hosts 5.5% of total world population. Ocenia and Antarctica are the continents that contain 9% and 6% of land mass respectively and house less than a percent of people on this earth.

Finally, it seems that Asia is the only continent that supports a larger proportion of population than the percentage of land it has.

◆ ◆ ◆

29. **The graphs below show the average exam marks achieved by students at English, Japanese and Italian language courses in a university. The passing marks are 50 and maximum marks are 100.**

Summarize the information by selecting and reporting the main features, and make comparisons where relevant.

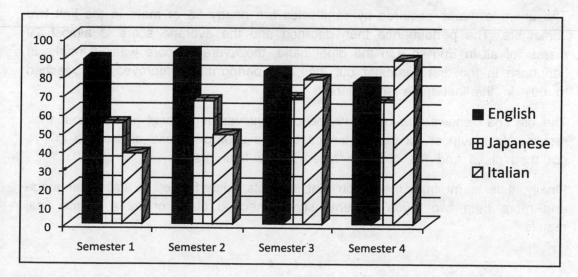

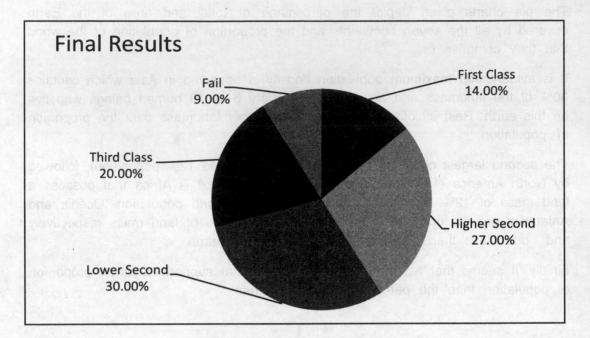

Final Results

First Class
14.00%

Fail
9.00%

Third Class
20.00%

Higher Second
27.00%

Lower Second
30.00%

The graphs show the performance of students who study three languages at a university.

The most striking point of the bar chart graph is the students' performance in Italian language. The average marks were below passing standards for the first two semesters but the last two semesters' performance outnumbered that of English language.

The average marks acquired by candidates are nearly 85 or more in the first two semesters. The performance then declined and the average score is almost 70 marks for all in English. On the other hand, the average score was 50 marks in Japanese in the first semester but then, the performance improved and reached to 60+ in the last three semesters.

The pie chart shows that only 14% people achieved an overall first class in their results. Next, almost six out of ten candidates scored second class, one in five got third class and 9% students failed in the final results.

Finally, it is learnt from the graph that students outperformed in Italian language and more than two thirds students scored second class or more in the final results.

◆ ◆ ◆

30. **The table gives information about the average hours spent per week in front of the computer (for internet surfing, playing games or business purposes) by people of different age groups in China.**

Summarize the information by selecting and reporting the main features, and make comparisons where relevant.

Age (years)	Male	Female
10-15	10	8
16-20	24	23
21-25	12	10
26-30	9	9
31-50	8	9
51+	7	8

The table reflects the number of hours spent per week on computer by people of various age groups in China.

The most striking point to be observed is that Internet usage was at its highest for those aged between 16 and 20, with the figure for males being 24 hours and females just one hour less. However, it is quite surprising to note that the youngest age group spent far less amount of time on computer. Boys of 10-15 age spent 10 hours whereas girls gave only 8 hours.

From 21 onwards, the hours spent reduced dramatically. By the ages of 26 to 30, males and females spent the same amount of time online with 9 hours each, after which females reportedly spent slightly longer hours online than males for the remaining two categories, falling to only 7 hours for men and 8 hours for women for those aged 51 or older.

Overall, it can be seen that the highest period of computer usage for both males and females between the ages 16 and 20. It is also seen that males younger than 31 spent more time than females on the computer.

◆ ◆ ◆

31. **The table shows the percentage of people with mobile phones who use various features on their phone.**

   Summarise the information by selecting and reporting the main features, and make comparisons where relevant.

	2006	2008	2010
Make calls	100	100	95
Take Photos	50	75	85
Send/Receive Text Messages	80	85	90
Play Games	20	55	52
Internet (surfing and email)	02	35	88
Play Music	10	24	44
Record Videos	02	11	50

The table illustrates the various functions available on mobile phones, showing the percent of users that took advantage of these features over three different years.

The most noteworthy aspect is that with the exception of a slight fall in 2010, all owners used their mobile phone to communicate with others. The second most common use was for text messaging, which steadily increased from just over three quarter of all users in 2006 to 90 percent of users in 2010.

Using the phone as a photo camera increased to 85 percent in 2010 from 50 percent in 2006. Playing games on the phone increased dramatically between 2006 and 2008, but then fell slightly in 2010 to end at 52%.

The largest increase in the table is between 2008 and 2010 for those browsing the internet, which was almost out of use in 2006. Video and music usage also increased, with video overtaking music in 2010.

In total, the usage of all the functions used on mobiles increased over the years with the exception of games and making calls.

◆ ◆ ◆

32. **The table shows the average life expectancy for males and females in 1900, 1950 and 2000.**

Summarise the information by selecting and reporting the main features, and make comparisons where relevant.

	1900		1950		2000	
	Male	Female	Male	Female	Male	Female
France	37.8	39.9	63.0	68.0	74	81
Norway	46	49.2	63.2	68	73.9	82
Italy	52	55.4	69.3	72	73.1	79.4
Spain	44.2	47.1	65.1	69.1	74	81.2
Poland	53.2	55.8	70.4	73.2	75.2	81.2

The table provides information on the lifespan of people from 5 different countries in three different time periods.

The most notable point is that in all countries, women generally lived longer than men, and in most cases the gap between the genders increased from the beginning to the end.

The countries that had the longest average life span in 1900 and 1950 were Italy and Poland, although by 1990, Italian life expectancy fell to the lowest age level as compared to all countries, for both males and females, with figures of 73.1 and 79.4 respectively.

The variations between France, Norway and Spain narrowed from nearly ten years difference at their peak in 1900 to only a year's difference for women and a month's for men.

Overall, it can be seen that statistically, Polish people had the highest life expectancy for both males and females for all three time periods.

◆ ◆ ◆

33. **The table shows the number of people in Canada in each earning level.**

Summarise the information by selecting and reporting the main features, and make comparisons where relevant.

The Ultimate Guide To IELTS Writing

Number of people in each income bracket in Australia					
	2005	2006	2007	2008	2009
Total, All income Groups	23,715,662	24,469,250	24,225,280	24,667,900	24,294,240
$ 20,000 or less	9,792,350	7,318,580	7,033,990	6,966,060	7,075,270
Between $20,000 and $50,000	8,916,970	9,667,540	9,235,740	9,307,050	9,390,030
Between $50,000 and $150,000	4,672,200	7,093,510	7,516,340	7,914,340	7,985,540
Over $150,000	334,140	389,620	439,210	480,450	473,400

The table offers details on income levels in Australia and the number of Australians who were included in each income bracket from 2005 to 2009.

In 2005, the number of people in each income level followed a decreasing order with an increase in income, with nearly 10 million earning $20,000 or less, falling to only slightly above one third of a million earning over $150,000.

By 2006, the pattern changed as the number of people with the lowest income fell by nearly one quarter, whereas those earning between $20,000 and $50,000 increased by almost one million and those in the next income level increased dramatically to over 7 million. There was also an increase in the number of people in the highest income bracket, which rose by over 50,000.

In 2007, the largest increase in numbers was observed in those earning between $50,000 and $100,000, and in 2008 and 2009, figures remained relatively stable, with those earning between $20,000 and $50,000 representing the majority.

To sum up, there were variations in the number of people in each income level. However, the middle class and the rich class of people had increased in numbers in Australia.

◆ ◆ ◆

34. The table below shows the percentage of cars of different age from the date of their purchase in four different countries.

Summarize the information by selecting and reporting the main features, and make comparisons where relevant.

Age → Country	New to 3 years	4-5 years	6-8 years	9-12 years	13 years and more
New Zealand	26	32	34	9	2
Japan	79	16	3	1	1
USA	39	24	21	11	5
Britain	35	36	24	2	3

The table provides information on the percentage of cars divided in five age groups right from their year of purchase to 13 years and above in four countries.

The most eye catching figures are from Japan, where 79 percent cars are younger than 3 years. Only 16 percent cars were of age 4-5 years and rest were less than 3. It means that 95 percent cars in Japan were bought in the last five years.

Little over one third of cars were bought in the recent three years in the USA and the UK and almost a quarter of the cars were up to 3 years old in New Zealand. The next age group of 4-5 years is led by Britain with 36 percent cars followed by New Zealand with 32 percent and America with 24. The following column of 6-8 years is topped by New Zealand where a little over one third cars were of that age followed by UK and USA with little over one fifth. The rest age segments were not so dominantly contributed to, in either of the countries.

Finally, it seems that Japanese started showing great interest in owning a car in the last five years whereas every four in five cars was younger than 8 years in remaining countries.

♦ ♦ ♦

35. The table shows the reasons for studying English language for the people of Japan. The information is based on a survey that was conducted in year 2000.

Summarize the information by selecting and reporting the main features, and make comparisons where relevant.

	Reasons for studying English language	Percentage of People
1	Study Abroad	19%
2	Work Abroad	09%
3	Business Tours	39%
4	Have a foreign spouse	11%
5	Promotion in existing job	17%
6	Make new friends	13%
7	Travel abroad	56%
8	Training provided by the employer	03%

The given table provides information about the factors that compelled the Japanese people to learn English.

It seems that most of the Japanese learned English to facilitate their foreign travel and the least of them acquired English to meet the requirements of their employer.

Now, to be more precise, the prime occupational reason for taking up English studies was to use it on business travels and the figure stood at 39% which was far less than those who learned it for travelling abroad, which was at 56%. Nearly one in ten Japanese who studied English did so for working abroad, living with an English speaking spouse and making new friends.

Lastly, nearly one fifth of English learners in Japan did it for foreign education and 2% less did it to get promoted in their existing job.

Finally, it seems that the Japanese people studied English to make their foreign travels easier and to live with their English speaking spouse. However, some of them used it for their vocational purposes as well.

◆ ◆ ◆

36. **The table gives information about various free-time activities done by men and women of different ages in New Zealand.**

Summarize the information by selecting and reporting the main features, and make comparisons where relevant.

| Age Group → | 21-35 | 21-35 | 36-45 | 36-45 | 46+ | 46+ |
Gender →	Male	Female	Male	Female	Male	Female
Jogging	35%	23%	48%	31%	22%	31%
Baseball	87%	2%	64%	1%	29%	0%
Basketball	97%	22%	68%	15%	43%	3%
Football	78%	9%	57%	5%	27%	0%
Meditation	0%	7%	3%	12%	7%	42%
Fishing	12%	1%	32%	0%	45%	0%

The given table provides comparative data on six types of leisure time activities enjoyed by both the genders in various age groups in New Zealand.

The most striking feature of the table is the involvement of males of age 21-35 in active team sports. Almost all men participate in basketball, followed by baseball where the participation is 87 percent, followed by football where eight out of ten men spent their leisure time. The least preferred activities in this age group were meditation and fishing. There is a change in the trend as the age progresses as nearly one in three men did fishing and one in two opted for jogging whereas nearly sixty percent males still preferred sports. Lastly, fishing was the most popular for males of 46 and above at 45%, closely followed by basketball at 43%. Other activities were around one fourth of the total, except meditation which was at 7%.

On the other hand, nearly one fifth females of 21-35 group took jogging and basketball and other areas were not given priority. The same trend continued with some rise in jogging excepting meditation where a 5 percent rise was seen. The eldest women's most popular activity was meditation (42%) followed by jogging (32%) and other activities were given negligible attention.

Finally, the table reveals that as the age progressed, both men and women took more interest in passive activities with an exception of jogging.

◆ ◆ ◆

37. **The diagram below shows information about the Eiffel Tower and Petronas Towers.**

   Summarise the information by selecting and reporting the main features, and make comparisons where relevant.

	Eiffel Tower	Petronas Towers
Country	France	Malaysia
Complete in the year	1889 (tallest building of the world when completed)	1998 (tallest building of the world when completed)
Time taken for construction	2 years	4 years
Cost of Project	US $ 1.5 million	US $ 1.6 billion
Height	986 feet	1,489 feet
Floors	3	88 – sky bridge on the 42nd floor connects both towers
Building Material	Wrought Iron	Concrete, Steel, Aluminium and Glass
Weight	10,000 tonnes	300,000 tonnes
Number of lifts	2	78
World's tallest building status	1889-1930	1998-2004

The table gives comparative data on two popular and tallest buildings of the world: the Eiffel Tower and the Petronas Towers.

The Petronas Towers are the younger of the two and were constructed in 1998. On the other hand, the Eiffel tower was erected 109 years before them. The Petronas towers were completed in 4 years and are made of concrete, aluminium, steel and glass and are almost 1500 feet high. Compared to that, the Eiffel Tower was constructed in only 2 years, was made of wrought iron and is almost 1000 feet tall.

The Eiffel Tower enjoyed the status of the world's tallest man made structure till 1930 whereas the Petronas Towers lost their claim in just 6 years of being completed. Moreover, the total construction cost of the former was 1.5 million US dollars which was negligible compared to 1.6 billion US dollars spent for the younger building.

Lastly, the Eiffel tower has 3 floors, 2 lifts and weighs ten thousand tonnes. Compared to that, the Petronas Towers have 88 floors, 78 elevators and weigh three hundred thousand tonnes.

♦   ♦   ♦

The Ultimate Guide To IELTS Writing

38. **The table below presents the perceptions of Chief Executive Officers (CEOs) and their partners/spouses as too the main sources of stress in the CEO lifestyle.**

Summarize the information by selecting and reporting the main features, and make comparisons where relevant.

Perceptions of Pressure in the CEO lifestyle: Top Ten Rated Sources of Stress (Percentage)		
Factors perceived to produce stress	Perceptions of CEOs	Perceptions of Spouses/partners
Time pressures and deadlines	52	60
Demands of work on private life	48	23
Demands of work on relationship with family	45	29
Work-related travel	39	37
Work overload	37	62
Interpersonal relations	25	21
Long working hours	24	62
Taking work home	24	32
Inadequately trained subordinates	24	17

The table describes the perception of a number of issues about stress of Chief Executive Officers (CEOs) and their spouses or partners.

Firstly, the three main sources of stress as far as CEOs were concerned were time pressures and deadlines (52%), demands of work on private life (48%), and demands of work on relationship with family (45%). The four main sources of stress that their spouses or partners included were their work overload (62%), long working hours (62%), time pressures and deadlines (60%) and work related travel (57%). Time pressures and deadlines are tangible factors that both groups were aware of. In addition, spouses tended to be more specific in identifying work overload, long working hours and work related travel as problems. However, CEOs focused more on 'demands of work' as a whole.

Finally, the main difference is in the numbers nominating long working hours as a source of stress; 62% of spouses, compared to only 24% of CEOs.

♦ ♦ ♦

39. The following table gives statistics showing the aspects of quality of life in five countries in year 2000.

Summarize the information by selecting and reporting the main features, and make comparisons where relevant.

Country	GNP per head (Calculated in2000 and inUS $)	Daily calories supply per head	Life expectancy at birth (years)	Infant mortality ratio (per 1000 live births)
Bangladesh	140	1,877	40	132
Pakistan	570	2,086	50	124
Vietnam	690	2,950	56	97
Bhutan	580	2,296	49	87
Japan	13,160	3,652	74	12

The table shows four economic measurables of the standard of living in five Asian Countries in 2000.

It is quite evident that Japan offered the best quality of life, had the highest GNP and the best daily supply of calories. In addition, it also had the longest life expectancy and the lowest infant mortality rate compared to all other countries in the table that had an average quality of life.

Pakistan, Vietnam and Bhutan were almost similar in their range of economic indicators. Vietnam had the highest quality of life amongst the chosen set of nations. However, its infant mortality rate was higher than that of Bhutan.

Bangladesh had the lowest quality of life in all aspects in the given data. Its GNP was almost one hundredth of Japan. Its daily calorie intake and average life span of denizens were almost half than those in Japan. On top of it, the infant mortality rate in Bangladesh was ten times higher than Japan.

Finally, it is observed from the given aspects that the countries except Japan were struggling with the quality of life but Japanese people were blessed with an excellent life.

♦ ♦ ♦

40. **The picture below shows how credit card transactions are carried out.**

Summarize the information by selecting and reporting the main features, and make comparisons where relevant.

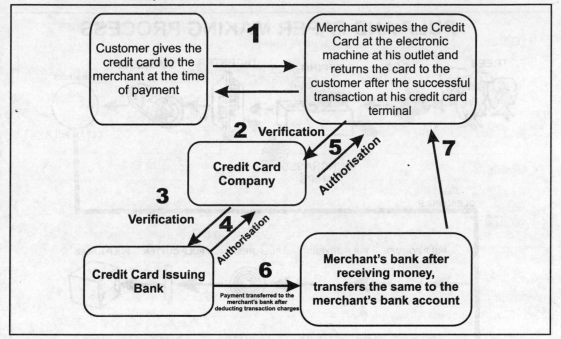

The given flow chart describes how a credit card transaction is carried out at a retail outlet between a merchant and a customer.

Firstly, the card is swiped at an electronic machine at the vendor. The information about the swipe then goes directly to the Credit Card company and from that, it is forwarded electronically to the issuing bank for verification. Once the verification is positive, a confirmation is sent from the bank to the credit card company, which passes on the same to the merchant's outlet where the swipe machine is located and the transaction is complete.

Next, the issuing bank then transfers the money from the customer's account to the merchant's bank account. However, the issuing bank deducts the transaction charges from the amount and also transfers the same to the Credit Card company as per their internal business agreement. After that, the merchant's bank credits the same amount in the merchant's bank account.

◆ ◆ ◆

41. The diagram shows how paper is made from trees.

Summarize the information by selecting and reporting the main features, and make comparisons where relevant.

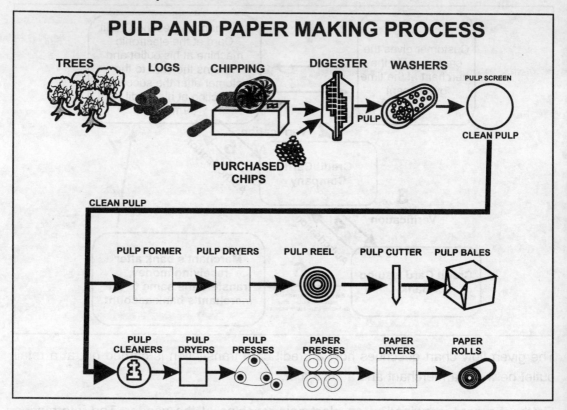

The given diagram describes process of making paper. It is seen that the wooden chips that are either made from wooden logs from trees or purchased from the market, go to the digester. The digester converts wooden chips into pulp, which goes to washers for washing. After that, the pulp is screened and the clean pulp is used for two purposes.

The first purpose is to create rough paper for boxes. The pulp goes to pulp former followed by pulp dryers and reels of pulp are made. The reels are then cut and paper bales are made out of it.

The second purpose is to make refined paper for printing. The clean pulp then goes to pulp cleaners and then to pulp dryers. After that, the pulp is pressed and paper is formed through pressing, which is dried and then the dried paper is rolled as a finished product.

♦ ♦ ♦

42. **The figure shows how coffee is made from the coffee fruits.**

Summarize the information by selecting and reporting the main features, and make comparisons where relevant.

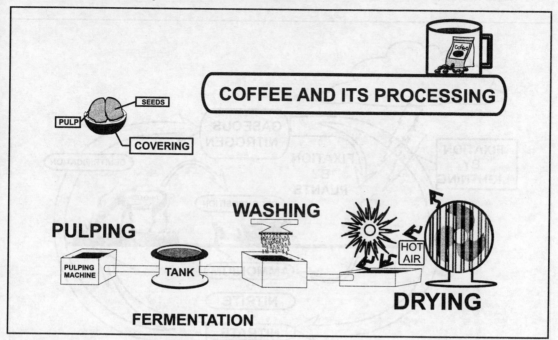

The given diagram describes how coffee is made out of the fruit. According to the diagram, a coffee fruit needs to undergo a four step process before being converted into a dry state of the powder that we use.

The first picture describes the coffee fruit which contains covering of the fruit that contains coffee pulp which covers the seeds of coffee.

Firstly, fruits are picked and sent for the process pulping in a pulping machine. The second stage is fermentation. The pulp of coffee fruits is fermented in a tank. After the process of fermentation, the material is taken out for washing.

The fermented and washed pulp is taken for drying, which is the final step shown in the diagram. The material is dried with the help of Sun. In addition, hot air is blown from machines or fans as shown in the figure to support the process of drying of the material.

◆ ◆ ◆

43. **The diagram below shows the cycle of Nitrogen Gas in the atmosphere.**

Summarize the information by selecting and reporting the main features, and make comparisons where relevant.

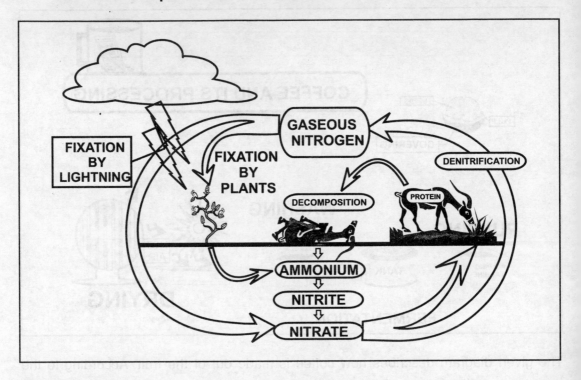

The diagram describes the Nitrogen Cycle. It shows how the gas is provided to living organisms and then returned to the atmosphere.

It is clearly seen from the diagram that most of the gas exists in the environment around us. Firstly, the lightening contributes some nitrogen in the form of nitrates to the soil. The nitrates in the soil are then absorbed by the plant roots. When plants or animals die, proteins are decomposed by bacteria into amino acids which are in turn broken down into ammonium, then into nitrates. Simultaneously, nitrogen in gas form is fixed by the vegetation, followed by a transforming process into ammonium, with the help of bacteria.

The ammonium from decomposition gets transformed in a cycle, from nitrites, then to nitrates, and then into protein. The nitrites are changed into nitrates by bacteria present in the soil. Some of the nitrates are degraded into nitrogen gas in the denitrification process. The Nitrogen in gas form then goes back to the atmosphere.

◆ ◆ ◆

The Ultimate Guide To IELTS Writing

44. **The diagram shows various stages of milk processing.**

Summarize the information by selecting and reporting the main features, and make comparisons where relevant.

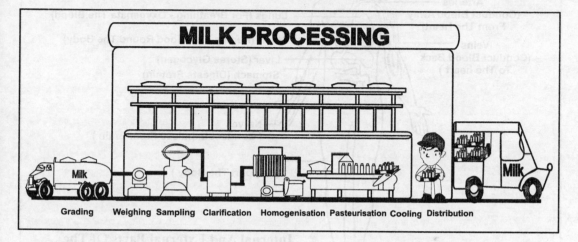

The given process diagram provides information about how milk is processed at a milk processing plant. It also shows different types of processes or procedures the milk goes through before it is sent for distribution.

First, milk is received at the milk plant in tankers. It is then taken inside the plant where it has to undergo three different procedures. The processes are; grading, weighing and sampling. After these processes are over, the next step is clarification of milk, which also takes place in milk processing plant. Following which, homogenisation of the clarified milk takes place.

After that, the homogenised milk is forwarded for the pasteurisation procedure which takes place in the plant and the last procedure that happens under the same roof is cooling of milk. Once the milk is cooled, it is packed and loaded in the milk van for distribution to various places.

◆ ◆ ◆

45. **The diagram shows internal and external parts of human body and their functions.**

Summarize the information by selecting and reporting the main features, and make comparisons where relevant.

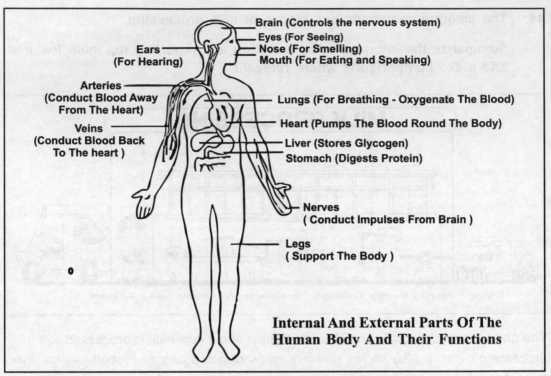

Internal And External Parts Of The Human Body And Their Functions

The picture shows external and internal parts of human body.

First, if we look at the external organs from top : eyes are for seeing, nose is for smelling and mouth is for eating and speaking. Ears are used for hearing the sounds around us. The figure also shows legs that support the human body.

Now, let us look at the internal organs given. From the top, brain is located inside the head that controls the nervous system of our body. In the middle, a pair of lungs breathes the air and also oxygenates the human body. Heart is located on the left, which pumps the blood around the entire human body. The diagram also shows arteries and veins. Arteries take the blood away from the heart to different organs of the body and the veins carry the blood from various parts of the body to the heart. Slightly below the heart, liver is located which stores glycogen and below that, stomach is shown that digests protein. In the left hand of the given picture, nerves are shown which conduct impulses from the brain.

◆ ◆ ◆

46. **The diagrams given below show changes that took place in Indigo Cottage from 1990 to 2010.**

   Summarize the information by selecting and reporting the main features, and make comparisons where relevant.

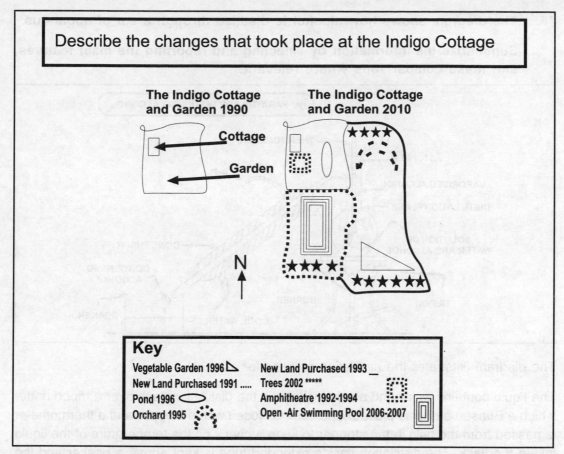

Describe the changes that took place at the Indigo Cottage

The Indigo Cottage and Garden 1990

The Indigo Cottage and Garden 2010

Cottage

Garden

N

Key

Vegetable Garden 1996 ◺　New Land Purchased 1993 —

New Land Purchased 1991 .....　Trees 2002 *****

Pond 1996 ⬭　Amphitheatre 1992-1994

Orchard 1995 ⌒　Open -Air Swimming Pool 2006-2007

The given diagrams depict a number of changes that took place at Indigo Cottage between 1990 and 2010.

The first and the major change happened in the expansion. Two adjacent plots were purchased in 1991 and 1993, respectively. The first plot was located to the southern side of the original plot and the second plot, which is almost of the size of the new plot, is located at the eastern border. Overall, the purchase increased the size of the original plot by four times.

Besides the expansion, an amphitheatre was added to the cottage from 1992 to 1994. In addition, the cottage also witnessed the planting of an orchard in the northern part. A pond was added to the garden in 1996 and in the same year a vegetable garden was also developed on the other side of the plot from the orchard. In 2002, few trees were planted along the southern edge of the garden. In 2006-07, an open air swimming pool was built in the land purchased in 1989.

In the end, it seems that the Indigo cottage was expanded and well-developed in the last two decades.

◆　◆　◆

48. **The diagram shows how alcohol is distilled through a set of apparatus.**

    Summarize the information by selecting and reporting the main features, and make comparisons where relevant.

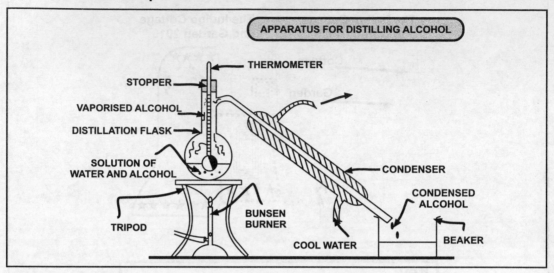

APPARATUS FOR DISTILLING ALCOHOL

THERMOMETER

STOPPER

VAPORISED ALCOHOL

DISTILLATION FLASK

SOLUTION OF WATER AND ALCOHOL

CONDENSER

CONDENSED ALCOHOL

TRIPOD

BUNSEN BURNER

COOL WATER

BEAKER

The diagram illustrates the distillation process for alcohol.

The liquid contains water and alcohol is kept in the distillation flask over a tripod under which a Bunsen burner is placed. The flask is closed with a stopper and a thermometer is passed from the hole in the stopper to keep a check on the temperature of the liquid inside the flask. The distillation flask's extended tube is kept above a beaker and the supply of cool water is arranged around the condenser in the tube that leads to the beaker.

Once the Bunsen burner is lit, it starts heating the liquid, which is a mixture of alcohol and water in the distillation flask. After sometime, because of the heat, the alcohol from the liquid starts evaporating and converts into vapour. The vapour then passes through the tube which is covered by a condenser. Here, the cool water converts the vapourised alcohol into liquid form. Finally, the condensed and pure form of alcohol gets collected in the beaker at the end.

◆ ◆ ◆

49. **The following diagram shows how electricity can be generated from tidal flow.**

    Summarize the information by selecting and reporting the main features, and make comparisons where relevant.

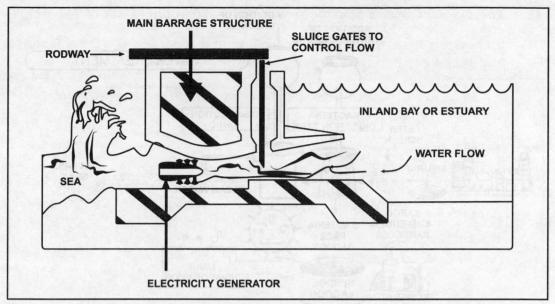

The given picture illustrates the method of generating electricity from the waves of sea.

The main barrage structure is first created under a roadway. Under the main barrage structure, a gap is created where an electricity generator is placed just above the base. The generator meets the tides in the hollow gap between the main barrage structure and its base.

When the sea waves start hitting the shore, the electricity generator converts that energy provided by the tides into power and the same can be transferred ahead. Here, Sluice Gates are also seen, which are created along with the main barrage structure and they separate the structure from the inland bay or estuary. However, at times, when the flow and force of sea waves increases, to protect the water from getting into inland bay, Sluice gates are also created. They close immediately in a situation where the water flow needs to be controlled.

◆ ◆ ◆

50. **The diagram shows how liquid domestic and industrial waste is recycled in a European Country.**

   Summarize the information by selecting and reporting the main features, and make comparisons where relevant.

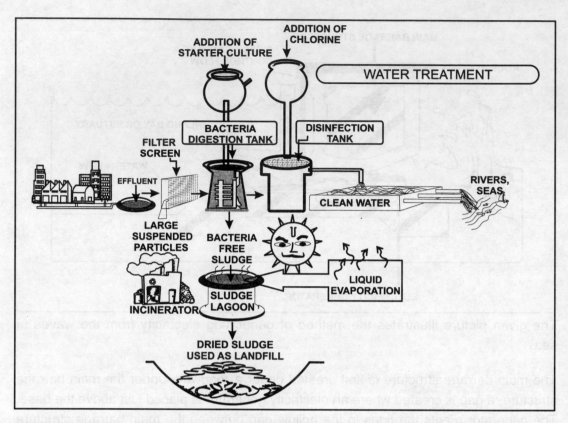

The given picture shows how the domestic and industrial garbage in liquid form is recycled in a European Country.

The collected liquid is known as effluent, which is passed through a filter screen first. Here, the large suspended particles are separated and are sent to incinerator. The remaining liquid is then transferred to the digestion tank where bacteria starter culture is added to the liquid to remove micro organisms.

The bacteria free sludge is them dried in the sunlight in the sludge lagoon. After that, the dried sludge is used as a landfill and buried in the designated landfill site.

The remains in the bacteria digestion tank are transferred to the disinfection tank. Here, the liquid is disinfected with the help of chlorine and then the clean, disinfected water is released in rivers or seas.

Finally, the process shows that the added solid and semisolid waste is taken out of the water and the cleaned water is then given back to the source, i.e. rivers and oceans.

◆ ◆ ◆

Section 2

General Training Task 1

This section contains:

- ### 7 step improvement course to get a high band score in General Training Writing Task 1

- ### Structure of a high band answer

- ### 5 points to follow when you write General Training Writing Task 1

- ### What you should do and what you should avoid in General Training Writing Task 1

- ### 50+ sample answers of IELTS General Training Writing Task 1

---

7 step improvement course to get a high band score in General Training Writing -Task 1

Step 1 ➤ Introduction to General Training Writing Task 1

The General Training writing task 1 asks the candidates to write a letter in about 20 minutes. Candidates must write at least 150 words.

We should also understand the structure of the letter topic that is asked in exam.

In IELTS General Training Task 1, the question provides the reason why the candidate is writing the letter, the person to address the letter to, and three specific points that have to be mentioned in the letter. To answer part 1 effectively, and achieve a high band score, candidates should make sure that they include the following points in their answer.

1.   Use the correct register (tone) of the language and correct letter format.

2.   Cover all three points given in the letter topic.

Step 2 ➤ Types of letter topics

The letter topics can be classified in two categories; formal and informal.

What is a formal letter?

In the context of IELTS, a formal letter is the one that you write to an unknown person, or someone who is at a higher or respectable position than you or who is elder to you and is not your family member or neighbour.

What is an informal letter?

In the context of IELTS, informal letters are the one that you write to someone whom you know personally like your friend, family member, neighbour, classmate or colleague/ co-worker.

What is the difference between a formal letter and an informal letter?

Formal letter	Informal letter
No contractions, see the examples below	**Contractions should be used; see the examples below**
I am, I will, I would, You are, He is	I'm, I'll, I'd, You're, He's

The Ultimate Guide To IELTS Writing

Usage of more passive expressions, see the examples below	Usage of more active expressions, see the examples below
Your response will be highly appreciated, It would be great if all the details are provided to us.	I will be happy to have your reply on that. I need some more details.
More usage of expressions that contains modals	**More usage of expressions with verb**
I would like to attend the orientation session.	I'll meet you before I'll leave for the meeting.
I would appreciate	I want
I look forward to receiving your reply	Hope to hear from you soon

Step 3 ➜ Structure of response that can get a high band score

Salutation	Dear Sir (formal) Dear Friend/Hi/Hello Steve (informal)
Paragraph 1	Reason for writing letter + elaborate the first bullet point given in the question. (Please note that some question may ask you to introduce yourself first, in that case, you should write the reason of writing letter at the end of the first paragraph or in the beginning of the second paragraph.)
Paragraph 2	Elaborate the second bullet point given in the question
Paragraph 3	Elaborate the third bullet point given in the question
Closing Line	If you want the recipient /addressee of the letter to take some actions after reading the letter, you should use the following closing lines:- I look forward to hearing from you. I look forward to receiving your response on it. (Formal)Hope to see you soon. Hope to hear from you soon. Can't wait to receive your reply. (informal)
Salutation	If your letter begins with 'Dear Sir' or 'Dear Madam', the salutation at the end must be 'Yours faithfully...' and if your letter begins with Dear Mr. Smith (name of the recipient/addressee of the letter) the salutation at the end must be 'Yours sincerely'.
Name	Writing xyz is a bit artificial according to me, you should write your name at the end.

Step ➤ 4 Learn to express different feelings in the letter.

The letter may ask you to fulfil a specific purpose of the letter. The purpose can be making a complain, sending a request, asking or providing information, giving a feedback, inviting someone or accepting invitation, applying for a job and so on

I would like to give you some useful expressions that can help you in expressing different kinds of feelings in the letter and can help you in fulfilling the purpose of the letter.

Dissatisfaction/dislike

Formal	Informal
I am dissatisfied from...	I wasn't satisfied from...
I am unhappy about...	I'm unhappy with...
This is not expected from a reputed restaurant like yours.	I didn't expect such a bad response from you.
I am writing to express my dissatisfaction about...	I'm writing this to tell you that I am not satisfied.
This does not suit me	I don't think this suits me

Satisfaction/happiness

Formal	Informal
I am delighted about...	I'm very happy to know that...
Your work was very impressive Your work has really impressed me a lot	I enjoyed going through your work
I am extremely elated to...	I'm really happy to...

Giving suggestions

Formal	Informal
Could I suggest that you should hire professionally trained staff in your organisation...	I feel you must hire well-trained employees
It would be really great if you could improve the quality of your services	You should try to give better services.
I would appreciate if you provide the latest facilities	The facilities are out of date
Please avoid doing....	You should give up ...

Making a Request

Formal	Informal
I would like to receive detailed information on…	Please send me detailed information on…
I am very interested to reserve a place in….	I'm keen on booking a seat for...
I would recommend that you bring that letter with you	Please bring that letter with you

Expressing gratitude/being thankful

Formal	Informal
Thank you very much for…	I'm thankful to you for…
I would be grateful to you if you…	I'll be thankful if you
……. is highly appreciated	I appreciate that…

Making an apology

Formal	Informal
I regret that...	I'm sorry that...
Please pardon me for...	I feel sorry for...
Please accept my apologies for …	I apologise for…

Expressing requirements/needs/wants

Formal	Informal
I would very much like to...	I want to...
What I am looking for is...	I'm looking for...
What would suit me best is...	I think this suits me best

Expressing annoyance/anger

Formal	Informal
Even though you were instructed that...	I instructed you very clearly about
Despite the fact that I ordered something else...	Why have you sent me what I didn't order…

Step 5 → How to begin the letter?

As I said earlier, it is important for you to write the reason for writing the letter. You should begin the letter with the reason for writing the letter. However, if you are asked to introduce yourself, you should add the reason of writing the letter after your introduction.

There are some starting lines that you may use to get a higher band score in letter writing.

Formal
I am writing this letter to express my dissatisfaction about…
I am writing this letter to draw your immediate attention to…
This letter has been written to express my deep grievances on…
I am sending this application for the post of…
I am writing this letter in connection with…
I trust this letter finds you in the best of your health and spirit.
I am sending this letter to complain about…

Informal
I hope this letter finds you in the pink of your health.
Hey, I hope you are cool...
I hope you are great and enjoying your time there.
I'm glad to hear from you.
It's nice to learn that you're…

Step 6 → Follow the '3-point rule'

The 3-point rule says that if you have to complain, add maximum three aspects or points, and describe them accordingly. For example :-

You went to a supermarket to buy something. However, when you came home, you found that they charged for certain items that you did not buy.

Write a letter to the supermarket manager. In your letter,

- **where and when you went there**

- **what items you did not by**

- **what you expect them to do**

Here, in the second point, you may write only one item or you can go up to maximum 3 items. Some students write a long list of items so that they can write more words and can reach to 150 word mark soon. But, such a tendency in letter writing will not get good bands to those candidates.

If you are asked to complain about the services of a hotel or a company, again, add maximum of 3 points and describe them properly.

If you are asked to give suggestions to someone or a company, do not write more than 3 suggestions.

Step 7 ➜ Writing the letter in appropriate tone

Maintain a proper tone in the letter is very important for all the candidates. Some candidates make the mistake of being too polite in a complain letter or they become too aggressive in the same.

For example, if you are asked write a complain to the local council regarding the problem of garbage or litter in your area, your tone should not be too polite or too offensive:

"I would really be happy if the councillor takes some keen interest in this problem and obliges us by solving the same at his earliest convenience."

The language in the paragraph above is too polite, which is not appropriate for the situation.

"The councillor should know the problems of the people of his area. If our problem will not be solved in three days, we will march towards the office of local council and we will not let any government vehicle pass through the roads in our locality."

The language in the paragraph above is too aggressive, which is also inappropriate for the situation.

Rather, you should write:

"I strongly assert that this problem must be addressed at the earliest. I am also sending a copy of this letter to the local newspapers.

◆ ◆ ◆

5 points to follow when you write General Training Writing Task 1

Point 1 ➤ Preparation (2-3 minutes)

Read the situation of the letter carefully. If required read it twice. Also, go through all the bullet points given.

Decide whether you should write formal or informal language.

Decide the purpose of the letter i.e. request, complain, job application, giving or asking for suggestions or information.

Point 2 ➤

Look at the three bullet points and prepare points on each of them so that you can elaborate them in your writing.

Point 3 ➤

Make a list of useful expressions and words that you can use in the letter. This list should be based in the tone of the language required and the purpose of the letter.

The first three points should be completed in 3-4 minutes.

Point 4 ➤ Start writing the letter (14-15 minutes)

When you have already invested a few minutes and worked on the graph, you should not find any difficulty in writing the response. As per my experience, 15 minutes are more than sufficient.

While writing, you should also keep the word count in mind. You should count the number of words that you write for the first 2-3 lines and then take an average of the words written per line. For example, if you have written 25 words in 3 lines, it means your average word per line is 8 and you should write 20-22 lines in total in the response. I suggest you to download a sample of IELTS Writing answer sheet from   [http://www.ielts.org/PDF/114184_IELTS_Writing_Answer_Sheet.pdf] and use that to write your responses so that you will never have to waste your time in counting words per line in your actual exam.

Point 5 ➤ Editing (2 – 3 minutes)

Check your response for any errors in spelling or grammar. If you have repeated any word, you should replace that with a synonym.

What you should do and what you must avoid when you are writing General Training Task 1

You should do the following:

- Use appropriate tone of the language according to the demand of the letter i.e. you should use informal language when you are writing a letter to your friend and you should use formal language when you are writing a letter to an unknown person.

- Use three paragraphs and give equal weight to all the three bullet points in the question given. It is not advisable for you to write two paragraphs for the first bullet point and cover the next two bullet points in the remaining paragraph.

- If you want a high band score (6 or more) please try to use complex sentences in your letter.

- You should use linking words and connectors to link your information logically. (A list of such words is given in section 4 of this book)

- Always try to use expressions given in the preceding section of the book.

You must avoid the following.

- Please do not write unnecessary words in the letter. Also, please do not add anything which is not demanded in the letter. For example, some people have a tendency that first they ask about the health of the addressee and his/her family and other formal questions and then in the second paragraph they come to the point.

- Please do not copy the printed introduction that is given with the task in the question paper.

- Please write logically. Some candidates do not write logical points and they can lose marks for that. For example, I read a response written by a candidate which went like this; "I am eagerly waiting for you to come to India. When you come, you can stay at my home or if you wish, you can go to a hotel. I know a hotel here in Manali (Manali is a hill station in India), which has sea facing rooms." Now, it is obvious that you cannot see an ocean when you are staying at a hotel in a hill station.

- There is no need to write any address (neither the sender's address nor the receiver's address) in the letter.

- There is no need to write a subject in the letter.

- There is no need to write the date of writing the letter above the body of the letter. However, if the topic demands, you may add the date in the body of the letter.

50+ sample answers of IELTS General Training Task 1
Formal Letters
1. Complaint (13)

1. **You went to appear for an interview to another city by train. The train departed late from the station and you could not reach in time.**

   Write a letter to the railway officer of your city. In your letter

   - **when you travelled and why the train departed late**

   - **what happened as a result**

   - **how you feel about the problem**

Dear Sir,

I am writing this letter to complain about a serious delay created at the local railway station, which has cost me my new job. Last Sunday (25.10.11), I went to Mumbai by National Express to appear for a final stage interview. However, there was a small dispute between railway staff and the management at the time of departure. The staff went on an immediate strike which was called off only after six hours. Owing to this, I was late by seven hours when I reached Mumbai.

I was one of the two candidates to be interviewed for the job. As I reached late, I was informed that the other candidate was appointed. I tried hard to explain the problem to the authorities but the management's decision remained unchanged.

I feel frustrated as my career has been ruined. It is really pathetic to lose an awesome opportunity because of such a silly reason. I feel that all those involved in the delay should be penalized so that they understand their job responsibilities. I am sending a copy of this letter to the Railway Ministry and local newspapers.

I hope this letter will awaken the management to serve the community in a better way.

Yours faithfully,

Parthesh Thakkar

♦ ♦ ♦

2. **You are disturbed by the rubbish and litter problem in your area and street.**

Write a letter to the local council. In your letter

- **describe the situation**

- **inform them about the possible consequences**

- **give some suggestions to solve the problem**

Dear Sir,

My name is Parthesh Thakkar. I live in apartment no 27, Smith Street. I am writing this letter to complain about the garbage problem in my street. There is a public garden near the street which is visited by all sorts of people. They often throw litter there and this waste is then brought to the garbage bin of our street. In this process, some litter spreads to the nearby area also. To make matters worse, the council's rubbish collection van comes only twice a week.

This collected waste attracts numerous insects and rodents, which are a great threat to our health. Moreover, the rubbish spreads a foul odour in air, which disturbs us endlessly.

I think the council should keep an extra garbage bin near the garden so that the litter does not spread across our street. Next, the collection of rubbish should be done daily. I strongly assert that this problem must be addressed at the earliest. I am also sending a copy of this letter to the local newspapers.

Yours faithfully,

Parthesh Thakkar

◆ ◆ ◆

3. **You did a one day course in a local college but you are unhappy about it.**

Write a letter to the principal of the college. In your letter

- **details about the course**

- **why you are unhappy**

- **give some suggestions**

Dear Sir,

I am writing this letter to express my dissatisfaction with the one day computer course which I attended at your college last week. It was a 6 hour crash course organized for those who wanted to know about Microsoft Office programs.

I regret to say it but the course did not meet my expectations regarding three major aspects. First, it started about 45 minutes late and this time was not compensated for at the end. As a result, we had to sacrifice certain parts of the course. Second, the computers were very slow. The start up took at least 3-4 minutes then loading the programs on screen took more time. Last, the version of Microsoft Office used was very old. Now, 2010 version is readily available in the market but we got the 2000 version to learn with.

I think it would be better if you update the computers and the version of the program before you start the next batch. This will give some value for the money to the students who pay you for the course.

Yours Sincerely,

Parthesh Thakkar

♦ ♦ ♦

4. **You gave a renovation contract of your home to a builder but you are dissatisfied with the builder's work.**

   Write a letter to the builder. In your letter

   - **about the things the builder has not done well**

   - **the problems you are facing as a result**

   - **what you want the builder to do now**

Dear Mr. Mehta,

I was surprised to know that you have completed the renovation of my home earlier than your stated commitment. Yesterday, I checked the house, but, I must say I am highly disappointed with the work. First, the wall-paint of the living room is not done properly. Anyone can make out differences in the colour concentration on various spots of all walls. Second, the new tap of the lavatory is leaking. It seems that it is a defective piece.

Now, if I start to live the house, the awkward, variable texture of drawing room paint shall not give a soothing effect and is aesthetically disturbing. Next, the leaking tap of lavatory makes it impossible to use it. It also wastes a lot of water. Hence, I would not prefer to live in the house.

I strongly feel that you should rectify both these problems as early as possible so that I can release your remaining payment. I can extend the contract for 4 more days. I hope this time is sufficient for you to complete the work.

I look forward to hearing from you.

Yours Sincerely,

Parthesh Thakkar

◆ ◆ ◆

5. **You are a university student who lives in an accommodation on the campus. One day you find something wrong with your accommodation.**

    Write a letter to the Housing Officer. In your letter

    - **explain him/her what happened**

    - **why you think it has happened**

    - **what you have decided to do**

Dear Sir,

My name is Parthesh Thakkar. I live in room no. 11 in the university hostel. I am writing this letter to inform you about a problem of the locker. I have been living in the room for 2 months and using the locker since the beginning. However, yesterday, I found that the door of my locker was open. I immediately checked my possessions. Fortunately, nothing was stolen.

I think some notorious students might have damaged my locker because, in our hostel, a group of senior students often harasses juniors. This act appears to be a part of their mischievousness.

Now, I have decided to get the locker repaired and to put an extra lock on it so that I can ensure the safety of my money and personal possessions. I would like to know whether I can get the locker repaired individually or not and if I am allowed to put an extra lock on it. I request you to give me a speedy response because presently I am using my room partner's locker as my locker is broken.

I am waiting for your early and favourable reply.

Yours Faithfully,

Parthesh Thakkar

◆ ◆ ◆

---

6. You have ordered a book by post. Yet you have not received the book. Write a letter to the bookshop manager. In your letter

- give details of your order

- why you need that book urgently

- what you want them to do now

Dear Sir,

I am writing this letter regarding the book which I ordered last month. The title of the book is 'The ultimate guide to IELTS Writing'. I placed the order online and I also paid the price through my credit card. My order confirmation number is 00113PT07. I was promised that I would get the book within 15 days by post.

However, to my disappointment, I have not received the book even after 25 days of the order. I am going to take the IELTS next month and it is extremely important for me to start preparing from the book as early as possible.

I anticipate a prompt reply from you regarding the availability of the book. I want dispatch details if it is the case or I want information whether you are out of stock, so that I can get the book from another bookshop. I must say that I am disheartened with the delay from such a reputed bookseller as you.

I look forward to hearing from you.

Yours Faithfully,

Parthesh Thakkar

◆ ◆ ◆

7. You have recently shifted in a rental apartment with your family. However, there are some problems with the apartment.

Write a letter to the landlord. In your letter

- describe the problem

- demand the solution for the problem

- inform him what you will do if the problem is not solved

Dear Sir,

My name is Parthesh Thakkar. I have shifted into your apartment as a tenant only 4 days back. I am writing this letter to draw your immediate attention to two serious problems.

First, the heating system is not working properly. Owing to this, we had to get an additional room heater to protect ourselves from the cold. Second, the glass of the living room window is broken, which presents a risk of injury and increased chances of break-in because the apartment is usually unattended in the afternoon hours.

When I came to see the apartment, I was promised a hassle free accommodation. However, so far, this has not happened. Now, I insist that both problems should be addressed by you within the next 3-4 days. I can lend you the keys of the apartment if you want to send a repairman in the afternoon.

I am highly disappointed and disturbed because of these problems. And if these problems still persist, I will have to demand a refund of the deposit that I had paid you and shift to new premises.

I look forward to hearing from you.

Yours sincerely,

Parthesh Thakkar.

◆ ◆ ◆

8.   **You have rented a car for few days from an agency. However, there are some problems with the car.**

Write to the agency officer and complain about the rented car. In your letter

-    **tell him/her the problems of the car**

-    **what you want the agency to do now**

-    **how you feel about the problem**

Dear Sir,

Three days before I hired a Ford Icon (booking no PT1100) from your company. When I took the delivery of the car, I was assured of adequate performance of the vehicle. However, this has not come to be. Since the first day, the car has been showing some starting trouble. I thought I could manage with this issue but the car did not start today morning even after vigorous efforts.

Presently, the car is in the parking lot of my hotel. I think it needs to be towed away to a repair station. Now, I want a refund of my advance fare which I had paid you at the time of booking and, today, I had to hire a taxi to complete my work. So, I also want a compensation of $50.

This incidence has shaken my confidence in your company. It is really a pity for a reputed organization like yours to hand over a faulty vehicle. Is it not possible for you to get the vehicles tested properly before delivering them to the customers? I shall not hire your services again unless I get a proper explanation for this problem.

Yours sincerely,

Parthesh Thakkar

♦ ♦ ♦

9.   **You live in a room in college which you share with another student. You find it very difficult to work there because he or she always has friends visiting. They have parties in the room and sometimes borrow your things without asking you.**

Write a letter to the Accommodation officer of the college. In your letter

- **explain your problem**

- **ask for a new room for the next term**

- **request for some alternative arrangements immediately as your exams are starting next month**

Dear Sir,

My name is Parthesh Thakkar. I live in room no 11 in university hostel. I am writing this letter to draw your immediate attention to the problems created by my inconsiderate room partner, "James Bach". He always comes in the room with a group of friends. They all talk aloud and often they play loud music. At times, they arrange dance parties and they use my cupboard and other stuff without my consent.

Now, it is next to impossible for me to study in my room because I am always disturbed by the nuisance created by James and his friends. I put forward a strong request to you to change my room starting next term.

However, my difficulties do not get over with this. I am going to take my exams next month. I am under a lot of stress because I have not been able to study thoroughly. Hence, I need your kind permission to shift in my friend Steve's room (No 20) till I complete writing my exams. I do need a favour because it is a question of my academic career.

I am waiting for your positive and prompt reply.

Yours sincerely,

Parthesh Thakkar

♦ ♦ ♦

10   You read an advertisement about in the local newspaper about a discount sale at a particular shop. However, when you went to buy the goods you wanted, you found the sale had ended.

Write to the shop manager. In your letter

-       inform him/her where and when you went to the shop

-       what you felt when you came to know that the sale had ended

-       demand compensation for the goods that you wanted to buy

Dear Sir,

I am writing this letter to express my dissatisfaction with your shop. I saw an advertisement in the newspaper announcing a discount sale for laptops. The advert clearly mentioned that the sale is on till the 25th of this month. I went there on 24th afternoon to buy a laptop because the model I was looking for was on offer at an attractive rate.

However, to my frustration, I was informed that you had closed the sale earlier. I also asked for the reason but I received a careless answer that it was a management decision. I was really shocked to hear that. On top of it, I was given a fresh quotation of the laptops at market rates.

I think it is an unfair trade practice to quote low prices in an advert and then close the sale earlier than announced. I am enclosing a copy of your ad, the quotation given by your executive and my contact details. If I do not get the laptop at discounted rates, I will have to litigate you to get the product I want.

I look forward to hearing from you.

Yours faithfully,

Parthesh Thakkar

◆ ◆ ◆

11.   You have recently come back from an overseas holiday. You faced some problems with the hotel booked through your travel agent.

Write a letter to your travel agent. In your letter

-       details about hotel booking

-       problems that you faced there

-       give suggestions to the travel agent so that such problems are not repeated

Dear Sir,

I have recently come back from a tour of Australia through your travel company. I am writing to inform you that I faced some problems with the hotel in Sydney. I booked a four-day package in which a deluxe room was offered with breakfast and two meals a day.

However, when I reached there, I was given a mediocre room which did not have the facilities of a standard room. On top of it, I was charged extra for the meals they provided. When I sought a clarification, I did not get a satisfactory answer.

I think it appears that the hotel management masked some information in order to earn more from the customers. I strongly assert that being a reputed travel agent, you must clarify all the services, facilities and charges with your associate hotels so that you can provide optimum satisfaction to your clients. I am enclosing the bills of the hotel for your reference. I expect that you will compensate all the extra costs that I have incurred in Australia.

I look forward to hearing from you.

Yours sincerely,

Parthesh Thakkar

◆ ◆ ◆

12. **You and some friends had dinner in a restaurant a few nights ago. The service at the restaurant was terrible and the food was bad. You and two of your friends had severe stomachaches the following day. The food was also overpriced.**

Write to the manager of the restaurant . In your letter

- **explain these problems**

- **give details that you think are relevant**

- **ask the manager to do something about the situation**

Dear Sir,

My friends and I had a dinner at your restaurant on last Sunday. I am writing to you to complain about the food and the service.

The first problem was that, during and after our meal the service was bad. The waiter who delivered soup to my best friend had his thumb in it. Another waiter spilt some curry on my friend's lap and did not even care to apologize. In general, waiters were inconsiderate and the service was pathetic.

Finally, even though the reputation of your restaurant is good, the food was mediocre.

The sweet corn soup was very sour. The vegetables were overcooked and the dessert was stale. The food was definitely not good for the price. Also, I think some of the food was bad because two of my friends and I had stomachache the day after.

I strongly feel that we ought to be compensated. I expect you to refund the cost of our meal. A copy of the bill is attached here.

I look forward to hearing from you.

Yours faithfully,

Parthesh Thakkar

♦ ♦ ♦

13. **You recently stayed in a hotel in a large city. The weather was very unusual for the time of the year and the heating/cooling system in the hotel was quite inadequate.**

Write a letter to the manager of the hotel. In your letter
- **give details of what was wrong**
- **explain what you had to do to overcome the problem at that time**
- **say what action you would like the manager to take.**

Dear Sir,

My name is Parthesh Thakkar. I have just returned home after spending three nights at your hotel in Mumbai. My bill number is 1155. The staff members were friendly and cooperative and the location was very convenient. However, I feel I must express my disappointment about the room.

As we all know, Mumbai is experiencing a very warm summer this year, with temperatures around 40+° C last week, which is quite unusual. Because of this, it was very hot and humid in my room. On top of it, the air conditioning system was not working properly.

Because of the extreme heat, I had to keep the windows open and hence it was very noisy, as the hotel is on a main road. Consequently, I got very little sleep over those three days.

I think it would be a good idea to check the cooling systems regularly and appoint a full time technician to look after them. This would make your hotel more comfortable. Perhaps, you would consider giving me a discount if I come to your hotel once again.

I look forward to hearing from you.

Yours faithfully,

Parthesh Thakkar

♦ ♦ ♦

2. Request (7)

1.   You go to a gym to carry out exercise everyday. One day, you have forgotten your bag in the gym and the gym management has announced that they would keep the gym closed for a week for some renovation work. You need your bag as it has some important things in it.

Write a letter to the manager of the gym. In your letter

-   introduce yourself and describe your problem

-   give a description of your bag

-   tell them what you want them to do

Dear Sir,

My name is Parthesh Thakkar, I am a lifetime member of the gym (membership no PT 111). I am writing this letter to seek your urgent assistance as I have forgotten my office bag in the gym. I come to the gym every morning at 6 am and leave at 7 am. However, today, I was running a little late and in the rush, I forgot to take my bag from the locker.

My bag is a black attaché. It contains my office papers and along with them it also contains some essential documents like my driving license and passport. It also has my name written on the label, which is visible from the front.

Since the gym is going to remain closed for a week for renovation, I cannot enter the premises. However, I need to get my bag and hence I am requesting you to permit me to enter the premises or let one of your assistants go inside and get the bag for me. I am confident that you would surely cooperate with me in this matter.

I look forward to hearing from you.

Yours faithfully,

Parthesh Thakkar

◆ ◆ ◆

2.   You have booked a hotel. For some reasons you need to change the booking dates and details.

Write a letter to the manager of hotel for the same. In your letter
-   give details for the booking which you have made
-   inform changes that you want with your booking
-   state reasons for the changes.

Dear Manager,

My name is Parthesh Thakkar. I have booked one single-bed room in your hotel from 20th to 25th November 2005 for a conference that I am going to attend in your city. My booking reference no. is 11022PT. I am writing this letter to make some changes in the booking.

Firstly, the dates. I would like to extend the booking for two more days that is to the 27th November as the schedule of the conference that I will be attending is changed. It will now continue till 27th November.

Secondly, I would prefer to have a suite, as I will be coming with two of my subordinates because my company has decided to send my junior teammates with me as a part of their learning experience.

I request you to make the above-mentioned changes in my booking. I would be grateful to you if you acknowledge the said changes so that I can confirm the details with my director and teammates.

I look forward to hearing from you.

Yours faithfully,

Parthesh Thakkar

♦ ♦ ♦

3.   **You have just returned home after living with a family in an English speaking country. You now realize that you have forgotten a small bag of personal possessions in your room.**

   Write to the head of the family. In your letter

-    **describe the things you left behind**

-    **ask them to send some or all of them to you**

-    **offer to cover costs.**

Dear Mr. Thomas,

Hello, I trust this letter finds you in the best of your health and spirit. I am writing this letter to inform you about my bag which I have forgotten in my room. The bag contains some documents that I had prepared there as a part of my study assignment. It also contains some music CDs, photographs and some gift packs.

I request you to kindly send those things to me on my mailing address. I am in great need of documents and I do need photos as well. You can send them by courier or give it to a friend of mine who is coming back next week. He will approach you and collect the bag from you.

The Ultimate Guide To IELTS Writing

I would be grateful if you send the things to me at the earliest because I cannot proceed with my project without the documents. Lastly, please let me know the cost incurred with a courier, if that is the case, so that I can pay the same to you. I regret the inconvenience I am causing you.

I hope to get my stuff back at the earliest. Thank you so much.

Yours sincerely,

Parthesh Thakkar

♦ ♦ ♦

4. **You stayed in a hotel for some days in an overseas country. You have forgotten some things in the hotel room after checkout.**

Write a letter to the hotel manager. In your letter

- **inform him about your stay**

- **describe the things that you have forgotten there**

- **state what you want them to do now**

Dear Sir,

My name is Parthesh Thakkar. I stayed in your hotel from the 25th to the 28th of last month in room no 203. I really enjoyed your hospitality. In fact, I have recommended your hotel to many of my friends and colleagues.

However, I am writing this letter to inform you that I have forgotten a small pouch in which I kept a digital camera, a photo album and some audio CDs in your hotel at the time of checkout. I came to know this when I reached at the airport. I immediately called back the hotel and confirmed with Mr. Mark (manager) about my pouch but I could not come back to collect it because I was short of time.

Now, I request you to keep the pouch with you because I am going to visit your city again, next month, for a business project. I will collect my pouch from your hotel at that time. This will give me an opportunity to stay in your hotel again.

I expect your cooperation in this matter.

Yours sincerely,

Parthesh Thakkar.

♦ ♦ ♦

---

5. Your company sent you to USA for further training. You stayed for the decided time but you want to stay there for more time.

    Write a letter to the company manager. In your letter

-   what you have done during the training period

-   what benefits you have received from the training

-   why you want to overstay there

Dear Sir,

I am writing this letter to put forward a request to you for an extension of my stay here in the USA. You will be pleased to know that I have completed in-house training with 95% success. I have received a special complement in writing from my trainer for my performance.

I am grateful to the company management for sending me to the USA. I have learned many innovative strategies from the "Supply Chain Management" course right from inventory management to the retail dispatch of products. I am eager to apply new techniques for the benefit of our company.

However, I could not complete the 15 day on-field training owing to extreme weather conditions. This is the reason I need your permission to overstay here and complete the training for two reasons. First, it is necessary to observe how the strategies are applied. Second, the company will not issue us a certificate of training until I complete it.

I look forward to hearing from you.

Yours sincerely,

Parthesh Thakkar

♦ ♦ ♦

6. You want to study a course in a local college. You already wrote a letter about the same to the principal of the college but you have not yet received any reply to your letter.

    Write a letter to the principal. In your letter

-   details of the course

-   why you want to study in that college only

-   request him/her to give an early reply

Dear Sir,

I am writing this letter to seek details about the management courses. I want to acquire a post graduate diploma in marketing management because I have an in-borne interest in the field of marketing. I had already written a letter about the same, but, unfortunately, I have not received any details of the course.

I am keen to study at your esteemed institution because it is a reputed and renowned college in the field of management courses. It also possesses an impressive record of lucrative campus placements. On top of it, a cousin of mine completed the same course in your college five years ago, and she has motivated me to make sure that I study at your academic institute.

Lastly, I know that the new batch is going to start from next month. In this case, if I do not get the course catalogue, I may not be able to apply for the admission, which could ruin my dream of acquiring an education at your institution. Hence, I again request you to send me the details of the marketing management course at the earliest.

I look forward to hearing from you.

Yours sincerely,

Parthesh Thakkar.

◆ ◆ ◆

7.   **You are going to study a short-term course at a university in New Zealand.**

    Write a letter to the accommodation officer of the university. In your letter

-    **introduce yourself**

-    **describe the type of accommodation you want**

-    **inform the length of your stay and ask for the cost of accommodation**

Dear Sir,

I am a 27-year-old pharmacist from Gujarat state in the Republic of India, and I have been accepted to take a one-month training course at Auckland University College starting next January.

I would be grateful if you could either find me accommodation for the month or give me a list of addresses that I could write to. I would like, if possible, to have a room in a family house because I would like to have the chance to practice my English at the same time. I will need a room with a bed and a table so that I can study there as well. I would prefer to live near the college since I will be in Auckland for a short time and will not have time to learn my way around.

I will need the accommodation for five weeks from 28th December to the 3rd February, as I would like to arrive a few days before the course begins.

Could you also please tell me how much an accommodation of this kind will cost and whether the price quoted includes meals?

I look forward to hearing from you.

Yours sincerely,

Parthesh Thakkar

◆ ◆ ◆

3. Applying for a job (3)

1. **You recently saw an advertisement in a local newspaper regarding some vacancies in a local departmental store / supermarket.**

   Write to the recruiting officer. In your letter
   - **the post for which you are applying**
   - **give details about your experience**
   - **why you want to get this job**

Dear Sir,

I am writing this letter to apply for the post of a customer care executive in your supermarket. I saw your advert in yesterday's newspaper indicating that you have two vacancies for the said post.

I completed my graduation in management with distinction 2 years ago and since then I have been working in a departmental store. I have handled all types of work in customer care in my present organization and I have received regular incentives for my work performance.

I have a keen interest in retail sector because it is one of the fastest growing sectors of our country, which offers handsome growth opportunities to individuals and organizations. In addition, I can also work more hours for your supermarket because I live nearby. Finally, I am confident that I would be able to provide a constructive contribution to your supermarket.

I look forward to hearing from you.

Yours Sincerely,

Parthesh Thakkar

◆ ◆ ◆

2. **An organization has given an advertisement for a part time volunteer job for local children.**

   Write a letter to the administrator of the organization. In your letter

   - **introduce yourself**

   - **why you think you are suitable for the job**

   - **state when you will be able to join that job**

Dear Sir,

My name is Parthesh Thakkar. I am a graduate in social welfare with more than 15 years of experience. Presently I am working for an NGO for the development of rural children and their education. I read your advertisement about the requirement of a part time volunteer in yesterday's newspaper. I am writing this letter to express my interest for the same.

I think I am suitable for your organization as firstly, I have an in-borne interest to do something for children. And, second, I have desired qualifications and experience in the same area, which will enable me to contribute creatively.

However, I will be able to join you next month because I am going for an overseas assignment next Monday, which will last for 25 days. I will be privileged to offer my services to your organization and the needy children of our town. I would appreciate a positive response before I leave for my assignment.

I look forward to hearing from you.

Yours Faithfully,

Parthesh Thakkar

◆ ◆ ◆

3. **You read an advertisement from a club of your area which wants to help old people.**

   Write a letter to the club administrator. In your letter

   - **why you want to help**

   - **write about your experience**

   - **explain how you can help**

Dear Sir,

I am writing this letter in response to your advertisement in the June issue of your magazine, "The Social" about helping the elderly people of our city. Many old people in our city are suffering from numerous problems. I want to help them so that they can have a reason to smile in the last phase of their life.

I have already worked for five years as a part time volunteer for an NGO which runs two old age homes. I used to go there for 2-3 hours a day on weekdays and 5-6 hours a day, on weekends. I have offered assistance in collecting funds via donations and charity. I have also helped them in resolving some medical issues.

I think I would be able to offer my services as a medical adviser because I am a pharmacist. I would also like to help them in developing some regular exercise regime, which can keep them fit and healthy. I am also keen to attract some donations from my corporate contacts for the organization.

I hope to get an opportunity to help the elderly people of our city.

Yours faithfully,

Parthesh Thakkar

◆ ◆ ◆

4. Asking or giving information/suggestions/feedback (13)

1.   **You recently saw a program on television. You would like to comment on the same.**

Write a letter to the satellite channel. In your letter
-   **introduce yourself and write the name of the program you are writing about**
-   **give your comments on the content and quality of the program**
-   **give suggestions about the program**

Dear Sir,

My name is Parthesh Thakkar. I am a regular viewer of your satellite channel. I am writing to comment on the program I saw on 21st October, Friday. The name of the program is 'The Great Indian Laughter Challenge'.

First of all, I am very thankful to you for telecasting such a unique program where comedy artists of our country come and perform on the TV stage. The performers were absolutely outstanding. I laughed a lot and I felt fresh after viewing this program.

However, there are two things, which, I think should be improved. Firstly, the judges: I do not doubt their ability but I believe that the evaluator should be experienced in the same field so that the selection of the winner can be well justified. Secondly, the time.

The program should be telecasted at 9-30 pm instead of 10-00 pm as the latter is relatively late.

Finally, I hail the endeavours of the people behind the making of this program. I wish this program to be a grand success. Lastly, I hope you will consider my suggestions and implement them.

Yours Sincerely,

Parthesh Thakkar

◆ ◆ ◆

2. **You regularly attend meetings where many people who belong to different countries take part. You have met people of a large number of countries and have had a wide experience of them.**

   Write a letter to the editor of a local newspaper. In your letter

- **why you attend such meetings**

- **what activities are being done in such meetings**

- **how this information can be useful to the people of your country**

Dear Sir,

I am writing this letter to introduce you to a unique forum where I regularly take part. I am studying in an Australian University, where there is an open discussion platform for foreign students created by the student union. I attend all the meetings regularly because I gain a lot of knowledge from it and it is extremely helpful to all overseas students in Australia.

The forum meets monthly at the university where all overseas students come to share their ideas and seek solutions for their problems. We also call some ex-students who are now settled in Australia who share their experiences of living and working in Australia. I have now compiled a good database on studying, living, working and settling in Australia.

I firmly believe that looking at the current rush towards Australia in our country, this information will be very useful to all the people who want to study and/or settle in Australia. I am sending an article for you to publish in your newspaper. Should you have any questions about the article, please contact me.

I look forward to reading the article in your newspaper.

Yours faithfully,

Parthesh Thakkar

◆ ◆ ◆

The Ultimate Guide To IELTS Writing

3.   **You have recently come back from an overseas holiday. An employee at the airport helped you when you were in trouble.**

     Write a letter to the airport manager. In your letter

-    **describe your problem**

-    **how the employee helped you**

-    **tell the manager to give a reward to that employee**

Dear Sir,

I am writing this letter to share a memorable experience I had at the Heathrow airport last month. I went to London by flight no BA 4459 on 25th of January this year. After landing at the airport, my bag didn't come out of the luggage counter on to the conveyor belt. I was really shocked as the bag was full with valuables.

However, to my better fortunes, Mr. Alex Mathew who was in-charge of the luggage section immediately came to my rescue. He took the description of the bag and started tracing it. His quick efforts became successful and I got my bag within 20 minutes of complaining.

I give full credit to Mr. Alex for resolving my problem. Had he not been prompt in attending to my complaint, I would not have got my bag. I did offer him some cash reward but he politely denied it. This incident has given rise to an idea in my mind that wouldn't it be inspiring for the airport staff to be rewarded for such good work by the management. I request you to reciprocate his good behaviour with some kind of a reward so that he keeps serving the travellers better.

Yours Sincerely,

Parthesh Thakkar.

♦ ♦ ♦

4.   **You live in Canada. In a magazine, they printed some information about your home country. However, there were some mistakes in that article.**

     Write a letter to the editor of the magazine. In your letter

-    **describe the mistake**

-    **give correct information about the same**

-    **give some more topics to them to publish**

Dear Sir,

I am writing this letter to you regarding the article published in the June 2012 issue of your magazine about "Gandhiji". I appreciate the endeavours of the authors but there was one mistake in the article. The article indicated a wrong birth date and birth place of "Gandhi", which I think should be corrected in the next series.

I am sending you some books written on "Gandhiji" for you to refer. Also, I am sending you a list of some useful websites and an English translation of the autobiography of Gandhiji, which will surely provide all the information you require.

Further, I think it would be a great idea to pay more attention to the principals of nonviolence and truthfulness as they were reintroduced by him to the world rather than focusing on the events that happened in his life. The material which I am sending you along with this letter will surely enable you to understand the philosophy of Mr. Gandhi. However, if you want to know more about him, I would be happy to offer my services to you.

I look forward to reading the next issue of your magazine.

Yours Faithfully,

Parthesh Thakkar.

♦ ♦ ♦

5.   **You live in the USA and your family has a spare room to rent out to a student.**

      Write a letter to the accommodation officer of the University of America. In your letter

-     **describe the room**

-     **describe the type of tenant you want**

-     **give information about your family and rent that you expect to charge**

Dear Sir,

I am writing this letter to inform you that I have a spare room in my house to let in a student. I live in a double storey house where the basement room is on offer for a tenant. The room is spacious; has all the facilities including a television and central heating. Also, it has a separate door so the student can have independence.

I prefer an overseas student preferably a female and from the Indian sub-continent so that she can easily befriend our family. Moreover, I would also prefer a graduate student because, I think they are more sincere and responsible. However, the latter is not a compulsory criterion.

I live with my wife and daughter. Presently, my wife lives at home to look after my daughter who is 2 years old. I am expecting a monthly rent of $500 which excludes the telephone bill (subject to the usage) and the cleaner charges which are $40 a month for the room.

I look forward to hearing from you.

Yours faithfully,

Parthesh Thakkar

♦ ♦ ♦

6.   **You live in a foreign country where a particular TV program about your country is being organized. You want to participate in that program.**

   Write a letter to the TV program organizer. In your program

-   **why you want to participate**

-   **what aspects about your country you want to cover in that program**

-   **at what time you will be available**

Dear Sir,

I am writing this letter to express my interest to participate in the program "Amazing India". I saw your advert on television indicating that you are going to start a series of programs on India. I think this is a good opportunity for me to introduce my home country to the people of Canada.

I am keen on providing useful information on yoga and meditation techniques which are being practiced in India for ages. I have lots of books and other reference material on these topics. I am confident that the information will be useful to all Canadians in improving their physical health. On top of it, these practices can lead to peace of mind, which is the ultimate goal of the humanity.

Presently, I am going back to India to conduct a seminar on latest meditative techniques in the 21st century. I will come back to Canada on the 11th of the next month. I will be pleased to open doors to the opulence of ancient Indian knowledge for all the viewers.

I look forward to hearing from you.

Yours faithfully,

Parthesh Thakkar.

♦ ♦ ♦

7. Your local library is under renovation. You are asked to give your suggestions about the changes you want in the library.

Write a letter to the librarian. In your letter

- what you like about the library
- what you dislike about the library
- what changes you want in the library

Dear Administrator,

My name is Parthesh Thakkar. I am a member of the library. I adore spending time at the library because it is very spacious, has a great collection of books and the atmosphere is peaceful.

However, the staff of the library is a concern. They at times leave their tables and do not pay enough attention to members' queries. Moreover, although the library has been donated a water cooler, it does not function on most days, and because of that, we have to carry our water bottles at times.

As the library is being renovated, I recommend three changes. First, the location of your cabin should be in the centre so that you can monitor what is happening in the library. Second, the library should start a small cafeteria in the unutilized, free space near the water cooler. Finally, the computers should be isolated in a separate room to ensure their long life.

I hope that you shall consider my recommendations and implement them.

Yours faithfully,

Parthesh Thakkar

♦ ♦ ♦

8. You are going to work for a company in Canada. The company has offered you a facility to find and provide an accommodation for you when you reach there.

Write a letter to the personnel manager of the company about your requirements. In your letter

- how long you are going to stay there
- what your requirements are for accommodation
- when you will require the accommodation

The Ultimate Guide To IELTS Writing

Dear Sir,

I have signed an employment contract with Sunsys Inc. in which I will have to work for the Toronto branch of the company. My contract is valid for three years, which can be extended in the future.

I am looking for a two BHK apartment because I am coming there with my wife and my child. Also I want it nearer to the company headquarters so that my daily travelling time can be minimized. I also request to find out an accommodation within proximity of the downtown so that we can have an easy access to all the essential amenities.

My contract with the company commences on the 1st January 2013. However, me and my family are planning to land on 21st December in order to adjust to the winter conditions of Canada before my job begins. Should you have any questions about my requirements, I would be happy to answer them.

I look forward to hearing from you.

Yours Faithfully,

Parthesh Thakkar.

◆ ◆ ◆

9. **You are accepted as an overseas student by a university. You want some information before you go to the university.**

    Write to the student officer. In your letter

-   **ask him/her about the accommodation**
-   **the transportation facilities**
-   **the class schedule.**

Dear Sir,

My name is Parthesh Thakkar. I am accepted by the University for the MBA course commencing this January. I am writing this letter to seek some information regarding my study and stay in USA. First, I would like to know about the accommodation. Would you inform me whether the university offers halls of residence to MBA students? Or are there other accommodation options available?

Apart from this I would also like to know the transportation facilities available there. I have tried to find out on the internet but I could not get the required data from it.

Lastly, I am deeply concerned about my class schedule. I received a letter from the university last week that the class schedule has been changed. The letter also indicated that the students should communicate with the students' officer for the same. I would appreciate if you could provide me the required information at the earliest.

I look forward to hearing from you.

Yours Faithfully,

Parthesh Thakkar.

◆ ◆ ◆

10. **You are a history teacher at a high school. You saw an ad in a local newspaper about the local museum which coincides with what you are teaching in your school now.**

   Write to the museum administrator. In your letter

- **introduce yourself**
- **inform him/her that you want to bring your students to visit it**
- **ask suitable timings and any other requirements to visit the museum**

Dear Sir,

I teach history to the students of Grade 8 to 12 at New Era School. I am always on the lookout for some innovative and experimental ways to teach history to the students so that I can arouse their interest in the subject and improve their comprehension through direct experience.

I was pleased to see your advertisement in yesterday's newspaper, which mentioned that you have added fossils of Dinosaurs and other species contemporary to them to your collection. Coincidentally, I am teaching about Dinosaurs to my Grade 8 and 9 students these days. I was wondering if I would bring my students to your museum to see those articles because, I think it will be extremely helpful to them in understanding the subject. .

There are a total of 100 students whom I would want to bring in there during the next week. I have already acquired the permission of my school authorities. Now, I would like to take your consent for the same. I would also like to know about the group entry requirements so that they can be taken care of in advance for your comfort and mine too. I am sure this visit will be helpful, enjoyable and informative for all the candidates.

I look forward to hearing from you.

Yours Sincerely,

Parthesh Thakkar.

◆ ◆ ◆

10. **You are a foreign student. You want to join a club or society so that you can enjoy your time when you study there.**

   Write to the Student Union manager. In your letter

- **introduce yourself**

- **write about your hobbies and interests**

- **ask for information about clubs and societies**

Dear Sir,

I am a new student from India doing masters in Information Technology at the University of London. I started my study here in this spring intake. While studying, I found that the union runs some clubs for students. I am writing this letter to seek more information for the same because I am keen on socializing with others.

I am very good at some sports activities like cricket and golf. I have participated in many domestic tournaments in my country in both these sports. On top of it I do like to study and understand cultures of different countries and interact with people from varying backgrounds.

I request you to send me information about the clubs, their activities, enrolment charges and contact details of the management authorities. I am eager to know and to join some of the clubs so that I can stay connected with my hobbies and with the people of this country and from other nations as well.

I look forward to hearing from you.

Thanking you in advance,

Parthesh Thakkar.

◆ ◆ ◆

11 **You are a professional and you are planning to work abroad. You have come across an employment agency on the Internet that hires people from your country to send to other countries.**

   Write a letter to agency. In your letter

- **write reasons why you want to work abroad**

- **describe what kind of company or organisation you want to work with**

- **state your expectations from the job**

Dear Sir,

I completed my Bachelors in Physiotherapy two years ago. I am working at a rehabilitation centre since then. However, I have now realized that chances of professional growth for physiotherapists are limited in my country. Therefore, I am writing this letter to express my interest in an opportunity to work abroad.

I have done my apprenticeship in a government hospital. Owing to that I have adequate experience in working at different levels as a physiotherapist. On top of it, I do have extra certification in treating children with Cerebral Palsy. Thus, I can work at any level and at any institution.

I prefer a government recognized institution that can offer me an attractive pay scale which goes in line with the field. I would love to work for a rehabilitation centre but I cannot work in underdeveloped areas because basic necessities are often not provided there.

Finally, I am enclosing my detailed resume for your reference and I request you to intimate me if there are any options available for me.

I look forward to hearing from you.

Yours Sincerely,

Parthesh Thakkar.

◆ ◆ ◆

13 **You are going to an English speaking country for some months.**

write a letter to a rental agency. In your letter

- **the type of house you want**
- **facilities you require**
- **for how long you need the accommodation**

Dear Sir,

I am writing this letter to inquire about the availability of accommodation for me and my family. I am going to stay in the UK for 15 months as I have a job with a company located at Wembley. I am looking for a 2 BHK flat located in Wembley or in areas with close proximity to my company's office.

I require all the basic facilities like furniture, cooking range, water, electricity, gas, lift, parking and central heating because it is not possible for me to either bring all the facilities or to acquire them upon arrival because my stay is not permanent. However, I am not looking for a luxurious accommodation; I don't think I can afford more than £1000 per month.

I have signed a 15 month contract with my company and hence I need the accommodation for the same period of time. However, I may stay longer over there because my contract is renewable. Finally, I request you to give a prompt reply with suitable options so that I can directly arrive at the designated accommodation.

I look forward to hearing from you.

Yours sincerely,

Parthesh Thakkar.

♦ ♦ ♦

5. Inviting someone or accepting an invitation (2)

1. **You are going to arrange a special party at your home next week. You want to invite a local artist who is a playback singer.**

    Write a letter to him. In your letter

-   **explain the occasion to him**

-   **invite him to the party**

-   **tell him why you want him to perform**

Dear Sir,

I am going to organize a small but special party on my daughter's tenth birthday on next Sunday. The party will be held at the club hall of our society. I am going to invite around 200 people for the party.

You might not know that my family members including my daughter are great fans of yours. She has purchased all your albums and she often listens to them. This is the reason I would like to invite you to the party. I have already talked to your secretary and booked the time slot for the day.

My daughter has always wanted to see your live performances but she has not yet gotten the opportunity. Now, on this occasion I want to give a surprise to her by arranging your performance on her birthday. I am confident that she and all the guests will be very happy to see you performing live on the stage.

We all look forward to watching you on the stage.

Thanking you,

Yours faithfully,

Parthesh Thakkar.

♦ ♦ ♦

2.   **You are invited to give a presentation about your country by an educational institute in USA in a seminar. You have been looking for such an opportunity for few months.**

Write a letter to the institute. In your letter

- **accept the invitation**

- **tell them your schedule**

- **inform them what equipments you will need and what things you shall bring to distribute to the people who will attend the seminar.**

Dear Sir,

I was immensely pleased to read your invitation. I accept it wholeheartedly and express my gratitude toward you. You might not know but I have been searching for such an opportunity since a long time.

I have booked my tickets. I am going to land at the New York Airport on the 27th of next month at 5.00 am (flight no DA 555). I will live at a close friend's house and he is coming to receive me at the airport as well. I will meet you at the University office on 29th at 11 am where I would like to inform you about the content of my presentation based on Gandhiji. Moreover, I would also like to see the presentation hall and other arrangements.

Finally, I will require a computer projector because I have prepared the entire presentation on my laptop, which I will bring with me. I also request you to arrange for the pointer and a cordless mike. In addition, I am going to gift a copy of Gandhiji's autobiography and a copy of my presentation to all the guests.

Should you have any question, please write back to me.

I look forward to meeting you at the University.

Yours Faithfully,

Parthesh Thakkar.

♦ ♦ ♦

Informal letters like those written to friends, colleagues, neighbours or relatives (14)

1. **You recently have completed a course in a training centre in Canada. Your friend also wants to do the same course.**

    Write a letter to him stating. In your letter

    - **what you did during the course**

    - **why you recommend this course**

    - **what the possible benefits of this course are.**

Hi friend,

I hope this letter finds you in the best of your health and spirit. It's nice to know that you're also interested in the SOLARIS course which I've just completed here in Canada. I selected a 6-month certificate course. In these 6 months, I've learned a lot. I've got both classroom and practical training here.

I suggest this course because this is an employment oriented course. It's a software program prepared by Sun Microsystems and installed in mid and big size organizations. This institute gives you an opportunity to work as an apprentice in its client companies, which, in turn gives you practical exposure and that's the second reason why I insist upon this course.

After completion, you can get a job in any of the client companies who are using this software. In addition, the company sends details of successful students to all its clients. I'm sending you the catalogue of the course. I want you to study it properly. You can always ask me for further information.

I look forward to meeting you in Canada.

Yours truly,

Parthesh Thakkar

◆   ◆   ◆

2. **Your friend will be staying at your home, but you can not be there with him because of some reasons.**

    Write a letter in which you explain. In your letter

    - **how he/she will get the keys**

    - **how to use the electrical appliances**

    - **recommend some interesting places to visit**

The Ultimate Guide To IELTS Writing

Dear Sam

Hi there. I hope your tour will be safe and enjoyable. It's unfortunate that I won't meet you at my home but, don't worry, I've made all arrangements. First, when you arrive, go to flat no. 205. Mr. Thomas, who is my neighbour, will give you the keys to my flat. He might ask you to call me for confirmation. Please cooperate with him.

When you enter the flat, put on the main switch, which is in the box right over the front door. There's a microwave, a washing machine, a water heater, a television and a refrigerator in my home. I've written operating instructions on a piece of paper and pasted it near the respective appliance so that you can operate them easily.

Once you get yourself set, call a taxi to move around in the city. If I were with you, I'd have shown some interesting places like the riverfront, kite museum and town hall. I'm confident that you'll appreciate all of them. However, if you need any assistance, you can either call me or contact Mr. Thomas.

Enjoy your stay.

Bye,

Parthesh Thakkar

◆ ◆ ◆

3.   **Your Friend is coming next month but you have some urgent work and hence you cannot receive him/her at the airport.**

       Write a letter to your friend. In your letter

-     **apologize to him/her**

-     **explain the situation**

-     **suggest for arrangements.**

Dear Tom,

I'm feeling very happy that you are arriving next month. I'm very eager to meet you and I'm sure we shall have a great time catching up. However, I won't be able to receive you at the airport. I'm extremely sorry for that.

Today morning when I went to my boss to give a leave application for next month, he informed me that there would be an inspection from our foreign parent company which would last for seven days and no employee will be given holidays during that period. To my misfortunes, there is a clash between the inspection period and your arrival.

However, I'm going to make some arrangements for you. If you wish, I can take the services of an escort company. Their executive can pick you up from the airport and can drop you at my town. We can meet at my home when I come back from my office. We'll have a good time together because your stay is longer than the inspection period.

Again, I apologize, but, I know that you'll understand my problem.

I'm getting impatient to see you.

Bye,

Parthesh Thakkar

♦ ♦ ♦

4. **You have left college but you didn't say goodbye to your friend who lived in the room with you because he had a course at that time.**

    Write a letter to him. In your letter

- **apologize and tell him how you spent the day when you left**

- **tell him how you got home**

- **invite him to visit you.**

Dear Austin,

I hope you've successfully completed your computer course. I've reached home and I'm missing college very much. I also apologize for I couldn't meet you when I left because everything happened so quickly that I hardly got time to do anything and you were at class then.

A cousin of mine came to the college and he wanted to go on a tour on the way back home. He gave me a surprise by getting us a tour plan with pre-booked tickets. I'd no choice left! We enjoyed a lot though. I'm sending you some photographs of my journey with this letter.

I think it would be great if you visit my town before you leave for your home. My friends and family members will be happy to see you. We can also go on a small tour to the nearby historical places and the beach. Send me a reply if you want to come to my town. I'll arrange everything for you.

Look forward to meeting you,

Parthesh Thakkar.

♦ ♦ ♦

The Ultimate Guide To IELTS Writing

5. **Write a letter to your English speaking colleague who is going to shift at your accommodation as you are shifting elsewhere. In your letter**

- **tell him why you are shifting**

- **describe the accommodation**

- **inform him when he will be able to shift at the accommodation**

Dear John,

Hi!!! I hope you are fine there. I would like to inform you about your new accommodation in this letter. As you know that I got promoted last week, as a result, I will have to report at the bay area branch. Thus, my accommodation will also be shifted there.

The flat where I am living presently will be given to you because you are taking charge of my present position. The flat is really good, spacious and well maintained. I am sure you and your family will enjoy living in this accommodation. It has three bedrooms, a kitchen, and a hall. The area is also peaceful and all amenities are located nearby.

I am planning to shift at my new accommodation on the 20th of next month. I will hand over the keys to you on 21st so that you can also shift here as per your convenience. Moreover, I will be on leave during those three days so I can help you in your process of shifting if you want.

Finally, please let me know if you require any further information or assistance.

Yours sincerely,
Parthesh Thakkar

♦ ♦ ♦

6. **You have recently moved into a new home. You are planning for a party. However, you are worried about the noise which may disturb your neighbour.**

   Write a letter to your neighbour. In your letter

- **introduce yourself**

- **invite your neighbour**

- **describe the planning of the party and express your concern**

Dear Mr. Thompson,

Hello!!! I am Parthesh Thakkar; I am your new neighbour. I am a software developer working for Apple Inc. We are a family of five. I am sure we will share a good and cooperative neighbourhood.

I am going to throw a party this Sunday and I am writing this letter to invite you and your family for the same. The party venue will be my house. All my friends, relatives, colleagues and old neighbours will come. We will be pleased to have your presence at the party.

First, at 8.00 pm, children will dance to the tunes of a DJ. Meanwhile, we can socialize and get familiar with each other. The dinner will start at 9.00 pm; there will be both vegetarian and non-vegetarian options available. However, I have one concern. There will be some loud music at the party venue (which will be stopped when the dinner starts). I hope you will consider it. However, if you are concerned about it, then please let me know so that I can make necessary changes in the plan, well in advance.

I look forward to meeting you at the party.

Yours faithfully,

Parthesh Thakkar.

◆ ◆ ◆

7.   **You participated in a sports event as a team member in a foreign country. Now you have come back to your home country and you want to recommend the same activity to your friend.**

Write a letter to your friend. In your letter

-    **describe the activities you did there**

-    **provide details about the facilities given to you**

-    **give reasons why you recommend this activity to your friend**

Dear Raymond,

Hi! I'm just back from a fifty day sports tour to Britain. I went there to participate in a 20-20 tournament organized by York County. I was there in the capacity of the captain of my club team. We played nine matches with teams of different countries. You'll be pleased to know that we reached the semifinals.

It was indeed a memorable tour for all of us. We got five star hotels to stay, limo coaches to commute to different sports grounds and a tour assistant who took excellent care of us. We won lots of prizes for our good performance throughout the tour. I too won the man of the match award in three matches.

I feel it is a good idea if you can approach York County as a captain of your club. They arrange such tournaments every year. It can give you invaluable experience of playing against international teams in the UK. I am sending you a DVD with this letter, which contains pictures and video recordings of our tour and information about how to approach York County. Write to me if you need additional help from me.

Yours Truly,

Parthesh Thakkar.

◆ ◆ ◆

8. **You are going out of town for a week's period for some work. Write a letter to your neighbour. In your letter**

- **why you are going**

- **what you expect him to do**

- **and what he should do if a problem occurs**

Dear Mr. Singh,

Hello!!! I hope this letter finds you in the pink of your life. I'm writing this letter to you because I need your support. I'm leaving for Delhi to visit my aunt who has suddenly fallen ill. I'm leaving this Monday and I'll come back next Sunday. I need your cooperation in looking after my house.

I request you to keep an eye on the visitors and postman. I'm expecting a parcel from USA next week. If someone comes to deliver, please receive it and keep it at your home. I'll collect it when I come back. I've also informed my friend, Brij about my trip. He might come to see the house if he gets time. I'll also hand over the keys of my house to you so that you can let him enter my house.

In case, if you find anything unusual, please call on my mobile or Brij's mobile (9998886660) immediately so that he would be there as soon as possible.

I'll be very thankful to you for your help.

Yours sincerely,

Parthesh Thakkar.

◆ ◆ ◆

9. **Write a letter to your English speaking friend that you have changed your job. In your letter**

- **why you changed your job**

- **describe your new job and company**

- **update him/her about other news**

Dear Manjeet,

Hi!!! I hope you are in the pink of life there. You'll be happy to know that, finally, I've got the job I was looking for. My previous company was located at a great distance from my home, which was eating up almost 2 hours in commuting every day. This was affecting my work and my family life too.

My new company, Concepts Inc, an outsourcing organization, is located few minutes away from my residence. Moreover, I have been given a higher position and better wages too. My company has its clientele in USA and Europe. Here I work as a team leader. I'm given a separate cabin and a personal assistant. I'm very happy with my new job.

Well, I've got one more surprise for you. Guess what??? Mary, our old classmate has just arrived from Australia and she wants to meet you. I've given your contact details to her. She'll approach you soon. I'm sure you'll be pleased to see her after such a long time.

Bye for now.

Parthesh

◆ ◆ ◆

10. **Write a letter to your new neighbour because you have some problems about his car park. In your letter**

- **welcome him/her as a neighbour**

- **explain your problem**

- **give some suggestions**

Dear Mr. Peter,

Hello! My name is Parthesh Thakkar. I live in flat no 202, exactly opposite to your flat 201. First, I'd like to welcome you as my new neighbour. I'm confident that we'll share a happy and cooperative neighbourhood.

I'm writing this letter to draw your attention towards your car parking mannerism. I think you might not have gone through the guidebook which is given to every new member of our society. Well, I'd like to inform you that you park your car very near to the entry gate of our apartment. It might be convenient to you, but, because of this, I've had to park

---

my car on the road for the last three days. Let me also tell you that someone broke the side-view mirror of my car yesterday.

It would be really convenient if you could please park your car at the right corner of the compound. That's the assigned car park for your flat by the society management. I hope you understand my problems and follow the society guidelines. I'm also sending a copy of this letter to the chairman of our society.

I look forward to having your co-operation.

Thanking You,

Parthesh Thakkar.

◆ ◆ ◆

11.   **You are facing a problem with your neighbour who is leaving rubbish near your house.**

Write a letter to your neighbour. In your letter

-   **introduce yourself**
-   **explain the problem**
-   **provide an appropriate solution**

Dear Mr. Parker,

My name is Parthesh Thakkar. I live in the bungalow no 11, exactly opposite to your bungalow. I'm writing this letter to draw your immediate attention to the problem of litter near my house.

I've been observing that someone from your house (might be your new maid) is leaving litter near the gate of my house. Because of this, a foul odour is created, which brings about an unpleasant and an unhealthy feeling. On top of it, the waste also attracts all sorts of insects, which are harmful to me and my family members. Yesterday, I'd to pay a fine of 20 bucks to the local council for the removal of the litter left by you.

Wouldn't it be better if you inform your new maid to use the common dustbin of our society ? Also, you can call the local council's help line to get your rubbish collected (the number is 49760011). I'm a bit disturbed with the problem and I expect you to look into it and take prompt actions.

Yours Sincerely,

Parthesh Thakkar.

◆ ◆ ◆

The Ultimate Guide To IELTS Writing

12. **An overseas friend has invited you to visit his country. You are planning to visit him.**

   Write a letter to your friend. In your letter

   - **thank him for the invitation and accept the invitation**

   - **write details about your visit**

   - **briefly describe what you want to do there**

Dear George,

I was delighted when I saw your letter containing the invitation to visit your country. I'm thankful to you for that. I've been wanting to visit the UK since long and to my fortunes; you've provided an opportunity to fulfil my desire.

I'll arrive at the Heathrow Airport on the 10th of August at 8:30 am by British Airways flight no. BA-999. I'll stay in the UK for 18 days and my return ticket is confirmed for the 29th of August.

I'm pretty excited about the trip. I've made some tentative plans too. I'd like to visit some important attractions like the Tower of London, London Eye Museum, Millennium Dome and Madame Tussaud's Museum. I'd also visit the House of Commons if I get a chance. On top of everything, I'm eager to spend some time with you and catch up on all old memories.

Please let me know if you need anything from India so that I can bring it with me.

Looking forward to having a great time with you in London.

Yours,

Parthesh

◆ ◆ ◆

13. **You have recently shifted to Australia as an immigrant. Your cousin who lives in your native country is getting married next week. He/she has invited you to attend the marriage ceremony but you cannot attend.**

   Write a letter to your cousin. In your letter

   - **wish him/her on this occasion**

   - **explain him/her the reasons why you can not come to attend the marriage**

   - **invite your cousin to Australia**

Dear Mili,

I'm delighted to know that you are getting married. I and my family wish you a very happy and successful married life. May God shower his choicest blessings on you and your spouse!!!

I'm really upset to say that I won't be able to attend your marriage because I'm facing some troubles here. You know that I've come here just before a month; I'm still struggling to settle in here. I just got a good job last week and it is impossible to get a long leave so soon. What's more, my daughter is also not well for the last three days. She has been advised bed rest for the coming 4-5 days. Looking at the situation, it's indeed impossible for me to come back. I'm really sorry for that.

However, I'll be pleased to welcome you here in Australia. If you haven't made any plans for a honeymoon yet, I can arrange it for you. Don't worry about your stay because my home is always open to you. I'm sure that your trip to Australia could be a memory for a lifetime.

Look forward to hearing from you.

Yours,

Parthesh

◆ ◆ ◆

14. **An English-speaking friend wants to spend a two-week holiday in your region and has written asking for information and advice.**

   Write a letter to your friend. In your letter.

-   **offer advice for accommodation**

-   **suggest some activities of his/her interest**

-   **give information about what clothes to bring.**

Dear friend,

I'm pleased to learn that you're coming to Goa next month. I would be very happy if you stay with us. Otherwise I can arrange for a comfortable hotel stay if you so wish.

My city offers plentiful activities of your interest. I suggest you spend two days on the beach relaxing and sunbathing and some days for sightseeing in the city. There are some old churches and beautiful sea-side views that I'm sure you will adore. One place you really should visit is a fabulous dance club named "The Passion", as I know you're the kind of a person who just loves to dance at discotheques with great music and a fun-loving crowd.

You don't need to bring any warm clothes, as the weather is a bit humid and sunny at this time of the year. In the afternoons it is a bit warmer, so I recommend you to bring shorts and loose t-shirts.

Please inform me when you're coming so that I can receive you at the airport. I'm eager to share a lot with you.

Yours truly,

Parthesh

◆ ◆ ◆

The Ultimate Guide To IELTS Writing

Section 3

IELTS Writing Task 2 (for all students)

This section contains:

- **7 step improvement course to get a high band score in IELTS Writing Task 2**

- **Structures of a high band answer**

- **5 points to follow when you write IELTS Writing Task 2**

- **Structure of a high band answer**

- **What you should do and what you should avoid in IELTS Writing Task 2**

- **200+ sample answers of IELTS Writing Task 2**

The Ultimate Guide To IELTS Writing

7 step improvement course to get a high band score in IELTS Writing Task 2

Step 1 ➜ Introduction to IELTS Writing task 2

Candidates are asked to write an essay of minimum 250 words in about 40 minutes. Candidates are given a topic and then some instructions are printed below the topic. The standard sample task 2 in IELTS Writing can be like this:

> **Some people think that maintaining public libraries is a waste of public money since a computer system can replace their function.**
>
> **To what extent do you agree or disagree?**
>
> **Give reasons for your answer and include any relevant examples from your own knowledge or experience.**
>
> **Write at least 250 words.**

Please note that the last two lines are the instructions printed below every topic in IELTS Writing Test. This is the reason why they are not printed in the topics given in the book.

Step 2 ➜ Different types of IELTS Essay Topics

Now, let us look at the different types of essay topics that can be asked in IELTS.

1. Agree or disagree

2. Discussion

3. Compare and contrast

4. Cause and effects

5. Problems, reasons and solutions

6. Miscellaneous

Please note that the standard classification of essays can be done in different manners.

The Ultimate Guide To IELTS Writing

Some trainers divide IELTS essay topics in categories like Argumentative, Discursive, Persuasive and so on. However, the classification given above is customized to the needs of IELTS and TOEFL students.

Step 3 ➤ Structure of IELTS Essay topic

Dear friends, you may have heard of a structure of essay response or an essay script. However, here, I would like to give you a structure of essay topics that are asked in IELTS. This structure helps you immensely in writing a better response in your exam.

I have seen many students writing an off topic essay and getting less bands in their exams. My experience tells me that this happens because they do not analyse the essay topic properly and so they write improper or irrelevant arguments in the body of their essay. The explanation on different structures of IELTS essay topics will help you to write a relevant and to the point answer which will get a higher band score for you.

Structure of IELTS Essay topics can be of four different types.

<u>The first type of possible structure of essay topic is O, A and D</u>

Where O stands for observation (or a general statement), A stands for Argument and D stands for Demand in the essay topic

For example, look at the topics given below :-

The importance of academic subjects as compared to extracurricular activities is increasing every day. Some people suggest that sports classes should be sacrificed in High School so students can concentrate on Academic subjects.

Do you agree or disagree?

Giving detailed description of crimes in newspapers and on television has bad consequences. Some people therefore suggest that the government should impose restrictions on them.

To what extent do you agree or disagree?

The Ultimate Guide To IELTS Writing

Many people work from home using modern technology today. Some people think that only the workers benefit from this and not the employers.

Do you agree or disagree?

It can be seen from the topics that the first sentence in all of them talks about a general observation. Thus, those sentences are labelled as 'O' (Observation).

It can be seen from the topics that the second sentences in all of them presents an argument or a stand or position. Thus, those sentences are labelled as 'A' (Argument).

The last sentence in all of them demands something from the candidates. Thus they are labelled as 'D' (Demand).

Now, please note that this understanding will help you in writing an effective essay because the parts of this structure can help you in preparing the parts of your essay response.

Observation → Introduction

Argument → Body of the essay

Demand → Layout of the essay (number of paragraphs to be written in the body of the essay)

<u>The second type of possible structure of essay topic is A, A and D</u>

Where A stands for Argument and D stands for Demand.

Please look at the topics given below :-

Some people believe that immigrants should adopt the local culture when immigrating to a new country. An alternative view is that they can adapt to a new environment by establishing a minority community.

Discuss these two views and give your opinion.

Some people think that an employee should change his career or field of work at least once. However, others think that employees should never change their career and stay

The Ultimate Guide To IELTS Writing

in one job for their entire lifetime.

Do you agree or disagree with the statements given?

In both the topics given, it is seen that the first two sentences are actually two arguments opposing each other, and the last sentence (or question) is the demand from the essay topic.

In this case, the structure should help you in writing the essay in the following way.

The topic presented in Argument 1 and 2 ➜ Introduction

Arguments 1 and 2 ➜ Body

Demand ➜ Layout (number of paragraphs to be written in the body of the essay)

The third type of possible structure of essay topic can be A and D

Please look at the examples given below.

In some countries, married couples plan to have a baby at a later age due to the demands of their professional career.
Discuss the advantages and disadvantages of it and give your opinion.

Some people argue that public transportation should be made completely free of charge.

Are there more advantages over disadvantages of this decision?

It is seen from the topics given above that the first sentence in the topic is an argument and the second is the demand.

Topic presented in the argument ➜ Introduction

Argument ➜ Body

Demand ➜ Layout (number of paragraphs to be written in the body of the essay)

<u>The fourth and the last possible structure of essay topic is O (Observation) and D (Demand)</u>

Children from age 7-11 now spend more time watching television and/or playing video games than before.

What are the effects of this on children, families and society?

What are the possible solutions to this problem?

Many people complain about stress at work.

How can employers reduce stress at work and what can employees do on their own to solve this problem?

People prefer to use their own transport these days.

Why is this so?

What can be done to encourage people to use public transport?

The first sentences in the given topics are O (Observation) and the last two sentences or questions are the D (demands) of the essay topic.

The structure of your essay response for this type of structure should be

Observation → Introduction

Demand 1 → Body paragraph 1

Demand 2 → Body paragraph 2

Step 4 → Structure of essay response for various types of essay topics

In step one, we have seen different types of essay topics. I would like to give you three possible structures for those essay topics, which can be followed for different types of essay topics. These structures will certainly help you in getting a higher band score in your exam. However, please note that some answers will not follow the same structure. This is done to give variety to the students.

The first structure is for Agree Disagree and Compare and Contrast Type.

Introduction (1 paragraph) (3-4 sentences)	→ Background Information → Thesis Statement	
Body 1 (Agree) (2 paragraphs)	→ Topic Sentence	
	→ Firstly.........First Point	→ In addition......Support sentence
	→ Secondly.....Second Point	→ Moreover....... Support sentence
	→ Thirdly...... Third Point	→ For example... Support Sentence
	→ Finally....... Final Point	→ Also....... ....Support Sentence
Body 2 (Disagree) (1 paragraph)	→ However... First point	→ What is more... Support Sentence
	→ Secondly... Second Point	→ Further... Support Sentence
	→ Lastly... Last point	→ For example... Support Sentence
Conclusion (1 paragraph) (3-4 sentences)	→ Summary of Body → Writer's opinion	

The second structure is for Discussion type.

Introduction (1 paragraph) (3-4 sentences)	→ Background Information → Thesis Statement	
Body 1 (Discussion Point 1) (1 paragraph)	→ Topic Sentence → Firstly………First Point → Secondly… .Second Point → Finally…… Final Point	 → In addition……Support sentence → Moreover……. Support sentence → For example… Support Sentence
Body 2 (Discussion Point 2) (1 paragraph)	→ However… First point → Secondly… Second Point → Lastly… Last point	→ What is more… Support Sentence → Further… Support Sentence → For example… Support Sentence
Conclusion (1 paragraph) (3-4 sentences)	→ Summary of Body → Writer's opinion	

The Ultimate Guide To IELTS Writing

The third is for Problems/Solutions and Cause/Effects type.

Introduction (1 paragraph) (3-4 sentences)	→ Background Information → Thesis Statement	
Body 1 (Problem) (Cause) (1 paragraph)	→ Topic Sentence	
	→ Firstly.........First Point	→ In addition......Support sentence
	→ Secondly... .Second Point	→ Moreover....... Support sentence
	→ Finally...... Final Point	→ For example... Support Sentence
Body 2 (Solutions) (Effects) (1 paragraph)	→ However… First point	→ What is more… Support Sentence
	→ Secondly… Second Point	→ Further… Support Sentence
	→ Lastly… Last point	→ For example… Support Sentence
Conclusion (1 paragraph) (3-4 sentences)	→ Summary of Body → Writer's opinion	

Step 5 ➜ How to write introduction in Task 2?

Before we learn what to write and how to write in introduction, I think it is very important for you to understand the function of introduction.

Introduction fulfils three functions it informs the reader :-

1) About the topic

2) The aspects of the topic that are going to be discussed

3) The position/stand taken by the writer towards the topic in the form of thesis statement.

As I have told you earlier, the structure of introduction is background information + thesis statement. You should write 2-3 sentences on the background information. Now, background information should be made out of the observation given in the essay topic. If the observation is not given, you should refer to the topic presented in the arguments and prepare your introduction accordingly. I suggest you to study the sample answers given in the book and analyse the introduction of all the sample answers to increase your grip on writing effective introduction.

However, most students face difficulty in writing a good introduction. I want you to tell you that the process that most candidates follow while writing their answer needs to be understood and changed. What most students do when they read the essay topic is: first, they read the topic and immediately, one or two points about the task start flashing in their minds. This is the time, most candidates start writing the actual essay thinking that if they keep searching for more points, they may forget the initial ideas that have flashed in their minds. Now, one important point must be understood by the candidates that the points that they have thought earlier are usually relevant to the body of the essay and not the introduction. But, unfortunately, when candidates start writing their essay, they normally write introduction first. Thus, they find difficulty in writing a good and effective introduction.

Step 6 ➤ How to write the body of the essay?

We should understand that the function of the body is to discuss, explain, prove or illustrate the thesis statement given in the introduction.

While writing the body of the essay, students should keep the following things in mind :-

1) Write separate paragraphs to discuss or cover different aspects of the topic.

2) You must use proper linking words (as displayed in the structure) to link the ideas logically and effectively.

3) Present the points in logical sequence.

4) Use at least one complex sentence in each paragraph of the body.

5) Try to use variety of complex sentences in the body.

More explanation on preparing points for the body is covered in '5 points to follow' section, ahead in this book.

Step 7 ➤ How to write a conclusion?

We have already discussed the structure of the conclusion of the essay but we must also understand the functions of conclusion.

Conclusion has three main functions:

1) It gives a signal to the reader that the essay is ending.

2) It provides a summary of all the main points or presents the thesis (in different words). Here, one important point must be understood, the words used in this part should go in line with the thesis statement.

3) It completes the entire essay with a clear position of the writer and does not confuse the reader with any new information, topic or argument.

◆ ◆ ◆

5 points to follow while writing the task 2

Point 1 ➡ Preparation (10 minutes)

Read the essay topic for 3-4 times. Some students simply read the essay once and start writing their essay. This is a harmful tendency because you may have misunderstood the topic and you end up writing a response that is irrelevant.

Decide which type of essay topic is given, i.e. agree/disagree, discussion, problem/solutions, cause/effects or miscellaneous.

Also, underline the parts of the essay topic like O (observation), A (argument), D (demand) and label them as per the step 2 from the previous section.

Point 2 ➡

Based on your understanding of the arguments or demands of your essay, draw a line in the middle of the page in the question paper given in the IELTS exam or use a separate page (you can request the invigilator/supervisor to give you an extra sheet for this work).

Agree/Discussion 1/problem/cause	Disagree/Discussion 2/solutions/effects
Points	Points
Points	Points
Points	Points
Points	Points
Points	Points

Now, in case of agree disagree or compare contrast types of essay, decide your favour only after making points. Because after making points you can better decide that which side of the argument you can present with effective and logical points.

                                     The Ultimate Guide To IELTS Writing

Point 3 ➜

Review the points and remove any off topic or illogical or irrelevant point from the list.

Decide which point you would write first and write numbers before every point accordingly.

Also, make a list of useful words that can be of help while you would write the response so that at the time of writing, you do not need to pause for thinking a new word thereby breaking the link.

You should spend 10 minutes for the first three points mentioned.

Point 4 ➜ Write the essay (25 – 27 minutes)

After investing 10 minutes and following the above mentioned steps, it will be very easy for you to write the essay of 250 words in less than 20 minutes. I have done many experiments like this in my class and I have found that after following such steps, students can comfortably write 250 words in 15 to 20 minutes.

Point 5 ➜ Editing (3-5 minutes)

Check your response for any errors in spelling or grammar. If you have repeated any word, you should replace that with a synonym.

◆   ◆   ◆

What you should do while writing the task 2

❖ Use only formal language, informal language is not at all entertained in writing task 2.

❖ Please read the essay at least 3-4 times.

❖ Please follow the points given earlier before you start writing.

❖ Write at least 4 paragraphs in your essay where the first is introduction, the next two will form the body and the last will contain the conclusion of your essay.

❖ If you want a high band score (6 or more) please try to use complex sentences in your writing.

❖ You should use linking words and connectors to link your information logically. (A list of such words is given in section 4 of this book)

What you must avoid while writing the task 2

❖ Avoid using informal language and contractions like I'm, we're, short forms like govt., st. (for students) or slangs like chick or gals (used for girls), lad or guy (used for boys) that are normally used in chatting or in SMS. You will lose your bands if you write like this.

❖ Do not start writing immediately after reading the essay topic.

❖ You must not copy the sentences printed in the topic question. If you wish to add a phrase or a part of the topic, modify the sentence and add it using a different sentence structure than the one used in the topic.

❖ Please do not add any new point or example in the conclusion.

❖ Some candidates simply mug up readymade sentences for introduction. For example, if the topic in the essay is about pollution, they think if they can prepare 2-3 sentences on the same containing impressive language, they can get good bands. I have also seen some reference materials trying to motivate students to learn readymade sentences for various topics like education, computer, technology, childhood, parenting and so on. Such sentences are often irrelevant to the topic and thus, instead of getting a good score, you actually achieve less score in "Task Response" criterion for irrelevant writing. Thus, I strongly suggest to the students to not learn readymade responses.

◆ ◆ ◆

200+ sample answers of IELTS Writing Task 2

1. AGREE DISAGREE (106)

1. **People nowadays work hard to buy more things. This has made our life generally more comfortable but it is a pity many traditional values have been lost on the way to such materialism.**

   To what extent do you agree or disagree with the statement?

It is certainly true that today's lifestyle has become more materialistic than ever. Our needs have been rising by the day. However, to say that we have been losing our culture and traditions in a rush to earn more and to buy more is a conservative statement to make.

The basis behind the argument that we are killing our roots on the way to materialism is that a lot of people do not wish to change with time. Culture and traditions have a strong identity but they are like a flowing river, every minute the same and yet different. With open markets and massive industrializations both the buying power of and the options for the people have increased. Thus, they wish to make life more comfortable for themselves and their family and this does not mean that that they do not respect tradition any longer.

Moreover, the act of buying or possessing does not directly kill our values but there is a deeper disease called instant gratification where people want to do less and get more results. In general there is seen an attitude of irresponsibility which makes people selfish and manipulative in today's stressful working conditions.

It is possible that the pursuit to buy more results in wasteful expenditure and incidents of people dealing with their insecurity by going shopping. This extreme consumerism needs to be certainly checked.

Finally, I believe that we are not losing our culture and tradition but the way of executing them has transformed in our times. Living a good, well provided life rather helps us take pride in our cultural history and celebrate it by way of rituals, festivals and day to day behaviour.

On the other side

It is the biggest truth of our times that life has become materialistic as men and women crave to buy more and more things. In this state of mind, they consciously or unconsciously make their life surfacial and gradually get disconnected from their culture and traditions.

There are a number of reasons behind this; firstly, material possessions are tied to self-worth. People believe if they do not have the latest gadget or clothes of the newest fashion in town they just do not have an identity. They believe that they shall not be accepted in the social circle and shall get no respect from peers. This craving may lead to adoption of unethical modes to earn money to fulfil their ever increasing desires. Consequently, values are compromised and this is the first blow to the inherited traditions.

In addition to this, culture and traditions are rooted in a social framework to maintain the relationships within which is of great importance. But in today's life where each one wishes to assert their individuality and superiority with their buying power, there is little place for respect and tolerance. Thus, as social structures collapse, the culture is lost as well.

However, not all the people who work hard and buy things to make their life comfortable lose their culture. There are so many successful people who maintain a fine balance between all aspects of their life.

Finally, I opine that the desire of having more things inevitably leads people to compromise with their cultural ethics and principles. It takes a lot of personal courage and conviction to save oneself from such an outcome and lead a balanced life.

◆ ◆ ◆

2. **Parents and teachers make many rules for children to encourage good behaviour and protect them from danger. However, children would benefit from fewer rules and greater freedom.**

    To what extent do you agree or disagree?

It is the fundamental duty of parents and teachers to help their children evolve into responsible individuals by imparting them lessons of good behaviour. To ensure that their purpose is fulfilled, parents adopt every possible mode for bringing up their children in a better manner. One such mode is the imposing of discipline through rules. I personally believe that though children cannot be given a total rule-free atmosphere, yet there need to be lesser regulations and more freedom.

So many people argue that parents and teacher should make more rules and give less freedom to youngsters. Firstly, they say imposing strict rules is the only way of making juveniles more disciplined. Young ones who grow up in highly controlled environs behave unpredictably mischievous in the absence of guardians and may also have personality disorders as they grow up.

Secondly, they point out that stricter rules would make them more cultured, well-behaved and sophisticated adults in the future. However, I believe that parents and teachers are the role models for the young ones and so they try to shape themselves like their parents and/or teachers. Hence, any disparity in the behaviour may lead to less respect and diminished importance of rules in the minds of the children.

Finally, some people assert that restricting freedom helps in protecting them from the anti-social or harmful elements of the society. Contrarily, I think childhood is the age to learn the good and bad things around the world. Confining them may diminish their ability to deal with reality.

All in all, it is true that we cannot give total freedom to kids, as they do not know what is good or bad for them. According to my opinion, fewer desirable rules and greater freedom, serve the purpose of shaping the child into a good individual.

On the other side

It is the principal duty of parents and teachers to protect their children from danger, ensure good behaviour and mould them into good individuals. They should adopt all possible means to work towards this purpose. I think it is essential that we put in place certain rules of behaviour and limit the freedom children have.

Firstly, children are innocent and more vulnerable as compared to mature adults. Stricter rules ensure that children obey them and become more disciplined. This in turn, helps them in concentrating more upon the tasks allotted to them. Moreover, it ultimately leads to a better performance academically and socially. Secondly, firm rules also make them more cultured and well behaved that finally leads them to become better human beings.

In addition to this, restricting their freedom protects them from some evils in the society, for example, bad habits like smoking or drug addiction. These can otherwise drive them away from their basic responsibility of getting a good education for themselves.

However, some advocates of child freedom assert that confining the development of children to stern rules may give rise to a dislike in them towards their family and school. Next, it may affect them in their overall development because their basic nature is to play and experiment which is not fulfilled. Moreover, they also suggest that rather than imposing rules, parents and teachers should be well behaved to make their children like them.

To conclude, according to me, it is true that we should not snatch the total freedom of children. However, imposing desired rules and giving required freedom would certainly mould children into better citizens. Moreover, we can protect them from danger.

◆ ◆ ◆

3.　**Some people say that all secondary and higher secondary school students should be taught how to manage money as it is an important life skill.**

Do you agree or disagree with this argument?

It is indeed a fact that managing money is an important skill of life and it has to be acquired by every human being on this earth. However, the time of learning this skill is also extremely important. I think adolescence is an inappropriate age to grasp the insights of financial management.

There are various factors which support the thought that high school children should not learn the aspects of money management. Firstly, owing to their age, they are not mature enough to understand the fundamentals of managing money. Secondly, there are chances that if they develop interest in earning money, they may digress heavily towards increasing their financial wealth. This can lead to a reduction in importance given to moral values, academic subjects and tertiary education.

Thirdly, indulgence in earning money might prompt their vulnerable minds to adopt some illegal activities, which can, in extreme cases, ruin their careers forever. Finally, high school children already have many subjects to deal with and in this situation, addition of another complex subject will make their school life burdensome.

However, some people assert that learning how to manage money does have some benefits. Acquisition of these insights at an early age might help children to plan for their future. Moreover, they can understand the value of money and this indeed can help them in reducing overspending, keep them away from bad habits like addictions and motivate them to keep a check on extravagant demands from their parents.

Finally, even though learning about managing money helps school going children in understanding its value, they are relatively premature to grasp the fundamentals of it and hence, I firmly believe that it is not a good idea to teach money management skills to high school students.

On the other side

It is an undeniable fact that managing money is an important life skill, which has to be acquired by everyone. Thus, adolescents ought to learn the insights of financial management.

Learning how to manage money is amazingly beneficial for high school children. First, it is extremely good for their future, since they learn it at a tender age; they will be able to manage their wealth properly and appropriately. Second, they can understand the value of money and hence they voluntarily reduce their unnecessary expenses, keep a distance from bad habits and also do not rush to their parents with extravagant demands.

Third, they also learn how to budget their money and in such a state, they develop maturity, tolerance and also give more respect to their parents and guardians. Finally,

The Ultimate Guide To IELTS Writing

the insights about money management motivate children to plan funds for their future academic studies. Consequently, it also greatly reduces the financial burden on their parents.

On the other hand, learning money management at high school also has some drawbacks. Students at this age are generally immature and hence most of them cannot grasp the subject properly, which may lead to some improper or negative thoughts regarding money in their minds. Moreover, at this age, children need to pay attention to academic subjects. Adding one more subject will definitely increase their burden. Lastly, some of them might become money minded and in that state, they often show less respect to emotional, cultural and social values of life.

Conclusively, even though teaching financial management at high school level is difficult and may have some disadvantages of students digressing from their studies, I firmly believe that it ultimately helps them in planning the financial aspect of their lives and leads them to be sincere, mature and capable citizens of the future.

◆ ◆ ◆

4.   **Some people consider thinking about the future and planning for the future to be a waste of time. They argue that people should simply live in the moment.**

       Do you agree or disagree?

Planning and preparing for the future is one of the most important traits of human psyche. We have been taught how to plan for future in all business schools across the world. However, a view has been surfacing every now and then that we need to learn to stay in the present. My inclination falls in line with this view.

There are numerous reasons why I believe that living in the moment is true living. Firstly, living in the present moment is absolutely stress and tension free. Those who live in the present can enjoy and experience the moment so well that they are attuned to the right flow in their life and such flow almost always leads them to the right future. It is a fact that humans do not have control over nature, and so, we should live the journey of the life to the fullest. But, we keep planning for the future, which brings insecurity, stress and fear in all of us. It is rightly said by the spiritual mystics that living in the future brings in fear.

Finally, living in the present always makes people accept the things as they are. Such acceptance is essential if we need a happy and a healthy life. I have experienced that constant endeavour to plan for the future creates a feeling of non-acceptance of the present and if we reject the present, we simply cannot have a better future.

On the other hand, safeguarding the future is a notion that is widely accepted across the globe. I personally see nothing wrong with it. We ought to have goals and plans for the future. But, we must work and live in the now to let these plans manifest.

Conclusively, I firmly believe that having a future strategy is not bad, but, even to live up to that proposed projection, we must live in the present. Thus, I agree that living in the present moment is the best way of living one's life.

One more answer

All the holy scriptures across the world have always given us one mantra to live life to its fullest and that mantra is "live in the present moment". It is also quite obvious that those who have lived like this have never regretted anything in their life.

There are many reasons to support this. Firstly, I firmly believe that life exists in the now. Life, in its inherent nature is full of bliss and joy, and is completely free from stress and tension. To elaborate on it, I must say that the general orientation of the entire human race is based on fear of future. We fear about uncertainties that may happen in the future and hence we always try to 'control' things. In addition, we serve the fear and insecurity that emerge out of our thoughts and we constantly engage ourselves in planning for the future, preparing for the worst and in such a rush, we simply forget the moment in which we are alive. It is rightly said that whatever you are today is based on your thoughts of the past and your future will also depend on how you spend your present.

Moreover, it is also true that if the present moment is lived fully, it always guides us into the right direction. I would like to quote an incident that happened in Gautam Budhdha's life. Once, he went to a village and begged for some food at lunch. He ate some of it and gave the remaining food to those who came to hear his discourse and asked them to feed any needy person. At that time, someone suggested to him that he should pre-serve his food for evening. What if he did not get food in the evening? To this, Budhdha replied, "If I had worried about my next meal, I would have never left my home to preach people". This example speaks a lot about the subject of this essay.

In conclusion, I believe living in the present is the most enlightening, spiritual and won-derful way of living life. This is what all ascended souls have taught us.

◆ ◆ ◆

5.   **We are witnessing traffic jams across all the cities in the world. Some people say that increasing prices of petrol will help in reducing traffic jams and pollution.**

Do you agree or disagree? Also, give other possible solutions.

Traffic jams are becoming one of the most severe urban problems for the authorities of most cities around the world leading to many other difficulties such as road rage, in-creased stress levels and so on. To address this issue, an argument is put forward by some short sighted people that increasing the prices of oil can be a solution in this regard.

Raising the cost of petrol cannot be an appropriate answer to the problem of traffic jams for many reasons. First, majority of cities face traffic jams because of car users as middle and lower class people prefer to commute only by public transport. Now, the rich people are not affected by the higher fuel price because they can afford it. Therefore, car usage shall not see a decline. Second, higher petrol cost puts a great burden on the economy of developing countries that import oil. This increases the gap between rich and poor countries, which can be a cause of innumerable problems.

Third, owing to higher fuel price, landing cost of essential items like fruits and veg-etables will also increase, which will contribute in higher inflation levels across the world. Finally, there are other effective ways to help the problem of traffic jams such as inspir-

---

...ple to use public transport, developing infrastructure of the cities, introducing ...traffic management systems and so on.

...the other hand, some people argue that raising petrol prices will affect the spending capacity of the commuters. This will oblige them to reduce usage of private vehicles and depend more on public transport. They also add that the earned money can be used for other meaningful causes like welfare, infrastructure, education, healthcare and so on.

Finally, the argument about raising petrol prices apparently has some credibility. However, considering the negative effects of it, I firmly believe that it is not an ideal solution to reduce traffic problems.

◆ ◆ ◆

6.   **Some people think that private health care is better for the people. Others say that health care should be free of charge and run by the government.**

How far do you agree or disagree with the statements given?

It is one of the fundamental duties of the government to offer quality health care to its civilians. There has always been a debate about whether free governmental health care should be preferred over private healthcare. My opinion is that governmental facilities are always required but there should be no restriction on private health care.

Private healthcare offers competitive and qualitative medical services to the people. Here, highly qualified professionals are hired to work for the community to ensure a certain enhanced quality of services offered. Moreover, private sector units are profit making organizations that invest a good proportion of their profits in acquiring latest technology and research. This is highly beneficial to the patients in the long run. Finally, private companies offer better facilities like 24 hour emergency services, ambulance networks, high quality and super speciality hospitals and so on. Though, on the flip side, some private hospitals sometimes overcharge their patients to maximize profits.

On the other hand, government run health care offers cost effectiveness and better accessibility. It is available in the smallest of towns and villages of the country, where under-privileged people are benefitted by it. In addition, governments can get dona-tions and allocate funds to offer free health care to the civilians. However, it is often observed that public health care centres may not offer satisfactory services primarily because of the huge cost of free health care. Lastly, it is also seen, at times, that prompt-ness and professionalism in healthcare services are absent in government run facilities.

Finally, it is evident that both systems of offering health care have their own benefits and drawbacks and yet both are required in present day societies. Hence, I opine that pri-vate healthcare should not be eliminated.

◆ ◆ ◆

7. **Rich countries should not give jobs to the skilled workers (for example doctors and engineers) of poor countries as they are needed by their home country more than the rich countries.**

How far do you agree or disagree with the statements given?

Migration of skilled people to developed countries is not a new phenomenon. However, it has been rising dramatically for the last few decades. This may appear advantageous to the workers and the host countries but it is harmful to the economies of the poorer countries.

Developed countries get immense benefits by offering jobs to skilled workers of under-developed countries. First, rich countries have a well developed economy, which re-quires more highly skilled people for efficient operation of the country. Second, foreign workers work at lower wages compared to the native people. This is helpful to private organizations as they can cut their costs and offer reasonably priced services and prod-ucts in domestic and international market. Finally, authorities in some countries make it difficult for foreign workers to have legal rights so that they have no access to govern-mental aid.

On the other hand, this situation is indeed harmful to the underdeveloped countries because they spend lots of money in educating and training professionals like doctors, engineers, scientists etc. It is estimated that in India (as India consists of the largest pool of skilled workers and fresh graduates in the world) the government spends billions of dollars for tertiary education but when the time comes to serve the country, the skilled graduates migrate to foreign lands. This process is called 'brain drain' and it actually widens the gap amongst the economies of the world.

All in all, it is true that skilled people are needed everywhere. I feel they are needed more in their home countries because they should pay back to their motherland by living there and serving their community. Henceforth, rich countries should limit the number of foreign skilled workers.

◆ ◆ ◆

8. **Now-a-days modern modes of transport are available; still some people believe a bicycle is the best way to get from one place to another.**

   Do you agree or disagree?

It is true that modern advancements in the technology are introducing so many efficient, innovative ways in transportation. Bicycle is certainly a cheap, effective and clean way of commuting but it cannot be a vehicle for all people and all kinds of needs.

There are ample reasons why a bike is not, in itself, a complete answer to transportation. Firstly, it is manual and hence it is time consuming. In today's competitive era, time is an important factor in every individual's life. Secondly, it has less loading capacity i.e. it cannot carry more than one or two persons at a time. Thirdly, it is useful for movement in limited areas only. One cannot go on a freeway or a highway on a bicycle.

Next, it is also not suitable for all individuals like disabled and elderly people, and working women. On the top of everything, it is not suitable for our all requirements like travelling to long distances or overseas, for shopping or official meetings etc. Moreover, it cannot offer the privacy that a car can offer. We can read a newspaper or work on our laptop while going in our car but a bicycle does not offer such facilities.

However, some environmentalists in favour of the bicycle argue that it is a non-polluting environment-friendly vehicle. Additionally it is maintenance free, cost effective, convenient and comfortable to ride. Furthermore, riding bikes is a very good exercise, which helps us in staying fit and healthy.

To conclude, I believe a bicycle is a good, green and healthy way of commuting from one place to another. However it certainly is not the best way because it is useful for travel in a limited area. Also, it cannot fulfil all the different requirements of people as per their expectations from a mode of transport.

◆ ◆ ◆

9. **Some people think that maintaining public libraries is a waste of public money since a computer system can replace their function.**

   To what extent do you agree or disagree?

Technology in the present day world has revolutionized services and facilities in almost all facets of life. Public libraries have also benefited to a great extent by the use of computers. Some people present an argument that governments should not spend money in maintaining them as computers can replace them. However, this suggestion does not seem feasible enough for most countries.

There are many reasons why computers cannot completely replace public libraries in the near future. First, libraries contain books written in many different languages whereas majority of software programs are developed in English which creates problems for the programmer in displaying information regarding such books. Subsequently, it also creates problems for the users to use the books efficiently. Secondly, it is indeed difficult to read books on computers as it has implications for the health of our eyes. In addition, it is expensive because computers need infrastructure which may not be affordable in the rural areas of developing economies.

Thirdly, not all the people who visit a library may be computer savvy. Thus, it is extremely difficult for many members of public libraries to access the services and to get benefits from it. Finally, computers are also vulnerable to technical glitches. They do succumb to system crashes, viruses, hardware or software related problems and in such a situation, it shall become next to impossible to access any book in the library.

However, according to some people computers do have benefits to offer. One of them is, they save time and they need less space. We can store thousands of books in a small 3.5 inch hard drive. Also, life of books is longer in digital form compared to their versions on paper. Most importantly, with the help of computers, books of the library can be accessed by people beyond geographical borders.

Finally, considering the points on the either side of the given topic, I conclude that computers should be used to facilitate library functioning but in the near future they should not completely replace the public libraries.

◆ ◆ ◆

10. **Some people argue that there should be a common punishment for committing a certain crime for all criminals who carry it out. On the other hand, others suggest that the conditions under which the criminal commits a crime should be taken into consideration before deciding the punishment.**

How far do you agree or disagree with the arguments presented?

Crime and punishment has been a raging debate since the early days of mankind and to easily resolve the issue would be to attempt a difficult task. The idea that there should be a common and fixed punishment for a crime for all criminals who carry it out may seem reasonable but I opine against it.

All criminals who commit a certain crime have very different backgrounds, reasons and methodologies. It is impossible that the extent of cruelty inflicted on the victim in one instance is exactly the same as in another. The history of the criminal, his or her motives and the way in which the crime is executed have to be taken into account at all times to be able to decide the quantum of punishment. In the absence of this, severe injustice may be done to some criminals while others may be let off lightly.

Next, is there ever a possibility of deciding the certainty of a crime, in the first place? For example, are all murders or all robberies equal? When we cannot come to decide the fixed definition of a murder, a robbery and so on, how is it possible to come to a punishment suitable for all instances of the same?

On the other hand, giving a fixed, common punishment for a crime to all the criminals who are found guilty of it could be useful in reducing the judicial hours spent on a case hearing. Also, when the punishment is not same for all, it gives a lot of room to the lawyers to get a reduced sentence for their client. So, when this possibility does not exist, such malpractice shall cease to exist as well.

In the conclusion, I opine that though the fixed, common punishment for a certain crime looks simpler in practice, we should not implement it at all in view of the reasons given above.

◆ ◆ ◆

11. **Some people believe that a country becomes more interesting and develops faster when its population includes a mixture of different nationalities and cultures.**

     To what extent do you agree or disagree?

It has been observed since the ages that a country which has welcomed different cultures and religions has evolved great traditions and added much to the richness of the world that we live in. I strongly agree that a country certainly becomes more interesting and develops faster when its people come from different cultural backgrounds.

Though there are many wonderful facets of this phenomenon one can go on to list, I will concentrate here on the ones that are most important. First of all, cultural diversity leads to a richness of experience in food, clothes, residential designs, education and art. In being exposed to so much variety, a person's mind gets more opportunities to open up and grow. Secondly, business opportunities abound as well. With a diverse population come diverse needs and not only is there the creation of a large domestic market but international trade relations can also develop in a healthier manner.

Thirdly and most importantly such a place inculcates a sense of tolerance. There is understanding of different belief systems and peaceful coexistence as narrow-mindedness. I believe that people who live in an environment characterised by cultural variety are more spiritual than others and certainly more open minded and friendly.

At times belief systems might clash and there is greater chance of disharmony here as compared to another society where everyone is united by a singular belief. But these can be tackled with the good governance systems and this small drawback should not prevent us from bringing up our children in a richer and ever-inspiring environment.

Therefore, I strongly agree that a country is more interesting and its development is furthered when its population comprises of people of different nationalities.

◆ ◆ ◆

12. **Some people think that the government should knock down old buildings and make way for new buildings.**

Do you agree or disagree?

Owing to fascinating developments in the field of construction, there at times is visible a huge disparity in buildings that are old and new. Hence, some people come up with an argument that the government should knock down old buildings to allow the construction of new ones. The idea does seem modern yet upon deeper thought is not feasible and I disagree with it.

Knocking down all the buildings and constructing new ones at a given time is not at all possible at any place whatsoever. The old coexists with the new. A building is usually designed to last a hundred years and to tear it down when all it needs is a little maintenance is a waste of precious money that can be used for all other kinds of infrastructure development. Also, some parts of cities are heritage locations preserving which is mandatory for us if we wish to take pride in our culture and traditions. They are walk-in museums of a life gone past, the beauty and complexity of which is there for us to appreciate and learn from.

Further, it is not always possible to predict that the current designs of buildings will pass the test of time and remain equally acceptable and efficient in future. All in all, a small proportion of old buildings may be risky or may not be 'fit' for today's life style in terms of comfort and can be therefore razed to the ground.

There is no doubt that at times old structures need a lot more maintenance than the comfort they provide for us or with the growth of the city come to be on a location which makes circulation of traffic difficult. In this case, the old certainly should make place for the new so that space can be better utilized and we can save the human and material resources that need to be spent on endless maintenance tasks.

Conclusively, to simply knock down old buildings and build new ones is not a good idea according to me. I think it is a mockery of the concept of development.

◆ ◆ ◆

13. **Technological development in earlier times brought more changes to the life of ordinary people than recent technological developments have brought.**

Do you agree or disagree?

Technology has always been doing a wonderful job of bringing prominent changes in the life of people. Human beings have been constantly working on newer innovations to facilitate their life on earth. It is often argued that the changes that technology brought in our ancestors' lives were better compared to the changes that it has brought in today's life. In my opinion it is impossible to compare any two eras of human life in this manner.

Each technological development alters life in unimaginable ways. What the invention of the train track did for locomotion in the times gone by, the Boeing 707 has done for our times. If telephone changed communication in the time of Graham Bell, the mobile has done as much the same in today's era. If anaesthesia killed pain, the vaccine for polio has saved millions from otherwise inevitable handicaps.

In talking about such things usually what happens is that the technology we already have been using for a long time is taken for granted and something historic or exceptionally modern is considered better than what exists in the present. However, it is also true that the technology which is being used in the present was considered more advanced in the past.

There is always scope for improvement in a given technology and place for new inventions and discoveries. But no advancement in the present is better or worse than what happened in the past or comes about in the future. Therefore I do not agree with the proposition given here.

The Ultimate Guide To IELTS Writing

14. **Computers do not help children in learning more efficiently. On the contrary, the use of computers has a negative effect on children's physical and mental development.**

To what extent do you agree or disagree?

Computers are an inevitable part of almost all walks of human life now and learning is highly influenced by these machines in the present. I completely agree that they help children to learn more efficiently.

Computers facilitate learning in innumerable ways. One of them is the visual and auditory applications. They make learning easier and even amusing for children. With every passing day, computers are enriched with new software applications that incredibly aid learning and expression. For example, students of geography and cartography are always thrilled to see earth on screen with the help of Google earth.

Moreover, it can also be of great help when one is connected to the World Wide Web or as we commonly call it the internet. Students can get loads of information related to their subject. Internet enriches their knowledge and improves their academic performance.

However, some people argue that usage of computer is harmful to the body of children. It is scientifically proven that excessive usage can damage their eyes and can cause muscular disorders. Also, long hours on the internet might mean harmful lack of social contact. But, like we give children a lesson in responsibility in all other facets of life it is important that the parent and teacher in us guide them to a balance in their daily routine. While taking care that their upbringing is enriched with the opportunities computers present them with, the young generation is to be saved from physical and psychological problems that come about with extreme behaviour.

Thus, I reiterate that computers are integral to children's learning process and with adequate precautions, we can certainly minimize their drawbacks and optimize benefits.

♦ ♦ ♦

15. Some people believe that international news should be included in the syllabus of secondary school students.

Do you agree or disagree?

The composition of the secondary school curriculum has always been attracting a range of suggestions from people belonging to various fields. However, not all are worth following and the view that international news as a subject should be added to secondary school studies is one of them.

My opinion is that news from other countries has little influence on the native culture, language and lifestyle. It is difficult for children of a secondary school to comprehend the effects this because they are at an impressionable age. In addition, many a times, it happens that they misunderstand the news thereby getting negative inspiration.

Moreover, news comes from all walks of life and it is indeed difficult to exclude a specific aspect of it because things are interrelated. Finally, secondary school studies are often burdensome for most students. They fall short of time to complete the academic syllabus assigned to them. In this case, adding a difficult and complex subject like international news may cause them to deviate from their goals.

On the other hand, some people argue that studying international news can help students to stay aware of the latest trends in all walks of life like politics, sports, lifestyle, education, technology and so on. They also assert that such updates can broaden their knowledge and enhance their learning capabilities.

Lastly, according to me, adding international news in secondary school certainly has more disadvantages than ways in which it could be helpful. It is a complex, difficult, demanding and burdensome task for children at a crucial period of their development and hence I opine against it.

◆ ◆ ◆

16. Some people argue that strict punishment for driving offenses is the only effective way toward improving safety on the road.

Do you agree or disagree?

We can see that numbers of vehicles on urban roads are increasing every day. With this, there is a huge increment in number of driving offenses. Amongst other traffic management policies, governments of many countries have made sure that there are in place very strict laws and stricter punishments for offenders. I completely agree with this.

It is my opinion that stricter punishments are the most effective measure in improving road safety. It is said that fear of punishment brings discipline and bad driving habits are no exception. Strict punishment can be in the form of a heavy fine, suspension of license or imprisonment. All these can certainly make drivers cautious and compel them to drive safely with all required precautions.

This step ensures safety as it brings about a sense of responsibility in the driving habits of people. Consequently, society can benefit enormously from it because injuries and casualties can be minimised and loss of infrastructure and government spending shall be reduced as well. In the long run, insurance companies may reduce their premium amounts as they get fewer claims for accidents. On top of it, we can have a happy, safe, mature and responsible society.

However, some people assert that rather than imposing strict punishments, we as a society and our governments should focus more on traffic education. They add that governments should stiffen the procedure of getting a driver's license in order to have qualified and well trained drivers on road. Apparently, all these arguments look good but increasing driving offences across the world make it necessary that stricter punishments be meted out to offenders.

Therefore, I agree with the notion that offensive driving must be penalized heavily in order to bring safety on the road and a sense of accountability in drivers.

♦ ♦ ♦

17. **Many people work from home using modern technology today. Some people think that only the workers benefit from this and not the employers.**

   Do you agree or disagree?

Modern technology is indeed a blessing to the mankind. It has facilitated human life in uncountable ways. Working from home is one of the convenient options that is being exercised by millions of people these days. This innovation is helpful to employees and employers. However, in my opinion, employees get higher advantages from it.

Firstly, employees do not have to travel all the way from their home to office. This saves their time and money and helps them pay more attention to their work and their family. The next benefit is of convenience. They do not have to work at fixed times as they are working from home and the work schedule can be adjusted to their comfort. Finally, employees who work from home can also look after their family in a better way.

Employers on the other hand are also benefited from the system of working from home. First, they do not have to purchase a huge office space to accommodate their employees. This saves cost for employers. Second, slightly reduced salaries can be paid to employees who wish to work from the comfort of their home thereby bringing savings to the employer. Finally, employers can hire people from across the world as this opportunity frees them from all geographical ties.

However, employers cannot monitor their employees all the time and hence, work productivity may be affected. On top of it, in today's rapidly changing world, employees need to be trained regularly. This is difficult if employees do not come to office on a daily basis. Thus, this system may not prove advantageous for the employers in all cases.

All in all, I conclude from the above paragraphs that working from home using modern technology is indeed a good option but it offers more convenience and benefits to the employees rather than the employers.

◆ ◆ ◆

18. **Some animal species, such as the dinosaurs, became extinct as a result of natural causes. Thus, extinction is a normal part of the world's evolution and actions should not be taken to prevent the disappearance of today's endangered animals.**

Do you agree or disagree with this statement?

There is no doubt that before man came onto the evolutionary stage a lot of species such as the dinosaurs were already extinct owing to natural causes. Extinction is a normal part of nature. Yet to think we have no role to play in the extinction of some of the endangered species in the present times is not right. Human action is responsible for a lot of environmental problems.

No species before the human being was blessed with as evolved a consciousness as we have. Thus, if we have the mind to create, discover and invent, we also have the power to destroy, exploit and wipe out. First of all, excessive cutting of forests has led to changes in weather patterns which make it difficult for many species to survive. This process of deforestation also leads to loss of habitat of the species and slowly their numbers start to decrease. Secondly, greed and mindless pursuit of passions like hunting or killing for the purpose of use in the fashion industry are responsible for destruction of nature as well. Thirdly, industrial and other kinds of pollution disturb the ecological balance of our environment. As a result, water, soil, air are so full of pollutants now, that not only other species but the human kind is at high risk too.

It is true that extinction and death are parts of the natural cycle of life. But mindless and irresponsible human action is leading to the unnatural and untimely death of many species. This can be prevented if we spread awareness about the importance of caring for our environment.

Thus, I disagree with the notion that we should not try to prevent the extinction of plant and animal species because it is only occurring due to natural causes.

◆ ◆ ◆

19. **Public celebrations (national days, festivals) are held in many countries. Some people say that these celebrations are a waste of money and we should spend money on more important things.**

Do you agree or disagree?

Public celebrations are a part of every nation's political history and cultural traditions. We celebrate days of national importance like the Independence day or the Republic day and also festivals such as Christmas, Id, Diwali etc. A lot of people now feel that these celebrations are a waste of money and we should spend on more important things like health, education, infrastructure etc. In my opinion public celebrations are important as they bind people together but wasteful and extravagant expenditure for the same should be avoided.

A day like Independence day is not only to celebrate but also to look back and feel grateful for the free world that we live in. We honour those who gave us the gift of freedom and in this manner teach the next generation about our history. Moreover, a festival like Christmas or Diwali is an occasion for an entire country to have a yearly holiday and at the same time a reason to celebrate with friends and family. This is very important for our psychological well-being and social existence.

However, with the free market economy some dirty trends have come into our lives. Instead of concentrating more on the importance of the occasion people tend to commercialize the event. This in turn leads to overspending by those for whom shopping is a status symbol and a way of being in tune with the modern times. This not only creates problems in the social relationships but also causes distress at an individual level. Also, governments can use such occasions to display their might in terms of new warfare weaponry that they have acquired. This gives rise to tensions at the international level.

Thus, in my opinion, observing public celebrations is very important but we should take care that the event in not commercialised or used for petty social or national gains.

◆ ◆ ◆

20. **Some people believe that the government should not spend too much money on the outer space exploration.**

   Do you agree or disagree?

We have always tried to find out if we are alone in this infinite universe or not. For this, we have spent immense revenue and so far, we have not met with success. Hence, some people come forward with an argument that governments must spend less on space exploration. Considering the rising needs of people and their problems, this argument does hold some valid ground.

Governments must limit their spending on outer space exploration for many reasons. First, the cost of such projects is in trillions, which is higher than GDP of many developing countries in the world. Secondly, there is no assurance of success of such projects. In such instances, all money along with precious fuel and other valuable material can go to total waste. Finally, we all know the most infamous accident of Space Shuttle Columbia, in which, NASA lost billions of dollars and highly qualified astronauts.

On the other hand, it is always important for us to know more about space. It is extremely necessary to learn and to understand the space in order to better comprehend our Earth and its possible future. Moreover, we can also protect our Earth from possible threats like comets or any other acute changes that may happen in outer space. Finally, such exploration may become successful in future and we may come to know about other planets where life is possible.

All in all, I strongly believe that we ought to find out more about outer space but certainly not by sacrificing the needs of people of our Earth. Their basic needs must be satisfied by governments before allocating budgets for outer space exploration.

◆ ◆ ◆

21. **Some people say that the government should control the amount of violence in films and on television in order to control violent crimes in society.**

   How far do you agree or disagree with this statement?

Controlling the intensity of violence that is depicted on television screen has always been a question of debate. It always has its supporters and protestors. However, in my opinion, it is good to not to show too many destructive scenes to the viewers of televisions.

Those who assert that government should not control violence come forward with the following arguments: Firstly, they say that television is a reflection of events happening in the society and those who produce shows take inspiration from incidents happening around them. This may appear convincing. However, it is also proven that showing violence can leave a negative and destructive impact on the minds of the viewers, especially children because they are emotionally more vulnerable and their minds are more impressionable.

Secondly, they say that too much violence is always shown in other media like cinema. Such violent movies also do good business and are watched by people. This argument looks convincing but if we look deeper, we realize that people go to cinemas for occasional entertainment only. On the other hand, they watch television regularly and with all the family members. In this situation, increased frequency of exposure to extreme violence is not suitable for all viewers.

Finally, they add that there should be no restriction on creativity and freedom of expression. It can be a promising point, but it is undoubtedly clear that freedom of expression and creativity must never be used to discomfort others and affect the psychology of our youth.

All in all, according to me, we must control the intensity of violence depicted on television in order to have a positive, less destructive and less crime inclined society.

◆ ◆ ◆

22. **It is generally observed that almost all high level jobs are done by men. Does it mean that the government should encourage a certain percentage of these jobs to be reserved for women?**

    Do you agree or disagree with this proposition?

It seems unusual but true because almost all high level and top position jobs are generally entrusted to men and not to women. However, I believe that reserving any proportion of top level jobs for women is not a wise proposition.

Introducing reservation for women in top level positions has plenty of disadvantages. First, such reservation will prevent deserving candidates from serving at higher posts. This will certainly create great frustration and disappointment in their minds. For example, in India, the system of reservation exists in civil services and in many other government sectors. This has generated huge discontent in the minds of government employees.

Second, such a system can bring incompetent candidates at important positions. As a result of this, it can hinder growth of the organisation, which ultimately leads to a negative impact on the economy of the country. Finally, a top level team comprised of some incompetent and some competent candidates cannot work with synergy and this can lead to hazardous results.

On the other hand, those who favour reservation for women argue that such a system lets women work with confidence and will brings sense of equality in them. They also add that women working at entry level positions shall get inspired by seeing other women in higher positions and this will encourage them to improve their own performance.

Finally, it is true that reserving seats for women in top level jobs may offer good opportunities to them. However, barring deserving candidates by reserving seats for the other gender will certainly have some unfortunate effects on the corporate sector. Hence, I think the government must not implement reservation for women in top level jobs.

◆ ◆ ◆

23. **Some people argue that if children behave badly, their parents should accept responsibility and also be punished for the behaviour of their children.**

Do you agree or disagree with the statement?

Bad conduct of children prevails in almost all societies of today's world. We have been searching for ways to inculcate discipline and obedience in children. However, expecting parents to accept total responsibility and receive punitive actions for the mistakes of children is not a good idea.

Expecting parents to undertake penalties for bad code of conduct of their children will create countless troubles. First, the fear of punishment and possible embarrassment will oblige parents to be extremely strict with their children. This, in turn shall affect the overall growth of children, as adequate freedom required for their development shall not be available to them.

Moreover, some children are stubborn by nature and their parents are therefore help-less in exercising control. Such children may lose their way completely and commit seri-ous acts about the consequences of which they are simply unaware of. In these cases, punishing innocent parents is inhuman. Such a system might give a wrong message to misguided juveniles who wish to seek revenge from their parents. Finally, it will always be difficult to prove the act of crime as children at times may commit mistakes in inno-cence or owing to lack of maturity or knowledge.

On the other hand, in today's fast life, many parents do not take adequate care and do not nurture their children appropriately. Hence, it may seem that punishing them for the mistake of their children will make them more responsible and sincere about their family and society.

Conclusively, according to me, giving punishments to parents for bad deeds of their children is not a good notion because it may spread negative messages in the society. What is more, it is a system that is extremely difficult to follow.

◆ ◆ ◆

24. **The importance of academic subjects as compared to extracurricular ac-tivities is increasing every day. Some people suggest that sports classes should be sacrificed in High School so students can concentrate on Aca-demic subjects.**

Do you agree or disagree?

We are living in a highly competent era where the importance of a good education is extremely high. This is the reason parents today motivate their children to pay more attention to academic subjects at school and not get involved in other extracurricular activities. It appears to be a valid move but it cannot diminish the importance of sports activity in the life of school going children.

Sports classes must not be compromised because they are helpful in many ways. Firstly, they offer good physical exercise and psychological relaxation, both of which are vital for the physical and mental growth of students. Secondly, sports teach plenty of important skills like team work, communication, strategy development and so on. It is indeed difficult to cover such aspects of life under academic subjects. Finally, sports in school always help in identifying talented children. This is very important because spotting talent for sport at a tender age can result in the creation of a legend in years to come.

On the other hand, some people argue that we should remove sports sessions because playing cannot help in improving academic performance of students. They also add that the economies of the world are growing in such a way that better academic degrees will be essential to survive and grow in the future.

All in all, I admit that academic subjects are becoming very important these days, but it does not imply that we should remove sports classes from schools. Thus, I disagree with the statement because I firmly believe that we need healthy, sporty and energetic graduates to lead the future world.

◆ ◆ ◆

25. **Computers these days can translate all kinds of languages with greater accuracy. Hence, our children will not need to learn more languages in the future.**

    Do you agree or disagree?

Technology is becoming extremely useful in dealing with linguistic problems. These days, we have readymade programs in the computer which can translate one language into another. Owing to this, a question is raised that should we teach different languages to our children if such wonderful technological support is available to us? The answer could be yes.

The need to learn more languages for children cannot be dealt away with completely because we now have the help of computers. To start at a very simple level, we all know that one word is used in different contexts and in different situations. Now, it is difficult to prepare such a program that can understand all the contexts of human behaviour. What is more, we also use intonation to convey meaning. Computers will thus have great difficulty in translating the actual meaning of conversations and there can be disastrous communication gaps.

Finally, excess usage of computers has its own disadvantages. It is also proven that excessive dependence on technology hinders the psychological growth in children and they may become incapable of resolving complex problems.

On the other hand, some people argue that children already study many subjects at school. If we facilitate them with the technology of translating languages, they will have less academic burden to deal with. Next, they also assert that translation software is becoming more competitive with every passing day. Millions of people are already using it in their everyday life.

In conclusion, I think using computers for translation is a good idea but children should be taught languages in order to acquaint them with different cultures and grant them a capacity which helps them wherever they are in the world.

◆　◆　◆

26.　**Forests are the lungs of the earth. Destruction of the world's forests can result in the death of the world we currently know.**

To what extent do you agree or disagree?

We all are aware of the fact that forests play a pivotal role in controlling the proportion of carbon dioxide gas in atmosphere and preventing soil erosion. By doing so, forests also help control the global warming and maintain the ecological balance of Earth. It is needless to say that destruction of forests will make human life a history for nobody to study.

Science has proven that plants, shrubs and trees inhale carbon dioxide and exhale oxygen. This process consumes additional carbon dioxide that is emitted by human activities like burning fuel, wood and other industries. Forests consume that carbon dioxide gas and keep a check on its proportion in the atmosphere. If the intensity of carbon dioxide increases, it increases the temperature of Earth and causes global warming. This leads to a faster meltdown of polar ice caps. Consequently, the sea level goes up and the available land will gradually sink in increased sea levels. The last and the most extreme and inevitable result of global warming is that this planet will lose most gases from its atmosphere and will become an ice ball, diminishing all possibilities of any type of life on this Earth.

The Ultimate Guide To IELTS Writing　　　　　　　　　　　　　　　　**183**

However, in today's world, we still see huge ignorance about this fact. Many a times, people concentrate on other less important things like reducing the use of fuel, electricity and other carbon emitting activities. Hence, they present an argument that in this manner we can resolve the global environmental crisis. This is a good step but cannot give us a large scale solution which the preservation of forests can.

Conclusively, I admit that forests are the only natural source we have that help us in controlling global warming. If we keep destroying forests for our selfishness, this planet will die soon.

◆ ◆ ◆

27. It is often said that children learn best by observing the behaviour of adults and copying it.

To what extent do you agree or disagree with this statement?

It is a proven fact that minds of children are impressionable and highly receptive. In my opinion, young children are always influenced by people around them and hence they subconsciously imitate the behaviour of these adults.

It is observed very commonly that parents may try very hard to inculcate habits in their children by telling them what to do and what not and yet the children do not imbibe any of them. In contrast, what is general routine in the house in terms of everyday behaviour is unconsciously absorbed by the children's mind and psyche. This is more intensely and accurately observed in language skills as children imitate every sound we make even when they do not know the meanings of any of the words spoken.

Moreover, a negative result of this process is that children adopt a lot of bad habits as well before they are old enough to know that such traits can never help them in any way in their life. Only when they grow up into youth and broaden their academic horizons, they can differentiate between good and bad.

On the other hand, there is an argument that each child is blessed with a basic instinct that is his or her individuality. Whatever the context of growing up, this instinct guides the child and is a stronger force than the behaviour of others around him or her. There is credibility to this argument yet the effect of environment cannot completely be negated.

Therefore, in my opinion, children learn a lot from observation of people around them and thus, it is our duty to see that we carry forth ourselves with responsibility.

◆ ◆ ◆

28. **Giving detailed description of crimes in newspapers and on television has bad consequences. Some people therefore suggest that the government should impose restrictions on them.**

   To what extent do you agree or disagree?

With the rise in the number of newspapers and television channels, almost all the crimes are covered with detailed information. There are divided opinions on the consequences of this description. Both views are discussed in this essay.

It is true that most people of the world access and rely heavily on electronic and print media. Hence, it is the responsibility of the media to serve the community with sensible and socially acceptable news because their reader class consists of vulnerable people like children, teenagers and even misguided beings. Such readers may get negative inspiration from crime descriptions and harm either themselves or other innocent people. It is very important to control crime rates in the world and the detailed descriptions of modus operandi of criminals may result in a contradictory situation.

On the other hand, some people assert that providing detailed descriptions of crimes helps in creating awareness in the people. They also add that this awareness is the key factor in preventing more crime and also helps people in protecting themselves from criminals. Moreover, the information about the crime may also be helpful in catching those criminals and bringing them to justice.

Finally, with the increase in crime in all parts of the world, it is essential for the media to give elaborated information to their viewers but I think they should differentiate and filter useless and provoking information from their coverage. By doing so, the media can play an important and fundamental role in keeping a check on the crime in society and also in building responsible individuals.

29. In order to improve a country's education system, young students should be allowed to openly criticize their teachers during class time.

Do you agree with this?

What are some other ways education systems could be improved?

In the times that we live in, open-mindedness and informality are considered more important than obeying value systems. Thus, we hear a suggestion from some quarters that students should be allowed to criticize their teachers openly, during class time. I do believe in open mindedness but I disagree with the viewpoint presented here.

If students were given the permission to criticize teachers during class time, first of all this could be used as a tool by disinterested students to waste precious teaching time. Secondly, learning can only occur when there is a feeling of respect for the teacher and with such openness there would be loss of respect and the teaching environment would be thereby spoilt. Thirdly, students are sometimes too young to grasp the intention of the teacher or the need of the subject being taught. In such a situation the criticism would not be of any help as it would only be a misguided judgment.

On the other hand, people who advocate such openness in the classroom say that this can make the relationship between the teacher and the student friendlier. However, I believe that if the teachers are well trained, they know the psychological aspects of teaching young children and thus, our education environment would be better served. Also, in the event of receiving some unwelcome behaviour from a teacher, there could be a system in place where the student or a group of students is allowed to submit a written complaint to the principal or any other authority that can then look into the matter and resolve it responsibly.

To conclude, even though the system of open criticism may appear democratic, I opine against this method considering its possible drawbacks.

◆ ◆ ◆

30. **It is observed that most governments pay a lot of money for the art projects. For instance, there are more and more paintings and sculptures seen in public places. Some people say that it is wrong and governments should spend more money on other important things of public interest.**

Do you agree or disagree?

Owing to the emphasis given to the aesthetics of our living environment, governments these days spend more money in improving the appearance of various parts of cities. We can see paintings, sculptures, carvings and many more artistic objects on display at crossroads, intersections and at different public places. This development is good, provided that it does not come at the expense of essential needs.

Such projects and artistic monuments are the call of the hour. First, tourism industry is promoted by almost all countries. To attract tourists, such sculptures and artistic monuments in public places are often useful. Second, they always remind us of our culture and the value of art. This is indeed helpful because they work as a bridge between us and our cultural values. In addition, they also help children in staying connected to the arts. Finally, such monuments also provide employment to many people who are involved in their design, construction and maintenance.

On the other hand, such artistic projects are often very expensive to build and to maintain. Governments have to allocate funds not only for the project but for its maintenance also, which, in turn, becomes more expensive. Next, almost all countries require funds for essential needs like providing better healthcare, infrastructure, education and other facilities to their citizens. It seems awkward if a citizen of a country does not have basic health care or primary education and the government is occupied in spending on artistic projects.

Finally, I believe that allocating funds for artistic projects is indeed good as it makes our living environment more aesthetic. However, such expenses must be avoided if vital services in the country are not properly developed.

◆ ◆ ◆

31. **Air travel is responsible for a lot of pollution in our environment. Some people think that prices of airplane tickets should be increased in order to reduce air traffic.**

Do you agree or disagree?

It is indeed an inevitable truth that air planes cause immense amount of air and noise pollution. This adds to the woes of global warming and its possible detrimental consequences. However, raising prices of air tickets to reduce air travel seems highly illogical.

There are many reasons why airfare hike will not suffice the purpose of reducing pollution created by flights. First, air travel is an indispensable mode of commutation which is now an integral part of our life. It is an essentiality for corporate executives, politicians and those who live or have relatives abroad or in other provinces. Second, air travel is used by the affluent class of the society. Therefore, a price hike in air travel would hardly hinder them from using it.

Third, these days, there are millions of people worldwide who earn their living from the airline industry. Hence, reducing air traffic will certainly mean that many of them shall lose their jobs. Finally, practically, it is not possible for any government to take such an action because of the laws and corporate freedom that most countries have implemented these days.

On the other hand, some short-sighted people argue that dearer air travel will help in reducing pollution caused by airplanes. They say that increased cost of air travel will compel people to search different options and this will help in a reduction of air flights. They also add that cost hike will ultimately result in only genuine flyers, which is a desirable situation from the environmental point of view.

In conclusion, there are chances that a few travellers may not opt for flights if the prices are higher, however, considering the benefits and its role in today's globalized world, this idea will not bear good fruits for anyone.

◆　◆　◆

32. **Public libraries provide a large collection of books to read. Some people argue that they should also provide other hi-tech facilities like computers, internet, CDs and DVDs.**

Do you agree or disagree with the statement?

Technology has now penetrated almost all segments of life these days. All facilities and services are now incorporating technology in different intensities. Users of public libraries should not be excluded from getting benefits of technology.

It is indeed desirable to introduce hi-tech facilities like computers, internet, CDs and DVDs in our libraries. First, users come to the library to read books and to gain knowledge. Many a times it happens that they may not get adequate resources on various subjects. In such instances, the internet becomes extremely useful. Users can search the net and can find out detailed information on almost any topic.

Secondly, these days, we can see that the world of publication has now changed and many books are being converted to CDs and DVDs format. In addition, books, documentaries and other useful reference materials are now being published in digital form. What is more, handling, maintaining and storing digital media is way easier than books. Lastly, the life of such material is often longer than books.

However, some people argue that a library should not offer such hi-tech facilities as many users of libraries are elderly people who are not tech-savvy and hence cannot use such facilities. Moreover, they say that such facilities increase cost of handling and subscription fee shall thereby increase.

Finally, I think, library's prime function is to offer material for reference and enrichment of knowledge of the people of society, irrespective of the form of materials. If the call of the hour suggests that hi-tech facilities should be included, a library ought to provide them to serve the community in a better way.

◆ ◆ ◆

33. **It is a fact that technological innovation is bringing about rapid changes and retraining becomes a lifelong necessity for most employees. Thus,**

The Ultimate Guide To IELTS Writing

some people say that industry should take over more responsibility for education to have competent future employees.

Do you agree or disagree?

In today's world, education has become a lifelong process for most people. We see new innovations almost every day and to incorporate those changes, people should be trained properly in order to extract desired benefits out of those innovations. This is the reason why it is often argued that industry should take over more responsibility for education. However, to me, it seems irrelevant.

Industries should not take more responsibility of education in the context of lifelong training of employees. First, most employees are already trained and educated in their tertiary or vocational education institutes. Thus, they only need updates or short crash courses on newer developments. Secondly, it is the duty of the employees to keep themselves abreast of latest developments and thus prove that they are indispensable for the organization.

Thirdly, industries spend millions on training their employees as they find fresh graduates unemployable and hence they are trained thoroughly before they start their work. Here, it is often argued by industrialists that it is the responsibility of governments to increase employability of fresh graduates by bringing required changes in the education system.

However, some people argue that industries must contribute in educating candidates. First, they say that industries make maximum use of skills that are learned by today's student because that student will be a future employee. Second, they also suggest that if industries take responsibility of education, they can bring desired changes in the system, which will reduce their on-the-job training costs. Finally, they assert that it is one of the ways to contribute to the society.

All in all, I strongly believe that the context of lifelong training of employees is not the responsibility of industries alone and thus industries may limit their role in imparting education to students in schools and colleges.

♦ ♦ ♦

The Ultimate Guide To IELTS Writing

34. **It is seen that awareness about environmental problems is very low among the younger generation in most countries. Some people argue that environmental awareness must be added as an essential subject in all courses in colleges and schools across the world.**

   To what extent do you agree or disagree with this argument?

It is indeed unfortunate that today's youngsters are not really well informed about environmental issues. I strongly assert that this ought to be reversed by imparting knowledge about this extremely important issue to all school and college goers.

There are numerous reasons why environmental education for all is essential. Firstly, understanding climatic problems at an early age makes children sensitive towards the same and when they grow up, they can stand for its protection whenever required. Secondly, it is often observed that ignorance is the prime cause behind most environmental problems and if children and teenagers are properly educated about climatic problems, we can reduce sources of pollution to a great extent.

Thirdly, we all know that prevention is the best cure and we can certainly prevent the occurrence of environmental hazards, which otherwise might happen sooner or later due to immense pollution and global warming. Finally, we study computers because we will have to use it; we study science and maths because they have practical applications in our life. Now, how can we not study about the environment based on which our entire humanity exists?

However, some short-sighted people might argue that students these days have to bear a lot of burden of other subjects. They also add that studying about atmospheric problems at an early age is boring and we should not make education undesirable for youngsters and children.

In conclusion, I strongly assert that we must teach about environmental issues to each and every student at primary, secondary and tertiary levels.

◆ ◆ ◆

35. **Whilst studying abroad provides an opportunity to broaden one's experience, it also presents the danger of negative influences from the host culture.**

How far do you agree or disagree with the statement?

Studying abroad is the flavour of the present era. Educational institutions receive international students from many countries. In my opinion, concerns of adverse effects of local culture on international students do not hold ground.

Students go abroad with a vision to study and acquire better quality education. Many a times, they have to pay a very high fee which is very difficult for them or their parents to manage. This brings about a sense of sincerity in them and negative influences are warded off. Next, staying in a foreign country makes students more tolerant towards the host culture and this, in turn, enhances their understanding of different cultures. Consequently, they become even more aware of good and bad in both cultures and can thereby become better world citizens.

Thirdly, students often stay in close touch with their families back home by way of internet, telephones etc. What is more, they also become friends with the students of their home country. All these factors ensure that they do not forget their goals and they do not go off track.

However, some people argue that the countries where international students go may have a free and bold culture. They assert that when a student from a conservative culture goes to a country where the level of freedom is very high, he or she is likely to come under negative influences of host culture. There is a possibility of there being one or two who do get misled but this cannot be taken to describe a general pattern.

In conclusion, I opine that international students come in close contact with the foreign culture and they do adopt useful aspects of it. However, most of them do not come under any kind of negative influence from the host culture.

◆ ◆ ◆

The Ultimate Guide To IELTS Writing

36. **Nowadays people have to work for longer hours under stressful conditions.**

Do you agree or disagree with this statement?

Suggest the ways by which the job conditions can be improved.

Working conditions in today's corporate world are highly demanding for almost all employees and the pressure of better performance is making life difficult for many workers across all sectors. I agree that in the present, people have to work longer and under highly stressful conditions.

There are many reasons to support this. First, almost all employees work toward certain targets set by their higher management. All companies are in the league to outperform their peers and to do this; they want their employees to put in better than their best. All conditions of achievement of a target cannot always be kept under control and therefore in the process there are times when employees have to work much more than their stipulated hours every day. Such work load is very stressful. Next, there are deadlines to many projects and in that sense not only the quality of the work but the time in which the same is executed also becomes important. This adds to the pressure immensely.

To address this problem, there are some solutions. One of them is that companies must limit working hours of all employees between 10-12 hours per day. This will give them adequate time to relax and to recharge themselves. Next, targets set by the management must be screened in the light of their viability. If targets are too difficult for the employees to achieve, frustration develops, which leads to a decline in performance. Finally, there has to be some legislation to support the employees to protect them from the exploitation they go through because of extended working hours.

All in all, I admit that we are in such an era where longer working hours and the pressure to deliver specific results have become an inevitable part of our work environment. However, with certain actions, we can limit the stress at work.

◆　◆　◆

---

37. **Some people think that men and women have good expertise only in particular fields. This means men are better at doing certain jobs and women are better at doing some other jobs.**

Do you agree or disagree with the statement?

Since our existence, we have been dividing mankind into two genders in countless ways. Ability of handling of different kinds of work by different genders is one of those ways of differentiation. However, with better awareness and education, it is proving to be untrue.

Today, both genders are capable of doing almost everything with great efficiency. To begin with, we can see that women are taking active part in the socioeconomic scenario now and doing really well in most jobs which were once perceived to be for men only. For example, engineering, technology, marketing, management and many more industries are now served efficiently by women. In the same context, we can see men are also doing well in areas which were once believed to be for women only. For example, parenting, housekeeping, hospitality industry, nursing, teaching etc. are now diligently nurtured by many capable men. All this has happened because of widespread awareness through education.

However, some conservationists still argue that men and women are respectively better at doing only specific jobs and not all. They say women are physically weaker than men and must work under consideration of their physical limitations. They also suggest that men are not as good care takers as women are and hence they should stay away from such jobs because nature has assigned specific duties to both genders to complement each other.

Finally, I completely disagree with the argument that men and women are better at doing specific jobs only. Thanks to today's education system such hypothetical boundaries have been erased between two genders and we have got a sense of equality to all humans on this earth, which, I think, is very important for the overall growth of the human race.

◆ ◆ ◆

38. **In today's societies, young people need more freedom to learn and explore the world on their own. Older people, on the other hand think that youngsters need to learn from their suggestions and experiences.**

Do you agree or disagree?

We live in a world that is constantly changing and developing. To keep the world in this flux, we need fresh eyes, which explore the world on their own without any preconceived idea. Hence, I think the expectation of today's youth of more freedom in this context is well justified.

There are ample reasons to support this. To begin with, teaching methods and content and patterns of delivering the same keep changing regularly. In this process, they develop radically in a generation's time. Now, in this scenario, when elders give suggestions, they are often based on their experience, beliefs and findings. However, many a times, their suggestions do not confirm to present day modes of learning and the new information available.

Moreover, today's education system makes youngsters more adventurous and prompts them to learn things on their own rather than being dependent on others for their learning. For example, if the likes of Bill Gates or Dhirubhai Ambani had followed the conservative advice of their elders, companies like Microsoft and Reliance would not have existed.

On the other hand, some argue that following suggestions of elders makes youth safe and secure. They also add that youngsters are vulnerable and may adopt improper directions in life, if not guided properly. Finally, they also say that old people are more experienced about life and hence their views are useful and more mature.

All in all, I do not deny the fact that suggestions of elders are indeed useful for youngsters. However, I strongly feel that for the comprehensive development of youngsters, they ought to be given the freedom they desire in order to make sure that more innovative, creative and intellectual citizens come to live in this world

◆ ◆ ◆

39. **Cooking food at home is a waste of time. Fast food restaurants help in living a modern and less stressful life.**

Do you agree or disagree with the statement?

We live in such an era where almost everything is available at our doorstep within minutes. Fast food home delivery services are also available across the globe. We can order almost anything and it can be at our home in no time. However, this does not mean that cooking food at home is wastage of time and energy.

Homemade food is far better than fast food. First, food cooked at home is always better, fresh, superior in quality and to the taste of family members. Second, food cooked at home has its own history of flavours and recipes which helps members to strengthen the bonding between each other.

Third, food cooked at home is often economical compared to fast food if the cost is calculated on daily basis. Finally, fast foods often contain high calories and fewer nutrients compared to homemade food which offers a wide range of nutrients and vitamins.

On the other hand, some people say that cooking at home is time consuming and should be replaced by fast food. They add that lifestyle today has become so fast that cooking food at home hinders other work and is a waste of time. They also argue that if good quality of food is available at a certain cost, cooking the same at home is not a good idea.

In conclusion, I assert that cooking food is not a waste of time at all. It helps us to stay healthy and energetic and strengthens family ties. Fast food is an alternative and is not a viable daily routine. It can be a break from the everyday home food in terms of taste but nothing more. It can never replace homemade food.

♦ ♦ ♦

40. **Some people think that modern inventions have more problems as compared to their benefits.**

Do you agree or disagree?

Inventions are always carried out to give comfort, facility and convenience to the people. However, many a times it is seen that these inventions create huge problems, as well, for the world, thereby raising a question whether they are really beneficial or not. Discounting a few exceptions and applications, I think modern inventions are indeed helpful to the people.

Those who say modern inventions have more problems come up with the following arguments. First, they say that it's modern technology that gifted us nuclear bomb which was used to kill millions of people in WW2. They are factually right, but they are forgetting the original intention behind inventing nuclear energy. We all know that it was meant to generate electricity from nuclear fusion. Now, if we instead invent bombs for massacre, it is our mistake and the invention cannot be blamed for it.

Secondly, they add that today's inventions are largely responsible for global warming and ozone layer depletion. They may have a point if we consider burning of fossil fuels in the process. Yet, modern day innovations actually do not play any direct role in harming the environment but it is our irresponsibility which is accountable for it.

Lastly, they assert that innovations like computers and internet have created a lot of problems for the youth today. Overuse of social networking sites, hacking, viruses, credit card scams are all a result of these. This is true but these facilities are meant to support human life and if some miscreants misuse them, we should try and control that rather than blaming the innovation.

Finally, I must say that misuse of innovations has created a myth that they have more problems than benefits. However, that does not imply that modern innovations are absolutely troublesome.

◆ ◆ ◆

41. **Air travel is preferred by rich people only. Majority of the people receive no benefits from the development of air travel as an industry.**

   Do you agree or disagree?

Air travel, apart from being an important mode of long distance journeying has always been a fascinating and exciting experience for humans. Initially, it was exclusive and expensive and out of reach of the common man and so it was considered to be a facility for the elite class only. However, stating that its advantages have remained limited to the rich class does not appear to be true.

Employment is the first reason why air travel has given its benefits to almost all classes of people. As an industry it provides immense direct and indirect opportunities to all sections of the society i.e. right from pilots, cabin crew, engineers, airport support staff etc. to loaders and technicians, ticket booking agents and even cab drivers. Most of these people may not fly regularly but earn their bread from it.

Moreover, air travel has now expanded its wings to include the middle class people as well. This has been possible because of increased competition amongst airlines and as a result, the end user is able to get a better deal. Hence, these days, many middle class people are increasingly opting for air travel.

On the other hand, some people argue that due to increased input costs and other expenses, air tickets are getting more expensive and hence air travel might just suit the upper strata of the society and so they believe that other people of the society are least advantaged by the aviation industry.

Conclusively, gone are the days where flying in an aeroplane was a rare, exclusive and only-for-the-rich kind of thing. According to me, air travel helps not only the rich class but all other classes of the society and hence I disagree with the statement given.

♦ ♦ ♦

42. **Many people believe that the most important things in life are free – they could not be bought because they are invaluable.**

   How far do you agree or disagree?

According to me, the most important things in life are those without which we cannot survive and grow. Hence, in that context, I think the statement holds valid ground.

These invaluable things cannot be bought by money. First, let us consider air, water and land. Without air, it is next to impossible for any living species to survive on this earth.

The Ultimate Guide To IELTS Writing

This is equally true for water and for land because, without them we cannot find the basis to exist.

Secondly, the love and emotional support that we get and we share with our loved ones can never be valued in terms of money. Finally, the religious, cultural and spiritual heritage that we have received from our ancestors works as a guide for us to live our life in a peaceful, progressive and sacred way. This heritage has come to us as a gift and can never be bought or reproduced by money.

On the other hand, some materialistic people argue that today, we can buy all comforts with money which are important in life. They also add that emergency life support services and systems which help save lives are bought by money and have saved countless lives. Lastly, they add that money gives us the power to buy materials which in turn impart a sense of achievement and happiness.

In conclusion, I do admit that money gives us freedom to buy luxuries which can make us happy momentarily but it is negligible compared to the love and happiness we get from our family, religious and social systems and the natural resources. Thus, I completely agree with the statement that the most essential things in life cannot be purchased by material wealth.

◆ ◆ ◆

43.   **Some people feel that certain workers like nurses, doctors and teachers are undervalued and should be paid more, especially when other people like film stars and company bosses are paid huge sums of money that are out of proportion to the importance of the work they do.**

How far do you agree or disagree?

It is an undeniable fact that doctors, nurses and teachers offer important contributions in today's society. Hence, it is argued that they are underpaid compared to celebrities and CEOs and should be treated more fairly. The argument holds ground yet the solution is not that simple.

What a certain profession gets paid is decided by multiple factors operative in the economy of a place. One important factor amongst these is that the value of a service is not decided upon the morality of its character but upon its demand. Films and media are a sector which most people watch to escape the drudgery of their life and to emulate these celebrities to feel that they too can touch the stars. Thus, the entertainment industry owing to its great demand is a big-budget and high-profit venture.

Secondly, entrepreneurship not only earns capital but creates it and therefore it sets its own standard of the price its services demand. Nurses, teachers etc. are trained professionals who come through a certain course of learning and start a job. The creativity inherent here is much less than the security promised. Thus, there is no doubt that company bosses have greater say in what they should be paid as compared to these professionals.

Finally, a profession cannot demand a price- it needs to command it. With the same degree two doctors can have very different career graphs. So, though as a general pattern, a profession may be paid less than the other but within its fold it is possible to rise to a higher grade with one's own perseverance.

In conclusion, no strict rules can ever be laid down with respect to the cost of services of a certain profession however noble or essential it may be. Thus, I disagree with the argument given.

◆ ◆ ◆

44. **Some people think male leaders always lead us to violence and conflict. Compared to them, female leaders are better because they have given us a well governed and peaceful society.**

Do you agree or disagree?

If we closely observe the course of history and review large scale violent events and conflicts, we can see that all such events were led and even motivated by male leaders. However, blaming the entire masculine gender for the same and labelling all males as incompetent or violent leaders is not a wise notion according to me.

There are many reasons why the entire male population should not be blamed for being blood thirsty. To initiate with, since the beginning of social system, man has been the bread earner and hence he had to face challenges that prevailed outside the home. Consequently, whenever anyone tried to attack or dominate it was the male who fought for the rights and independence. In this context, it is obvious that the male has both faced the perils and even sacrificed his life for reasons of liberation and freedom.

Moreover, according to history, there have been very few female leaders and rulers and they too were also prone to violence and domination over other countries and states. There are pertinent examples of the queen of England and the queen of Egypt in this regard who suppressed thousands and even claimed countless lives to fulfil their ambitions.

On the other hand, barring a handful of women leaders, history does not give adequate data to analyse and to reach a conclusion that women leaders always create a peaceful society. In addition, the world has not seen any great war or conflict post World War 2 and most female leaders we know have come into prominence after that era.

Finally, even though the feminine gender is known to be more peace loving and not prone to inflicting violence and provoking conflicts, I firmly believe that the male race cannot be held entirely responsible for leading humankind towards disputes and violence.

◆ ◆ ◆

45. **Some people believe that schools should only teach subjects which are beneficial to children's future career and therefore other subjects such as music and sports are not important.**

   To what extent do you agree or disagree?

In this era of globalization, competitiveness is considered as an essential virtue for the financial growth of individuals and societies. This is the reason some people assert that we should eliminate non-academic subjects like music and sports. However, they fail to understand that these subjects are vital to the overall development of children.

There are ample reasons which confirm that non-academic subjects must not be removed from the school curriculum. To begin with, subjects like sports give exercise to children, which is much needed for their physical growth. In addition, they can learn a bunch of practical life skills like interacting with others, team spirit, sportsmanship, planning, envisaging and so on. Hence, such activities are a boon for them.

Next, subjects like music and arts help students to broaden their horizons of creativity. They learn to be creative, to visualise and to relax. These subjects are of extreme importance because children are overburdened by academic studies. They get relaxation from such creative and artistic activities. On top of it, teaching music and sports in school days hones the innate talent of gifted children and paves way for a famous artist or sportsman of tomorrow.

On the other hand, some people say that non-academic subjects are not necessary because students get admission in higher studies or get jobs on the basis of their marks in academic subjects only.

To sum up, I do admit that academic subjects are always more important. However, that does not imply that we should limit the overall development of children and deprive them of sports and music. I strongly oppose the argument that non-academic subjects should be removed from the school syllabus.

♦ ♦ ♦

46. **The problem of obesity is becoming a serious issue all over the world. Some people argue that the price of fattening foods should be increased to reduce the growth of this problem.**

     Do you agree or disagree?

Overweight people are commonly seen everywhere in today's world. Consequently, diseases and disorders due to obesity are on an all time high and they keep mounting upwards every day. To curb this, some assert that the food that increases lipid levels should be made more expensive. However, this is not an ideal solution to this problem.

There are many reasons why rising prices of high calorie foods cannot solve the problem of obesity. First, we should look at the reasons behind obesity. Most people live a lifestyle where they have to sit on a chair throughout the day, in air-conditioned offices. This practically eliminates scope of any physical exercise from their life, which leads to weight gain. In addition, science has proved that overstress and irregular work patterns result in over eating and digestion related problems. Both these factors also lead to a rise in body weight.

Secondly, these days, prices of all commodities are rising and yet their consumption has not declined. The irony is, consumption of food containing higher fats is more in affluent classes, who are not going to be affected by any increment in cost of those foods. Finally, unreasonable rise in prices of food items may create inflation and cause several economic problems for the governments.

On the other hand, some people present a point that upping the cost of fat boosting foods may lead the consumers to think twice before buying the item. Hence, less consumption will certainly reduce calorie intake in the people and will help them in staying in shape.

All in all, some assistance in reducing obesity may be gained by raising prices of fatty foods. However, looking at the reasons behind rise in obesity and adverse consequence on economy, I opine that it is not a wise decision.

◆　◆　◆

47. **Recent studies have shown that overweight people tend to eat 'junk foods' that are high in unhealthy fats. Some people argue that an increase in the price of such foods will serve as a deterrent and thus reduce the number of overweight people.**

    Do you agree or disagree?

There is no doubt that societies around the world are trying to find a solution to unhealthy weight gain caused by consumption of junk foods. One solution that is put forth is that the prices of such food items should be increased to decrease their popularity. I completely disagree with this idea.

Firstly junk food like burgers, chips, pizza, soft drinks etc. are mostly consumed by people who are financially well off. Increasing prices would have no effect on them at all. Secondly, eating junk food is almost like an addiction as the body craves for these empty calories once it has gotten used to them. So, even if some people do find it expensive they still would want to buy it. Thirdly, increasing prices may have some negative effects on the economy of a country as all business is interrelated.

It is true that an expensive item does make the consumer think twice but I believe it can never bring a total solution to the problem. In my experience only when people- young or old, understand the harmful effects such food has on their body they try to reduce its intake. For example, I loved to have an aerated drink every day during summers but only when I became sluggish in my sports class I realized I had to give up this habit. My friend stopped eating French fries when his doctor told him that his asthma attacks were a result of overeating which caused unhealthy weight gain and reduced his stamina.

To sum up, considering the reasons behind the increased intake of fast food, I believe that increasing the prices of junk food is not going to decrease their consumption.

◆ ◆ ◆

48. **Traditional lifestyles of many people in developing countries are attracting increasing amount of international tourists. Such tourism discourages modernisation in these areas.**

   Do you agree or disagree?

It is indeed a fact that vernacular cultures and lifestyles are a major attraction for international tourists. They visit different corners of the world to see traditional lifestyles of the people of developing countries. It is often argued that such visits do not let a tourist spot modernise. This observation seems accurate to a great extent.

There are many reasons behind this. First, tourism has now become a major contributor of foreign revenue for developing countries. When international tourists come, they spend their money to see the traditional culture and lifestyle. Visitors come with curiosity and for the sake of maintaining their interest such areas need to stay as they have been because if they change and develop, they may lose valuable earnings from interna-

The Ultimate Guide To IELTS Writing

tional visitors. Secondly, most people in such areas have a strong attachment to their culture as they are identified with that. Thus, they also think that if they modernise, the existence of their tradition will be jeopardized.

Finally, it is often observed that even if some people want to bring in transformation to facilitate the development of their community, they are often suppressed by businesses that rely heavily on foreign visitors.

However, certain areas cannot develop for other reasons as well and tourism cannot be blamed for the same. Some areas are too isolated or underprivileged and thus, governments of these areas need huge sums of money for the required transformation. In addition, due to lack of infrastructure, no industrial development takes place, which, otherwise is capable of modernising any area.

All in all, it seems true to me that international tourism is one of the main reasons why areas with traditional lifestyle and culture cannot modernise themselves.

◆ ◆ ◆

49. Some people believe that teenagers should be required to do unpaid community work in their free time. This can benefit teenagers and the community as well.

Do you agree or disagree with this point of view?

Working for the society is always good and rewarding for all. Thus, the idea of inspiring teenagers for voluntary work can result in a win-win situation for both – the society and the teenagers.

There are ample benefits of teenagers volunteering for the community in their leisure time. First of all, teenagers learn to interact with a variety of people. By doing so, they can develop virtues like teamwork, compassion, interactive ability and so on. In addition, they develop tolerance and become considerate to all the classes and races of people in their community. Secondly, teens can attain sense of achievement and self worth by working for the society. This helps them to boost their confidence levels. Finally, teenagers develop deeper understanding of the culture, lifestyle and traditions of their own people.

On the other hand, there are certain drawbacks of the same as well. To begin with, such work is time consuming and within highly busy academic days, it is hard for school going teens to spare any time for volunteering. Moreover, teenagers are naive and vulnerable. Hence they can easily be drawn to illegal, improper and harmful activities. Such instances increase chances of their exploitation and they may fall victim to some criminal tendency. However, I think all such flaws are manageable with proper guidance and the backing of a legal framework.

In conclusion, I firmly believe that the notion of teenagers doing unpaid community work is indeed good. I would also like to add that proper monitoring and care ought to be exercised to avoid any untoward consequences.

♦   ♦   ♦

50. Many museums across the world charge an entry fee from all visitors. Some people argue that entry to the museums should be free.

How far do you agree or disagree with this argument?

Museums are places where we can find antique and historical articles to see, discover and learn from. This place has immense importance and hence to maintain it, there should be some entry charges.

People who favour free entry to museums put forward the following arguments. First, they say that museums hold our history, so everyone should have the right to see those articles without paying. This argument looks convincing, however, free entry to the museum will certainly attract vagabonds who lack all seriousness and may even damage the articles. An entry fee is a deterrent for anyone who is not interested in the artefacts but comes in for other mischievous motives.

Secondly, they also assert that historical articles are public property and thus they should be freely accessible to all the people. But, they forget that making something freely available actually reduces its importance in the minds of people. They take it for granted and do not pay adequate respect to the hours spent in collecting and exhibiting articles.

Finally, they argue that governments fund museums for their maintenance and expansion so they do not need to levy charges on the visitors. It is indeed true in some cases. However, it is not true always because maintenance of typical artefacts may be a tedious and expensive job which the government grant might not cover.

To conclude, though the argument of making free entry to the museums appears attractive, it is not feasible for the authorities to implement this in reality. Hence, I opine that museums should charge a token fee from all the visitors.

◆ ◆ ◆

51. **Today, there are a lot of websites providing news on the internet. Some people believe that these websites will totally replace traditional newspaper and magazines.**

To what extent do you agree or disagree?

Both - the number of news websites and the number of internet users are swelling at a rocket speed these days. There are innumerable people who get most of their daily news from websites and this community is increasing in number every minute. However, I believe that this development will never be able to diminish the existence of newspapers and magazines.

There are many reasons why news websites cannot replace newspapers. First, newspapers are cheap, easy to handle and carry. We can take them anywhere with us and read. Secondly, many people in the world today are not familiar with computers and internet. This proportion will never be zero in the coming centuries because millions of people today hardly earn their everyday living. For them, computer use is simply out of question.

Thirdly, newspapers and magazines are more reader friendly as one can glance through a variety of items with a flip of pages as compared to the internet where one would have to open several windows. Also there are many other distractions online that might prevent one from a rich newspaper reading experience which a well edited and composed print media format offers.

However, users who depend on the news offered by the net are rising every day because they are benefited in many ways. One of them is that they get instant news up-dates from the website in any corner of the world. Some of them even offer video clip-pings of the event. Moreover, this material can be forwarded, downloaded and even printed for the future references.

To sum up, I admit that news websites are offering immense benefits to the users. How-ever, they cannot cater to each and every person in the world, which implies that print media will survive on this earth.

◆ ◆ ◆

52. **Some people say that to solve today's global problems, every nation should have a good relationship with other nations.**

To what extent do you agree or disagree with this statement?

In this era of globalisation, many problems of one nation often spill over into other coun-tries and continents. In this situation, it is almost essential for the countries to have good relations with each other so that they can take corrective measures in cooperation with each other at the international level.

Having a cordial relationship with other countries is highly desirable in resolving issues that affect various nations. For example, we all know that Australia is severely affected by Ozone depletion but research indicated that most activities of Chlorofluorocarbon emission take place in the USA. Now, Australia can influence USA to find a solution to prevent Ozone depletion only if they have good relations with each other.

Secondly, this helps countries to develop an international network where they can po-lice antisocial elements and prevent terrorism from becoming a multi-national corpora-tion. For example, cordial relationships between USA, Pakistan, Afghanistan, India etc. could mean that the problem of cross border terrorism can be curbed and the world would be saved from attacks such as the one on the world trade centre and at Mumbai.

On the other hand, some conservationists argue that developing relations with other countries to solve problems is not a useful step. First, they say that it is a time consum-ing process where the affected countries may have to suffer a lot if they entirely depend

The Ultimate Guide To IELTS Writing

on the other country. Second, they also say that rather than relying on others, each country should be independent and efficient enough for the solution of problems affecting the world.

Finally, I must admit that we live on this earth as neighbours of each other and we must take collective responsibility to resolve problems that exist at the global level and for the same, it is vital for countries to develop good relations with each other for the better future of our world.

♦ ♦ ♦

53. **Some people say that schools do not make enough efforts in teaching young people to look after their health and they add that schools should undertake health education more seriously.**

   Do you agree or disagree?

In this era of satellite television and fast food, children are at a higher risk of diseases related to poor health or lack of nutrition. In this context, inadequate attention to health issues at school seems to be a contributing factor.

It would be excellent if schools pay more attention in imparting knowledge on healthcare to young pupils. To start, young children come to know the importance of preventive healthcare measures at a tender age. Consequently, they develop healthy habits, which, in turn benefits them as they can perform better at school in both academic and co-curricular activities. Second, they stay away from diseases and hence absenteeism at school is reduced. Moreover, they do not have to visit doctors frequently; this is indeed useful for parents and the government because the spending on child health care can thereby be reduced.

Finally, today's healthy child is tomorrow's healthy citizen; therefore, we can have a healthier society. This is of immense benefit to the whole world because healthier societies can grow better and can lead happier lives. On top of it, they give this heritage to their coming generations and hence, we can expect a disease free world in future.

However, some people say that schools are already under a lot of burden of teaching academic, sports, arts and other co-curricular subjects. Hence, they cannot spend more time in imparting health education to young children. Next, they also assert that it is the responsibility of parents to teach healthy habits to their children.

In conclusion, I completely agree with the notion that schools should place health education at a high priority level because healthier kids are the true founders of tomorrow's healthier society.

◆ ◆ ◆

54. **It is a tendency of human beings that they copy from each other. This spreads the popularity of fashion, lifestyle and consumer goods and helps these industries to grow.**

   To what extent do you agree or disagree?

Imitating others is a deep, subconsciously rooted trait in human beings. Even as children we learn the first lessons by imitating. To copy is not only to get an idea about how to do a certain thing but it is also done to achieve a sense of belonging in a social context. I completely agree that such a tendency helps the growth of fashion, lifestyle and the F.M.C.G. industry.

When people are introduced to a new and innovative product, possessing it is a sign of upward mobility and in this race the industry benefits as the sales rise. Add to it the attraction of a film star promoting a product and there is even more craze and hype generated around the thing. Everyone wants to be identified with a celebrity and therefore they want things which the star has.

Secondly, copying others at times is also a sign of a product that has mass acceptance. When companies build a reputation over time about maintaining a certain standard of quality in the produced goods, people learn from each other about it and that is how the client base increases.

On the other hand, some think that there is no originality in copying others and hence they always search for newer things. Some may try to improvise on the trend and yet others may opt for very unique items. This tendency needs lots of experience, courage and financial strength because the market usually supports products which have a mass appeal.

Finally, I second the notion that the tendency of imitating others helps the fashion and consumer goods industry to grow well. In the long run it also helps create a niche market for those who do not want to imitate.

* FMCG = Fast Moving Consumer Goods

◆ ◆ ◆

55. **Adults always say that life was better in their childhood and school days than it is now. Why do they say so?**

To what extent do you agree or disagree with this statement?

It is indeed true that adults in almost all the societies complain that their childhood was superior than the life today's children live. There could be certain reasons behind such a thought but as a whole, their argument seems one sided.

There are many factors that compel today's adults to think like this. One of them is the tendency to psychologically associate the experiences of the lifestyle to our identity. Most of us do this and hence when the generation changes, there are many who cannot accept the change because that modern ways cannot be identified with the life that they had lived before a few decades. Next, with advancing age, the pace of learning declines and people lose their adaptability to fit themselves in the changing lifestyle. This is troublesome for many adults and forces them to think that the life during their childhood was better.

Lastly, globalisation has influenced our lives tremendously. Today, no society can exist in an isolated manner as was possible in the olden times; the happenings of one affect the other as well. Thus, cultural notions are challenged frequently as you cannot shut your doors to the world. For example, oriental people think their culture is invaded by the western culture and occidental people think their economy is dominated by the skilled people of eastern countries.

However, as per my opinion, we live in a world which is continuously changing. We live in unending flux where nothing is permanent and in such a context, it is futile to label something as good or bad. We should accept the changes that come with time and do our best to move with them. Hence, the argument that life in the past was better is not acceptable to me.

◆ ◆ ◆

56. **The government spends enormous amount of money on renovations of old buildings in large cities. Some believe that this money is better spent on building new houses and road development.**

   To what extent do you agree or disagree with this argument?

Infrastructure development and maintenance of old buildings are the two aspects that always perplex most governments across the globe. It seems that maintaining structures that have historical and cultural value for the society is essential. However, apart from that, governments' funds ought to be used in new development as well.

I see many reasons in support of new construction. First, the need for new infrastructural development is increasing everyday in all parts of the world owing to the needs of the people to travel and remain connected with other parts for varied reasons. Secondly, new construction lasts much longer compared to older ones. This is so because they are made up of modern, sturdy materials which have been tried and tested. In addition, they are constructed with the help of latest technology, which not only enhances their life but also offers an excellent example of contemporary architecture.

Thirdly, newer constructions are created by keeping the needs of the people and future trends in mind. Hence, they can facilitate their users in a far better manner compared to what older buildings can. Finally, better infrastructure always facilitates economic growth. Thus, it is the need of the hour for all the governments.

On the other hand, there are certain buildings that attract attention and need funds. Some buildings have religious, historical and cultural value that need to be carried forward for the next generation and so it is extremely important for the governments to

The Ultimate Guide To IELTS Writing

spend a large chunk of money for their restoration and maintenance.

In closing, I admit that certain constructions need to be maintained. However, apart from them, it is not sensible for the governments to spend their revenue on old constructions. I assert that new development should be given higher priority.

◆ ◆ ◆

57. **Olympic Games were very important and respected in the past. However, some people say that technological improvements have reduced the importance of Olympic Games in this 21st century.**

Do you agree or disagree with this?

Olympic Games have been given paramount importance across the world since their beginning. To assume that the importance of Olympics is reduced because of technological advances is an improper notion according to me.

There are many reasons to support this. First, Olympics are now far better known and enjoyed than they were in the past because of the technological facility of live telecast. What is more, millions of people around the world watch these games and are bound to a common global stage. Secondly, with the help of improved technology, accurate measurement of performance of athletes is now possible. For example, we can now successfully measure hundredth fraction of a second and this enables us to conduct a higher grade of competition and deliver exact results with transparency and clarity for the participants and the viewers.

Thirdly, stricter surveillance and improved testing technology can prevent athletes from adopting illegal routes like drugs etc. Moreover, better security and safety systems keep criminals away and offer a tension free environment. Finally, sophisticated arrangements are now possible so that we can successfully organise games even under unpredictable weather conditions.

On the other hand, there are certain disadvantages of technological advances as well. Over and above the strength, agility and stamina of their bodies, athletes are now helped by body suits that cut friction, regulate temperatures and even affect the amount of

---

lactic acid produced in the muscles. Thus, any competition between athletes becomes meaningless if they have the ability to buy a technology.

In conclusion, I believe that technology is invented to support and facilitate human endeavour and its role in Olympic Games is no different. Though in some sports it might have reduced the element of challenge and fun, overall it certainly does not reduce the importance of Olympic Games.

◆ ◆ ◆

58.   When families have a meal together, it is considered as a social activity.

Do you agree that eating together is important to the people of your country?

It is said that man is a social animal. Humans like to share lots of things with others and eating together is one such activity. In my country a family meal is a joyous occasion and is accorded a lot of respect and importance.

Across all religions, ethnicities and communities eating together is a significant family event for everyone in my country. This is so for many reasons. First, by doing so, people meet each other and create warmth, togetherness and a sense of security. The stressful professional lives that we live in the present can give rise to a sense of loneliness and frustration at times. Meeting one's family and feeling accepted and loved takes away all the negativity. Secondly, all members seek and offer their opinions, experiences, solutions and assistance to each other on various problems or troublesome situations in life. Thirdly, there is inculcated a sense of tolerance for each other and group activity is fostered.

Finally, such activities always strengthen social bonds between the members of the family. Youngsters gain from the experiences of their grandparents while the latter are blessed with youthful energy in the presence of children. Thus, relationships are honoured and one is conscious of a sense of responsibility to the whole clan. Consequently, such familial bonding translates into a happy, safe society as well.

I firmly believe in the fact that eating together is indeed an important social activity, which is highly respected and followed religiously by the people of my country. In my opinion it should be made one of the essential rituals in almost all societies across the globe.

◆ ◆ ◆

59. **It is observed that people these days spend large sums of money on clothes, hair care and other beauty products. Some people see it as a necessary expenditure whereas others see it as wastage of money.**

How far do you agree or disagree with one of the arguments?

In this highly competitive era of 21st century, it has become indispensable for everyone to look good and presentable. Owing to the same, people spend enormous amounts of money on beauty care, garments and accessories. Such spending is often justified by many. However, such extravagant expenditure is not good in the long run for an individual or a society.

There are many reasons why a large sum of money incurred on aspects of vanity is not a good idea. First, such a tendency leads people to create an artificial identity that can be displayed to the world, which, in time may lead to severe psychological problems like split personality or even depression. Secondly, such cosmetic and superficial care is extravagantly expensive and creates a hole in one's pockets. At times, in a rush to spend money on looking beautiful and attractive, some youngsters adopt unlawful ways to earn money.

Thirdly, this has deep impacts on the social and cultural structure. As people live in a fallacy, they develop traits like lying, cheating and being jealous. Such tendency may lead to additional stress, tension and negativity in the society. Finally, excessive usage of beauty care products and treatments is indeed harmful to the skin and hair and may result in permanent damage to the body.

However, for some, looking attractive is essential. They say that to grow and flourish in this highly competitive era, one has to present oneself in an attractive manner in order to cast a good impression on people around. What is more, if we do not take enough

---

The Ultimate Guide To IELTS Writing

care of our appearance, the world will forget us and we shall lose our importance.

In conclusion, I admit that the idea of spending money behind body and hair care and clothing is not bad in its essence. However, squandering massive amounts of money, energy and time in their pursuit is a choice that will have dreadful consequences for the society.

◆ ◆ ◆

60. **Some people believe that richness is an important factor when we consider helping others.**

Do you agree or disagree with the statement?

It is a popular notion that money is a powerful tool when we want to help anyone and hence, it does hold great importance in providing the best possible aid to anyone in the world. In my opinion there are many other ways in which valuable help can be held out and money is not the only aid which one can offer.

There are ample reasons in support of my viewpoint. Firstly, everyone does not require financial assistance only. People do need helping hands to see them through tough times. For example, in cases of natural calamities like a tsunami or an earthquake, people need to be rescued, and what is required is disaster management and not financial help. When we offer physical help in saving a life, it is far more important than offering money.

The second important need is to help underprivileged, elderly or emotionally challenged people. I think money cannot offer much help in such cases. Those who need aid for education or basic health care or someone to talk to or in certain cases a shoulder to cry on cannot satisfy their needs with money. Finally, personal support requires spending quality time, which is the most precious thing to offer in this world.

On the other hand, some think money can be of paramount importance in helping others in various ways. We can give monetary support to those who need to access basic requirements like food, shelter, medicines, education and so on.

The Ultimate Guide To IELTS Writing

In conclusion, even though financial assistance can be hailed as a very important medium when we help others, I firmly believe that a helping hand in terms of personal support is far more valuable than money.

♦ ♦ ♦

61. **Employers now tend to prefer employees with good social skills in addition to good qualifications. Social skills are getting more and more important compared to qualifications.**

   Do you agree or disagree?

It is indeed a fact that the world is getting smaller with the help of technology and the need of the hour is not only adequate qualification but also the ability to present ideas in a convincing manner and establish good relationships. In such a situation, social skills hold supreme importance. Companies are doing nothing wrong if they give equal importance to social skills and qualifications.

There are abundant reasons why social skills are getting more and more important. Firstly, irrespective of the type of industry, today's corporate world is completely interdependent i.e. all workers have to rely on others in order to complete their tasks successfully. Here, employees with good interpersonal skills come out as winners in most situations. Secondly, businesses today demand lots of communication amongst each other, with higher management and with people connected to the company. Better group skills will enhance smoother functioning and will result in better efficacy of the organisation.

Lastly, public skills are extremely important to establish a trusting client base and therefore there is no doubt that a person having good communicative skills performs better than other employees.

On the other hand, some might say that academic skills are extremely important and should be given top priority while hiring someone. They believe that it's the technical knowledge and qualification that makes someone eligible for the job. They also add that person with only civil skills may harm others and the profitability of the company in useless conversations.

The Ultimate Guide To IELTS Writing

In conclusion, I fully agree with the notion that the trend is shifting towards appointing people with greater social skills though the importance of educational qualification cannot be undermined. One without the other cannot deliver results.

◆ ◆ ◆

62. **Some people think that an employee should change his career or field of work at least once. However, others think that employees should never change their career and stay in one job for their entire lifetime.**

Do you agree or disagree with the statements given?

A few decades before, being loyal to a job throughout one's career was an ideal situation for countless people. However, with the inclusion of technology and expansion in education and work practices, it seems almost impossible for any employee to stay glued to one field of work.

There are several reasons why changing the field of work is beneficial. Firstly, change in itself is challenging. It helps people to grow and encourages their ability to adapt. It also accelerates intellectual growth and skill development. Secondly, any change is a potential tool to open new avenues in work, which may lead to handsome revenue generation at the level of the organization and the individual.

Thirdly, any new dimension will also enhance inventions and innovations in the field of work, which further improves efficiency and quality of life for those who are involved. Finally, according to a survey, 4 out of 10 highly paid jobs in 2002 did not exist in 2012. It does not mean that those 4 jobs vanished; it means that new areas and work sectors opened that gained more income.

However, change has always created resistance in the minds of people. At times, it may give additional stress to the employees and some of them cannot withstand that pressure. In addition, changing the field often calls for skills enhancement, which can be a daunting task for many employees. Finally, those who cannot grow in the new area of work may succumb to it by falling victim to physiological distress or frustration.

To cap it up, I firmly believe that the entire world around us is in a flux. It keeps changing and hence, change is the only permanent thing in this world. Thus, I assert that employees ought to change their field or area of work whenever they get the right opportunity.

◆ ◆ ◆

63. **Some people say that working couples must equally share the household responsibility in all cultures across the world. However others simply do not agree with this view.**

    What side of the given views do you agree with?

It is obvious that both partners in a marriage have to work in today's fast paced and demanding life. However, such a situation has also created a need that both husband and wife should equally share the workload of the household. It is indeed the call of the hour according to me.

There are some strong reasons why I think the couple should support each other in household work. Firstly, it is quite evident that workload and working hours are increasing at the work place everywhere. In addition, challenges and stress at work are also rising to their all time highs in most workplaces. Now, in such a tough and demanding situation, it is nearly impossible for women to look after the house entirely on their own as in earlier times. In the ages past when women did not work the division of labour was very simple- house for the woman, office for man. But now with she having stepped into his domain he needs to step into hers.

Secondly, the true essence of life lies in sharing. If the woman is contributing with her efforts in earning for the family, she must be reciprocated by a helping hand in household responsibilities. Thirdly, men get an opportunity to become better human beings as they evolve an understanding of how the infrastructure of life is put together in the house.

On the other hand some people think that a woman is a natural nurturer and mother and the way she can set up and run a house a man cannot. There is no doubt that men and women have different instincts yet no task can be completely classified as meant for one or the other only.

Finally, I reaffirm my belief that men and women employed in full-time jobs should share the responsibilities of household chores.

64. **Police in the UK do not keep guns with them. As a result some people feel that citizens are less protected, whereas others feel that it reduces overall violence.**

   Do you agree or disagree?

It is the basic duty of police to protect the civilians from crime and to stop or prevent untoward incidents in the society by maintaining law and order. However so many of our legal codes are still traditional. I think the legislation should be changed and police should keep guns with them.

The people who favour that police should not keep guns with them present a few good arguments for it. Firstly, they argue that if police keeps guns with them they will be inspired to use it and this can lead to an overall increase in violence. This argument apparently looks good but in an era where criminals are using advanced weapons to commit crimes, if a policeman cannot protect himself, how can he possibly protect the civilians?

Secondly, they assert that by not keeping guns the police maintain the traditional and social environment of the UK and they can use other means to control criminals. This sounds fair; however nothing is permanent so the social climate is not constant as well. Criminals are changing their activities everyday and to cope up with them, police has to adopt new approaches to maintain law and order in the city.

Thirdly, they also say that police may misuse the weapons to settle their personal disputes with some innocent people. I admit this as a possibility. However the system can be made efficient enough to find out those who exploit their powers. Yet, we cannot allow 99% of people to suffer for the sake of this 1% possibility.

All in all, I firmly believe that prevention is better than cure. A weapon does inculcate fear in the minds of criminals and hence police in the UK must keep guns with them.

65. **There are several factors that motivate people to stay in workforce. Among them, money is the most important reason/factor for the same.**

To what extent do you agree or disagree?

It is an undeniable fact that almost all of us work or do jobs to earn money. The basic intention behind this is to sustain the supply of resources that we need to sustain a life. Hence, it is often argued that money is the most important factor for the people to stay in the workforce. To my mind such a notion is not incorrect.

It is indeed true that most of us work for the remuneration that we get in the form of a paycheque that comes to us at the end of the week or the month. Moreover, the salary also gives us a sense of being worthy because we can use that for our family's happiness and other needs. Furthermore, it is obvious that financial safety and growth are the most important aspects of any individual's life and owing to this I have seen people who stay in a job even if they are unhappy there. On top of it, some people are ready to take a job which obliges them to stay completely outside their comfort zone if they are paid more.

On the other hand, there is a niche segment of workers who do not have money as their first priority. There are people who work for less remuneration provided they get the opportunity to create, the comfort to work at their own pace and most importantly a sense of joy. In addition, factors like dignity, atmosphere at the workplace and the possibility to learn are more important than money for some people.

In conclusion, since money is one of the prime needs of all of us to survive and prosper in life, according to me, it is and it will be the most important factor for most workers to be committed to their respective workplaces.

◆ ◆ ◆

66. **Popular events like the football world cup and other international sporting occasions are essential instruments for easing tension as they aid the release of patriotic emotions in a safe way.**

Do you agree or disagree?

Since the existence of the first human societies, man has been dividing the world into warring factions based on regions, religions, races etc. Such divisionary policies have led to international disputes in modern times. Until recently humans used to settle such disputes by war. Nowadays international sports events have emerged as a safe and creative way to do the same.

International sporting events help in reducing tension between two countries or regions or races in so many ways. Firstly, they are organized in a grand manner and with a big pomp, thus, people come there basically to enjoy themselves. Secondly, in extending support for their home teams leads to a release of patriotic emotions without harming others and their sense of superiority is satisfied.

Thirdly, when such events are held, people of participating countries can meet each other and interact. This helps a lot in reducing tension as interaction is the first step in evolving tolerance. Next, sports teach sportsmanship- the better player always wins. This gives a chance to appreciate the good in others and recognise one's own weak-nesses.

However, in some cases, such events may turn violent if people of a losing team cannot digest defeat or are teased in an extreme manner. But such occurrences are few and far and cannot undermine the positive effects of competitive sport.

Finally, I firmly believe that although there are some chances of violent reactions on part of the spectators, international sports events certainly help in decreasing sectarian ten-sion. Next, this helps in making this world a better and peaceful place to live in.

♦ ♦ ♦

67. **Some people say that our culture and tradition are lost when they are shown to foreigners for the purpose of earning money. Whereas others state that we actually can save the culture and tradition by doing so.**

   Which opinion do you agree with?

The Ultimate Guide To IELTS Writing

Culture and traditions are the identity of an individual and that's why everyone has affection and respect for them. I think more diverse the culture and tradition the longer they can survive on earth. Thus, showcasing its qualities for the foreigners does not diminish it in any way rather helps it to grow further.

People who think that we lose our culture and tradition if we show them to the foreigners to get revenue put forward three arguments. Firstly, they say that by showing our culture we are exposing our strengths and weaknesses to them, and at times, our imperfections can be exploited by the foreigners. This according to me is more an imagination than an actual possibility. We can make the reverse come true if we exhibit our strengths thereby deeply influencing their minds.

Secondly, they assert that to showcase our culture and tradition for the purpose of earning money is a business and we have to modify the 'product' as per the demand of the customers. This leads to our culture being treated as a commodity. There is no doubt that professional concerns can bring in superficiality, yet in introducing our traditions to outlanders, we are actually creating an opportunity for our civilisation to diversify and become richer.

Finally, some advocates of culture and tradition also argue that foreigners may take active interest in them and may customise it as per their beliefs and convenience, which also leads to a deformity of the original culture. However, culture and tradition are lived and followed by people. The more people follow it, the longer it exists on this earth. For example, today so many western countries follow the principles of yoga and meditation.

All in all, I strongly believe that culture and traditions live in the minds of people. When we show them to others we can generate respect for them and thereby earn revenues that can help our culture and traditions to spread and last long on this planet.

◆ ◆ ◆

68. **The advantages of the spread of English as a global language outweigh its disadvantages.**

   Do you agree or disagree with the statement?

Many languages on this earth evolved with the growth of human civilization at multiple different sites that were disconnected to each other before the transport and communication revolutions took place. Now the world is interconnected and has become smaller so it is difficult to deal with such diversities and complexities of language. Hence, there is a need to tie populations of the world with the help of one global language. Presently, the English language seems to be doing this job.

There are some concrete reasons why the spread of English as a global language has more benefits. Firstly, when we have a common language, it becomes easier to communicate accurately and effectively. For example, in case of natural calamities like a tsunami or hurricanes that can affect more than one country, warnings of alert can be understood by all if communicated in English.

Secondly, new theoretical developments in the field of science and technology can be easily shared amongst all countries of the world if there is a common language in which they are conducted. Finally, the spread of English makes the world an easy and convenient place to access and live. This is a boon for those who travel and/or work for multinational companies.

However, some people argue that the spread of English has certain drawbacks. Many vernacular languages are dying because of it and this is not only a lingual loss but a cultural loss as well. Moreover, they also add that such invasion of English is a threat to the cultural and linguistic diversities that we have on the earth.

To conclude, it is true that the widespread usage of English as a global language dominates over local languages and their cultures. However, I think we need one common language for human betterment. Thus, I opine that the spread of English, as a global language has more benefits.

♦ ♦ ♦

69. **Some people believe that the use of animals for the purpose of experiments is cruel while others believe that it is necessary for the development of science.**

To what extent do you agree or disagree with the statement?

For centuries, the human being has always been exploiting natural resources for his betterment. As a part of development of science, many animals are used to carry out experiments. In my opinion it is an injustice to them and it is cruel.

There are many reasons to support this. First, every animal on this earth has an equal right to live with freedom. Captivating some animals for experiments is to snatch their freedom. Secondly, experiments lead to dangerous results including their death. In any case they suffer from immense pain. They are speechless hence they cannot express pain. This is indeed cruel because it is an offensive crime against nature.

In addition to this, every living animal has been given a specific role to play by the nature in ecosystem. When the animals are captivated, the eco-cycle of that area gets disturbed that has its own hazardous implications on the earth and human life.

However, some advocates of science argue that such experiments help in understanding so many things about them and their reaction to various substances help further the development of new medicines. They also assert that the current success of many medicines can be attributed to such experiments. Next, they say that science has also developed many vaccines for the safety of animals by experimenting on them.

Finally, according to me, although it is true that experiments on animals help scientists to develop more knowhow to serve the mankind and the animals, it is cruel to give pain to an innocent, speechless animal. It should be restricted only to the diseased animals or to selected species at least, with strict jurisprudence in order to prevent their exploitation.

◆ ◆ ◆

70. **It is observed that communication between family members in today's times is less as compared to the past. However, some people do not think so.**

Do you agree or disagree?

Modern life varies enormously, as compared to the past. Today's life is hectic and busy, which has given rise to a fear that there is less communication amongst family members now. However, I feel today's family members communicate more with each other than ever before.

There are many reasons why communication between family members has improved than in the past. Firstly, today's families are small in size. In addition, they live in apartments that are compact as compared to the big houses in the past. There is more interaction with fewer people and a common space. Secondly, because of better education, today's parents have changed their roles. They are becoming friends of their children and caretakers of their elders. Thus, the atmosphere at home is more relaxed and conducive to openness and sharing.

What is more, technology like mobile phones and the Internet helps families to be in touch whenever and from wherever they want. Tiny details of each other's existence can be easily shared and though two members may be living thousands of miles apart yet they can feel connected and cared for.

However, some conservationists argue that today's family members live like strangers under one roof. They say that because of hectic working schedules, many family members cannot even talk to each other for days. Next, they assert that today's new generation spends more time watching TV and passing time outside or on social networking sites.

All in all, it is true that today's busy and stressful life could lead to a reduction in interaction between family members, but in my opinion that does not happen with a majority of people. According to me, the level of communication between family members now is better than in the past.

♦ ♦ ♦

71. **Some people believe that school students should only do homework every day. Others think children should get to do extra work to succeed at school.**

    How far do you agree or disagree with this topic?

The general perception of success at school for most parents is good academic performance only. The parents believe that this can be attained by doing homework rigorously. However, there are many skills that are essential to learn in order to achieve success and concentrating only on academic homework might compromise the development of the child.

If we wish that children acquire a variety of skills, then only doing homework is insufficient. The school needs to allocate many other kinds of tasks to students in the form of compulsory newspaper reading, making reports on parts of one's city, learning a musical instrument or a sport etc. Such activities are conducted within the school in some proportion, but by giving children tasks to do on their own shall be a better learning experience for them.

Second important aspect here is the imparting of social skills. Children need to be guided about their role in the family and the society. If household tasks are relegated to them by the school they shall take them more seriously as compared to the event where their mothers tell them to do things around the house. They also should be taught about how a society works and how they can contribute in bringing about positive changes like keeping their neighbourhood clean, spreading the message of education etc.

However, some people favour doing homework only. They assert that this revision and practice are important to understand all the fundamentals of a subject.

All in all, I strongly iterate that doing only homework is deficient to get success at school. According to me, extra work for the development of practical and psychological skills is essential for children to grow up into successful, all-round individuals.

◆ ◆ ◆

72. **Serial drama on TV (for example soap opera or soaps) plays an important social role.**

Do you agree or disagree?

Due to the rise in number or television viewers, so many satellite channels are on air now and each telecasts daily soaps to cater to the mainstream entertainment. For them, it is business. However, for society, the soaps can play an important role.

Firstly, majority of the soaps are based on social themes of present day. Hence, people see a mirror on to their own reality and relate to the soap to be entertained, to learn from and even become conscious of things that they might not be doing in the right way. Also, on a lighter note the viewer gets to know recent trends in lifestyle, i.e. clothing, furnishing, fashion etc. and imbibe from it. What is more, by showing such lifestyle on TV, soaps can bridge the gap between urban and rural area and may help in slowing down the polarization process towards the cities.

Secondly, daily soaps can play an important role in spreading awareness about our culture and traditions from different regions. Each serial drama is set in a particular place and community and in this way others can get to know about their rituals, festivals and traditions. Even watching one's own culture showcased on television gives us a sense of belonging to a larger community.

On the other hand, there are certain disadvantages as well. First, when a serial becomes popular, their producers stretch it too long for monetary gains. To do this, they inevitably add negative characters and this may spread wrong messages in the society. Also, the celebration and depiction of rich lifestyle on TV, may misguide people into adopting unethical ways to earn more money to have a certain kind of life.

Finally, as per my opinion, daily soaps play an instrumental role in the society, as viewers' exposure to them is very high. However, governments should take actions to stop some serials which spread negative messages in the society.

◆ ◆ ◆

73. **Rather than promoting the quality of products, advertisements encourage consumers to buy the products in quantities.**

Do you agree or disagree with the statement?

The prime objective of any advertisement is to make the consumer 'aware' of the product. Later on, advertisements diversified their role to promote the products and show the products' distinguishing qualitative features over their peers and help the sales. Nowadays, advertisements of many products perform only one function namely to prompt the consumer to buy the product.

The reason behind this change is that advertisements today are perceived only as a means of increasing the sales. Hence, the companies force the ad makers to prepare the advert in such a way that the consumer wants to 'buy' more. It is a ploy to attract rather than a tool to inform. This is applicable to most FMCG (Fast Moving Consumer Goods) companies and their products.

Moreover, there are many ways in which they increase sales by offering various schemes, discounts, and free gifts via advertisements. These offers entice the consumer to buy only a certain product and not its competitor. This serves manifold purposes for the company as firstly, the consumer wills to use the product. Second, he or she is made aware of quality in the process and third, now he does not need to be attracted any longer if he is satisfied.

However, many product segments are still untouched by this trend. Segments like, auto-mobiles, capital goods, services sector still have to rely heavily on promotion of their quality.

Finally, according to me, it is true that today adverts inspire consumers to buy more rather than promoting the quality of the product. It does help in increasing the initial sales. However, if the quality is inferior, then, such products cannot survive.

♦ ♦ ♦

74. **Scientific research should be carried out and controlled by government owned companies rather than private owned companies.**

   Do you agree or disagree?

Scientific research is one of the most important contributing factors in the economy of any country. It has to be nurtured and developed properly. Hence, it is more advisable that government owned companies should control it.

There are many advantages of this. First is the 'motive'. The motive of the government is to raise the standard of living of the people and ensure their well being. Contrarily, a private company first thinks about its own profit. Second, the government agencies are bound by laws and have to operate within their limits while the private companies are usually seen to exploit the law to get the desired result. Third, government can fund the

---

research and can collect donations, which is not possible for private companies. What is more, help of governments of other countries can also be asked for, from the international level to hasten the process of research.

On the other hand, for private companies the research process is fast because they work under pressure to perform better. Next, the working environment is more professional, competitive and free from political influence. Hence the output can be efficient and result oriented. This is unlike the government companies where the job security is very high at times and that retards the growth as employees take their positions for granted.

To sum up, it is true that private companies offer better and efficient operative conditions. However, considering the chances of exploitation of the law by private firms, I assert that scientific research should be carried out and controlled by government owned companies only.

♦ ♦ ♦

75. **It is more important for a building to serve a purpose than to look beautiful. Architects should not worry about producing a building as a work of art.**

   Do you agree or disagree?

Since the early stages of evolution, human being has been building in order to get a place which houses him, a shelter that protects him and a site where he can work from. Civil engineering and architecture are the formal branches of the study of the science of construction. In my opinion the artistic facet of a building is outweighed by its practical use.

The usage of a building where day to day life takes place is the prime importance and varies from residential, commercial, storage, industrial purposes etc. Issues of space utilization where every square inch is important in urban locations, those of well-functioning services and adequate response to the environment are paramount for the comfort of those who shall inhabit the building.

Hence, architects should concentrate more on space management, ventilation, and convenient infrastructure that can enhance the efficiency of the people who will live and work in it. There are some cases where an office complex looks very elegant from outside but the people who work inside are not satisfied with the services and this troubles them each and every day. In addition to this, providing an artistic look to any building adds to its cost and maintenance. Moreover, at times, it does not obey the rules of structure and may succumb to pressures from the weather conditions or ecology.

However, for some buildings, more attention to aesthetics is essential, for example in the case of hotels, multiplexes, exhibition halls and museums. Here, art can be given due consideration by keeping all the structural rules in mind as these buildings serve the purposes of art and recreation.

All in all, I believe for any building, its function is more important than its looks because art is of no use if the building fails to serve the purpose.

◆ ◆ ◆

76. **Some people believe that air travel should be restricted because it causes serious pollution and uses up the world's fuel resources.**

To what extent do you agree or disagree?

Air travel is a product of continuous introduction of innovative technology in the field of transport. It is an essential mode of travel for majority of people. As it is the fastest and most time saving mode of travel, it contributes to the economic development. However, some non-essential flights are harmful to the environment and have serious disadvantages.

Air travel affects negatively in many ways. Firstly, all the aircrafts run on ATF (Aviation Turbine Fuel, a high quality petrol) and they emit carbon and other gases in the sky in the form of smoke. This emission contributes to global warming, which is a serious problem for the world. Secondly, they consume large quantities of oil, which is a valuable resource. This leads to a rise in the price of crude oil and depletion of oil reserves which can have hazardous consequences.

Thirdly, air travel also adds to noise pollution. This is harmful to all the animals and birds. Finally, more number of flights means we require more and bigger size of airports. To build such airports, we require huge land and for that many forests are cut, which is another threat to the environment.

On the other hand, in today's world, air travel is almost essential. So many industries and economies rely heavily on this. If air travel is completely restricted, the economic growth of the whole world will be inhibited. Moreover, air travel also gives employment to millions of people who are engaged with the industry.

Finally, I firmly believe that though air travel is harmful to the environment, it is essential for the growth of the world. However, non-essential flights like those of the tourist, leisure and exploratory variety should be restricted.

◆ ◆ ◆

77. Some people believe they should keep all the money they have earned and they should not pay tax to the state.

Do you agree or disagree?

A state is a system that is run by the people and for the people. A state fulfils many duties for its people and to run efficiently, it requires income. This revenue comes from taxes that people pay to the state. Thus, paying taxes is absolutely necessary for the people.

There are so many reasons to support this. First, a state is a system that funds the development of so many segments including schools, universities, hospitals and so on. Secondly, states develop and maintain infrastructure i.e. roads, bridges, parks and they also run public transport systems like bus, tram, rail and airlines. Maintenance of all the systems requires huge funding. Hence state authorities rely heavily on the tax that people pay.

If people do not pay tax, it becomes very difficult for the state to maintain and operate all the facilities and services. This leads to dissatisfaction in the people's mind. Such developments bring many hardships for the people across all sections of the society. Finally, the economic growth of the state stops and it can become a backward or underdeveloped part of the world.

On the other hand, some conservationists argue that governments do not utilize tax income in proper ways. Moreover, the money is generally wasted in scams and corruption. They also assert that the ratio of expenditure to earning is increasing everyday so they cannot afford to pay a big pie of their income in the form of tax.

All in all, I believe that it is essential for states to earn from taxes to keep the development of the country on track. That is why we must pay taxes because we are going to be reciprocated by the state in the form of facilities and services.

◆ ◆ ◆

78. **In today's world, the pressures of modern life are negatively impacting family life.**

   Do you agree or disagree?

In every human being, there exists a never ending desire to be different. To satisfy this craze, he has been innovating novel ways to live life. This innovated lifestyle is called modern life and it seems there is no end to it because everyday more and more people adopt modern life without thinking of its adverse effects on their family life.

The desire to live a modern life is harmful to family life in many aspects. First, to look modern, people spend hefty sums of money on clothes, jewellery, cosmetics and so on. It is obvious that everyone cannot afford such expenses. Hence, people start borrowing money to show-off. This debt disturbs their minds and brings imbalance in the family life. There are incidences of people committing suicide after being under debt. Second, at times they also get addicted to narcotics, as it is considered thrilling and modern. Such addiction has disastrous consequences for the family.

Finally, I have seen people who force their spouses to change and to become modern beyond their abilities or against their will. Such expectations either bring deformity in the personality or can lead to broken relationships. This is also the reason why extra-marital affairs are increasing nowadays.

However, modern life has few benefits also. First, people stay updated with all the latest developments in the society. Second, innovations also add to the intellect of modern people. Finally, modern life gives immense opportunities to creative people from the fields of fashion, entertainment, music and art.

Conclusively, as per my opinion, there is nothing wrong to be modern. However we generally try to pretend to be modern and anything beyond a limit is bound to have negative effects. Hence, I agree that those who live under pressure of a modern life affect their family life negatively.

◆ ◆ ◆

79. **Education is considered vital for the future of any society in today's world. Governments throughout the world should make education compulsory for all children between the ages of 5-15 years.**

To what extent do you agree or disagree with the statement?

Today's economies are mainly divided into three parts; developed, developing and underdeveloped. The difference between these parts can be largely attributed to education. Countries that had concentrated more on education for centuries are developed. Those who have been doing this for decades are now developing and those who have not focused on education are still underdeveloped. This fact suggests that education has to be made compulsory for the better future of any society.

There are numerous advantages of making education compulsory. First, all children become literate and skilled in various practical ways. They are prepared for technical or professional qualifications. Second, the pool of skilled youngsters works as a building block for many industries and help the economy of the country to grow.

Next, multinationals are motivated to invest in such countries, because graduates with technical skills are freely available. For example, India has a pool of literate, English-proficient youngsters. As a result of this, India has become an outsourcing hub of the world and this industry is contributing considerably to the Indian economy. Finally, making education a must reduces child labour as well. This is a positive sign for the future of any society.

On the other hand, some people argue that it is practically not possible for all the governments to make education compulsory because it requires infrastructure, funding and skilled trainers. However, such issues can be taken care of by inviting private industries in the field. What is more, governments can also borrow funds from international sources because it is an investment for the future.

Finally, I assert that education is the foundation stone for the well-being of any society and hence it has to be made compulsory throughout the world for all children between the ages of 5 to 15 years.

◆ ◆ ◆

80. **In many countries the television telecasts many foreign made programs. The dominance of imported entertainment is harmful to the cultures of these countries. Do you agree or disagree with this?**

Owing to the changes in lifestyle and advancement of technology, television has emerged as a prime means of relaxation and pastime in many societies. This has increased the demand of new programs with every passing day. In many countries, foreign made programs are shown to satisfy this demand. This development leaves some adverse effects on the viewing societies.

There are a few aspects by way of which the cultures of the viewing societies are affected. First, some people argue that watching foreign made programs makes the viewers aware of the cultures of developed countries. This argument looks good. However, it also implies that people start imitating foreign cultures and forget their own in the process and thus face the risk of losing their own identity.

Second, advocates of foreign made programs assert that such programs help people in improving their lifestyle. This statement is biased. Such programs always promote lifestyles and products that may not be in the reach of the people of the country in which the show is aired. False expectations thus build up, causing frustration in the long run.

Last, promoters of imported entertainment say that their programs satisfy the demands of people of watching television. This notion appears valid but it also means that local

---

TV companies have stiff competition and have to struggle to exist. Such development affects other areas of entertainment and even the artists.

Finally, I believe that foreign entertainment is harmful to the cultures of viewing societies as it can threaten the existence of cultures. I also assert that government should take some actions to stop the invasion of foreign cultures upon regional identities.

◆ ◆ ◆

81. **A century ago, when man landed on the moon, many people thought that it was a great contribution to the mankind. However, space travel has made little difference to people's lives.**

To what extent do you agree or disagree?

Man has the tendency of taking ambitious steps to satisfy his curiosity, thrill, thirst for knowledge and sense of achievement. The usefulness of space travel may be proved later on however, the material, effort and time spent for such projects is always an investment where returns from the same are a question.

Space travel has made some important revelations about our galaxy. With the assessment of samples from the moon and conducting of experiments in spacecrafts scientists have provided us significant information about the cosmos. There is constant speculation about the possibility of life on other planets and whether we succeed or not this exploration has helped us understand our life on earth in a better manner.

However, in the rush of proving that they too are not behind in any way, countries have developed space travel projects and have spent billions of dollars on them. Space travel requires expensive fuel and therefore valuable natural resources are used up in huge quantities. An attitude to race against each other is thus disastrous for the earth in many ways. If countries share this knowhow human kind can run a collective space programme thereby saving a lot of money that can be spent on the upliftment of the needy populations of the world.

All in all, I agree with the notion that space travel has given us some ambitious, cheerful, proud, historic, memorable and satisfying moments. Apart from that, it has made no contribution to the life of a common man. Countries should rethink their policy regarding the same.

◆ ◆ ◆

82. **Some people believe that we should not study history as it has little or nothing to tell us.**

   Do you agree or disagree with this statement?

Human beings have a tendency to look back before they take a stride forward. In almost all the aspects of life, for example, law, technology, research, family, society and so on we tend to check the past and then we decide our next course of action. Studying history in an academic curriculum cannot be separated from this phenomenon.

Learning history is vital in today's life. First, by studying history we can understand the lifestyle of the past and gain examples of dealing with different issues of life. This study offers great help in solving present day problems. For example, archaeological study of water canal networks in ancient India helped a lot in preparing current irrigation projects that made water distribution very effective and fruitful in the country.

Second, study of history is a vehicle to impart the information about our culture, tradition, religion and rituals to the new generation. History glorifies and confirms the greatness and effectiveness of a culture and religion to the learners in the present and also prepares them for their future life by telling them about the faults of the past.

On the other hand, some people argue that history cannot teach us anything because day-by-day we are advancing in our life and hence we must only look forward. They also assert that what has happened cannot be changed but we can always construct what is going to happen. Thus, we should always focus on the present and future because history is nothing but a chronological list of events that is taught in schools to bore the students.

Finally, I assert that we should study history because it is a significant storehouse of information that enhances our understanding of the present.

◆ ◆ ◆

83. **Some people think that it is impossible for females to be successful working women and good mothers at the same time. They also suggest that government should give salary to mothers who stay at home to take care of their children.**

Do you agree or disagree with the statement?

Women have made phenomenal progress in last few decades in most professional areas. However, there are concerns about women failing as a mother in the pursuit of being professional and there are divided opinions on whether they should be paid when they rear babies at home. I think they should be supported economically to nurture the future of the nation.

It is difficult for a woman to take care of her baby and fulfil all duties at her job as well. However, in our times it is not possible for everyone to sit at home bringing up children as the pressures of living in the modern world are intense. Thus, times are changing and we simply cannot pick one role over the other- she has to do both.

Considering the difficulties they face during the bringing up of their child, some people assert that they should be paid by the government as they rear the next generation of the nation. Hence, if there is any deficiency in that process, the country has to suffer from it in the future. They also add that now-a-days the birth rate is reducing in many developed countries because mothers find difficulty in fulfilling both the duties simultaneously and so they avoid conception. However, with government aid they can be encouraged to step into motherhood.

On the other hand, if the government were to pay those women who live at home and rear their children there are high chances of exploitation of the perks offered. Next, when women do not work, there is a loss to the economy.

Yet, according to my opinion, it is necessary to pay mothers because that support will aid the healthy development of our future generations.

◆ ◆ ◆

84. Nowadays children's writing and mathematical abilities are affected by computers and calculators. Some people argue that we should limit the use of these tools in schools.

Do you agree or disagree?

It is true that application of technology is affecting writing and calculation skills of students. There are divided opinions on the use of computer and calculators in schools. I think, benefits of technology outweigh its drawbacks.

Usage of electronic gadgets offers numerous positive results. First, they provide convenience by offering a faster pace in writing and calculation process that increases the exposure of students to more practice materials on the subject. Second, this usage makes students techno savvy. They get used to applying computers at a tender age. This helps them at the later stage in colleges and in jobs because these places use them extensively. Third, a computer offers editing, navigating and presentation facilities and it is a user-friendly tool. Students are thus motivated to gain benefit from it and enhance the quality of their projects.

However, usage of computers affects adversely also. To start with, they make a student dependant . Even for small calculations students feel the need to switch on their computers. This dependence inhibits natural growth of skills and abilities in candidates and makes them vulnerable. According to a survey, in a developed country, students are using computers and calculators to carry out even small calculations like '24 x 2'. What is more, they are so psychologically reliant on computers that they cannot learn, study and pass their exams.

Finally, although the usage of computers and calculators is almost inevitable, their increased applications do hinder writing and mathematical skills of students. Therefore, I assert that we should limit their usage in order to make our future generation more independent, intelligent and confident.

◆ ◆ ◆

---

85. **Technology like computers and mobile phones are widely in use. Writing letters will no longer be practiced in future.**

Do you agree or disagree with the statement?

Describe the importance of writing letters.

It is a fact that we are living in the most advanced technological era. There has been a revolution in communication with the invention of the computer and mobile. Because of this revolution, writing letters seems to be a thing of the past. However, it cannot be eliminated completely from use.

Latest electronic gadgets offer many options to communicate like email, sms, voicemail, chat and so on. Moreover, these options offer plentiful benefits. First is speed. We can send an e-mail or sms to any person anywhere in the world in seconds. Next is cost effectiveness. They offer longer, interactive and real time communication at a very low price. In addition, we can send large amount of data such as graphics, music and even video recordings. Finally, they offer better reproduction quality and data can be stored for ages in a CD or in the memory of a hard disc.

However, this revolution has not touched all regions of the globe yet. There are places where mobiles and computers are not available. What is more, a big proportion of people cannot communicate either in English or they cannot use new technology. For them, writing letters is the only way to communicate.

Moreover, as letters are written by hands, they create a natural effect on the reader that is not possible for electronic communication to generate because it is mechanical. Furthermore, there are certain personal, business and public communications that must be carried out on paper only.

All in all, it is true that the spread of electronic communication is immense and its usage is increasing. Still, according to me writing letters has its own significance that can never be eradicated.

◆ ◆ ◆

86. **To learn a language, you have to learn the culture and lifestyle of the country in which the specified language is spoken.**

Do you agree or disagree with the statement?

Language acquisition is a complex process. One opinion arises that we should also study the culture and lifestyle of the country in which the language is spoken. In this essay, arguments for both the views are discussed.

Different communities live with varying culture and lifestyles. Therefore, their language also differs from each other. It is also observed that different cultures use the same language differently. So, in order to acquire proficiency over a language, we must study the way of living and culture of the country because languages have various functions, styles and dialects. Moreover, every culture has different perceptions and applications of its language. Accordingly, styles and dialects are developed and keep changing constantly. Now, if a learner does not understand this aspect of language, his acquisition of that language remains superficial.

Moreover, study of lifestyle and culture always make the learner more comfortable with the usage of the language and in developing skills like reading, writing, speaking and listening. Furthermore, this results in effective and clear communication skills for the learner.

However, with the help of advanced learning tools like computers and Internet, it has become easy to learn any language without studying the culture or lifestyle of the native speakers. What is more, we are in an era of the development of a global culture and uniform lifestyle where the knowledge of a language does not require in-depth knowhow of the respective culture and lifestyle.

In conclusion, I assert that to develop proficiency over any language, learners ought to study the culture and style of living of the native speakers because without that knowledge of the language remains incomplete.

◆ ◆ ◆

87. **Some people state that the national teams and individual sportsmen and sportswomen should be financially sponsored by the government or a non-government body.**

How far do you agree or disagree with the statement?

It has been a trend for last few decades that sportsmen and teams are sponsored by corporate bodies and/or government. With the increasing extent of financial sponsorship, controversies over their worthiness are also rising. However, there is nothing wrong in sponsoring them, provided the drawbacks are taken care of.

There are plentiful benefits of sponsoring sportsmen financially. First, players can use the money to buy expensive but useful and latest sports equipments that can help in enhancing their skills. In addition, there are many costly software programs that can be then acquired to understand the game better and improve their performance.

Second, with the help of finance, teams can hire doctors, physiotherapists, and sports psychologists. All these professional services are highly expensive but extremely essential to the team members for maintaining their physical fitness, improving mental attitude and expanding professional life. Finally, this money is a boon for upcoming players who do not have enough financial resources to support their sports activities.

On the other hand, there are some loopholes in this process. To start with, players get handsome amounts as their match fees, prizes and other gifts for their participation in tournaments. Next, it is also seen that popular sports individuals earn millions out of private brand endorsement contracts and other events like inauguration ceremonies, parties, cultural programs and so forth. Finally, companies focus only on highly successful players of popular sports. Consequently, other segments are completely neglected.

In conclusion, I assert that if the authorities give desired importance and justice to all segments of sports, financial sponsorship can be a boon for the players.

◆ ◆ ◆

88. **The increasing housing problem in big cities has social consequences. Some people say that only governments can solve this problem.**

To what extent do you agree or disagree?

Owing to the rise in population and polarization of people towards mega cities from small towns, the accommodation problem is mounting in all metropolises. This leads to other social troubles for the people as well. To encounter this issue, both governmental authorities and individuals have to share the responsibility.

The government can take some important steps in solving the housing problem. To begin with, it should develop adequate infrastructure in big cities that help families and communities to live together peacefully and synergistically. Also, it has to keep a strict administrative check on the real estate sector. Next, migration towards cities from villages is a major reason for housing problems in large cities. To prevent this, government should develop small towns and villages and provide facilities like employment, healthcare, education, interconnectivity and transportation, water, irrigation and so on.

On the other hand, at the individual level citizens need to pay their taxes regularly for the government to be able to provide them with better infrastructure. Also, they have to take responsibility for the maintenance of their urban environment and build their houses or commercial units in accordance with governmental bylaws. Illegal occupations have to be stopped and individuals have to be willing to give up a part of their property if that is the need for the construction of a road or an under bridge etc.

Finally, it is true that governments can do a lot in reducing social problems that arise due to housing scarcity in big cities. However, people at an individual level can also contribute to solve the problems. Thus, I opine that It certainly has to be a joint endeavour of both, people and government.

◆ ◆ ◆

89. **People who are poor and those who come from rural areas find it difficult to access university education. Some believe that universities should provide some special facilities to help them.**

Do you agree or disagree?

It is a fact that poor and rural people face troubles in accessing the universities. To address this issue, people argue that universities should offer some support in the form of finance, reservation, accommodation, scholarship and so forth. This argument has credibility provided it does not create imbalance in the student community.

People who favour underprivileged students support their view with the following arguments. First, facilities help the students to acquire tertiary education and make them competent professionals. In addition, their qualifications help them in getting lucrative jobs. This scenario contributes in reducing the rich-poor and urban-rural divide. Secondly, such students can use other resources of the university like computer, library, halls of residence etc. to enhance their academic performance. Finally, these perks can prove to be a boon for hidden talents within the student community in the field of studies, sports or arts.

However, there are some disadvantages of offering facilities also. First, educational opportunities should be based on merit rather than community, region or economic status. In offering any kind of reservations, social imbalance and dissatisfaction is bound to occur. Second, there are chances of exploitation of the support offered to poor or rural people. Such incidences make the whole effort look worthless. Finally, universities must be supported financially by the government to maintain such facilities, which in turn becomes a tax burden on urban people.

All in all, there are mixed impacts of offering assistance to poor and rural people. However, our ideal motto should be to provide equal opportunities to all sections of the society to build a balanced world. That is why I assert that we should offer facilities to them but with effective safeguards so that the educational system is saved from any untoward effects.

◆ ◆ ◆

90. **Food can be produced cheaply by using improved fertilizers and machinery. At the same time, it has some dangerous effects on human health and may have negative effects on local communities.**

To what extent do you agree or disagree?

Owing to recent developments in the farming technology the food-producing process is getting more economical and productive. It does have some negative effects on human health and farmers. However, the rewards of this technology outnumber the problems.

There are numerous advantages of cost-reduction in the food production process. To begin with, reduced cost makes the food reach the indigent and poor classes of the society. This improves health standards as the crops supplement the diet of conventional food sources that are largely cereal based. Next, increased food yield enables a country to export crops to other nations and generate revenue to promote its own economic growth.

Finally, a cheaper food production process attracts more entrepreneurs in the sectors like farming, irrigation, manufacturing of fertilizers and farming equipments etc. This development creates higher employment opportunities in these fields and invariably benefits the local people.

However, there are some threats observed for human health and local communities. First, fertilizers may affect the composition of food and can reduce the nutritive value of the food. In addition, such food can have adverse effects on human immunity and can lead to diseases like cancer. Last but not the least fertilizers can alter the soil quality of the region thus, effecting disastrously the livelihood of local communities.

In conclusion, the topic raises some issues of health and well being of farming communities. However, they can be taken care of by improved research in science. Hence, in my view, cost reduction of food production process is a welcome development and has many advantages.

◆ ◆ ◆

91. **It is seen that while studying, university students stay away from their parents in most countries. Some people think it is good for the students.**

   To what extent do you agree or disagree?

It is indeed difficult to agree completely with either side of this proposition because both aspects of the topic have their pros and cons. Benefits and drawbacks of each are discussed below.

Living away from home has its own advantages for the students. First, staying at the university while studying gives a life of freedom and independence. According to me, freedom, if understood properly, always brings maturity and responsibility, which is a great improvement in the students' personality. In addition, their decision-making ability also strengthens. Second, study at home sometimes suffers because of social interference. What is more, students also have to follow the discipline of the home and that may hinder their studies. For example, medical students may have to go to the hospital even at midnight. If they live at home, other members of the family shall be disturbed.

Now, let us look at the other side of the argument. Students who live to hostels always lack the support and warmth a family can provide. They miss the guidance of their parents in important matters such as an event of failure in studies or selecting a specialization or a part time job. They often feel lonely at university and to overcome this loneliness, they may digress towards addictions. Next, many students feel that the environment of their home is more convenient and helpful for their study. Finally, parents can better assist financially when they live with their children. Such support enhances academic performance of the students.

In my opinion, living away from home while acquiring tertiary education often helps in overall development of students. However, I also assert that they should remain in close contact with their parents to sustain warmth and support for each other in order to prevent themselves from the drawbacks of living alone at the hostel.

◆ ◆ ◆

92. **Learning a foreign language offers an insight into how people from other cultures think and see the world. Considering this, it is often argued that teaching of a foreign language should be made compulsory in all primary schools.**

    To what extent do you agree or disagree with this view?

It cannot be denied that language conditions our mind. It is a mould by which we shape our perceptions and understand the world. Learning a foreign language always helps a person to understand other people and their cultures. However, teaching a foreign language at primary school level cannot attain this objective.

There are ample reasons why teaching a foreign language at primary schools is not sensible. First, to know other languages and other people, one should know one's own self. Childhood is the time to create this base for the children. They should learn their language first and know themselves and their culture. Second, childhood is a phase where students start developing their abilities to think and perceive. It is necessary for them to come to a certain level of understanding and then after that they should acquire a foreign language at a tertiary level.

Moreover, teaching a foreign language can also disturb students' learning and development of their understanding. Because they cannot distinguish easily between different cultures it can lead to a hazy perception of the world.

On the other hand, some people argue that if we teach a foreign language in primary schools, children develop a better approach towards the understanding of other people and their culture. Furthermore, they also argue that at a later stage, the minds of the students that have already been conditioned by the first language education, offer resistance to the new insights that a foreign language brings in.

Finally, in my opinion, it is true that a foreign language always helps in improving our understanding of other people and their perceptions. However, I think at primary schools, such an objective cannot be fulfilled, as it is not the proper time to learn a foreign language.

◆ ◆ ◆

93. **Some people warn that the era of the silver screen is coming to an end and that people will lose interest in going to the cinema.**

   Do you agree or disagree with this view?

The cinema has been a popular form of entertainment for many decades. Even the silent films of the early centuries were loved by the people around the world. Hollywood is now an enormous business and film stars like Angelina Jolie or Brad Pitt earn millions of dollars. This is a means of entertainment, which will never decrease in popularity.

People think that going to cinema will become out of date because of the increase in the production and popularity of DVDs and home videos. It's certainly true that we can all stay at home now and watch films in comfort. What is more, the cost of these films is much cheaper for a big family than going to the cinema. In addition to this, pirated CDs and DVDs also prevent people from going to movie theatres. Next, young people enjoy spending a night at home watching a DVD or a video. Furthermore, young children adore videos because they can watch them again and again.

However, the cinemas in my country and across the globe are still full every weekend and when a new film is released, we are keen on watching it on the silver screen. In fact, many small cinemas have been rebuilt into new multiplexes having six or eight screens and showing eight to ten movies a day. Moreover, they offer luxurious facilities and many other fun oriented activities that make for a joyful experience for the visitors. Finally, movies genres like horror, science fiction or thrillers can be enjoyed fully only on a cinema screen.

All in all, it seems that we are enjoying both the cinema and the facilities that technology can offer us and that each of these has its merits. In my view although people will watch DVDs and videos, they will never stop going to cinemas.

◆   ◆   ◆

94.   **Movies with spectacular car chases are a thrill to watch and fun too but they have led to an increase in car accidents on urban roads.**

Do you agree or disagree with the view?

What do you think can be done to make the youth more aware of road safety?

Movies tend to have a very high influence on young people who are swayed both by what they see and hear. In my opinion, it is true that car chases in action movies tend to an increase in the number of car accidents among young drivers.

There are so many reasons behind this. Firstly, in the process of imitation they drive too fast and take unnecessary risks to satisfy the sense of thrill, which is very strong in them at that age. Secondly, youngsters are so influenced by the films that they forget the difference between movies and reality. Most importantly, they do not realize that they lack the skills and experience to do this and in the process put themselves and others at risk.

There are a variety of ways in which young people can be encouraged to practice safer driving habits. To start with, the government should launch a "drive-safe" campaign to convey the fact that driving safely is not uncool. Secondly, every movie should make it clear that dangerous car chases are undertaken only in strict safety conditions with experienced drivers, and often most of those thrilling scenes are created on computers with the help of various softwares.

In addition to this, it should be compulsory for young people to take safety driving courses every year for the first five years that they have their driver's license. In this way, they are forced to perfect their driving skills or lose their license if they fail to do so.

Finally, as a part of this course, young drivers should go to the hospitals and see people whose lives have been destroyed due to stupid risk taking. It will help them to change their minds about copying action heroes and driving fast.

◆　◆　◆

95. **Some people think that paper money and coins will be replaced completely by credit cards and online methods of payment in the near future.**

   Do you agree or disagree with their statement?

It is indeed a fact that usage of plastic money and internet transactions have been rising constantly over the last few years. All over the world, majority of corporate and shopping transactions are now carried out without printed money. Thus, a belief has been created that such a trend will eliminate paper currency from usage. This seems convincing but shall not materialize according to me.

There are numerous reasons why paper money can never be completely out of usage. Firstly, even today, there are some places where credit cards and internet have not reached. At those places, printed money is the only way of monetary exchange. Secondly, all online and credit card transactions are accessible by the authorities and those who hide away their income never use such methods of money exchange. They always opt for cash.

Thirdly, usage of credit cards and internet has its own drawbacks like frauds, theft, misuse and so on. Such possibilities often oblige people to stay away from them. I would like to quote world's most renowned investor Mr. Warren Buffet, who once said, "In my life of 70 years, I have never ever used a credit card." His statement speaks a lot about the perception of plastic money in the minds of many.

However, it cannot be denied that usage of internet based transactions and various types of cards is becoming more common by the day as they offer convenience and ease of access. Moreover, we do not have to carry around cash and worry for its safety.

All in all, I admit that usage of internet and cards for monetary exchange is increasing and will continue to rise. However, considering their limitations, I opine that paper money will never be eliminated from use.

◆ ◆ ◆

96. **Once children start going to school, their teachers have more influence on their intellectual and social development than their parents.**

   To what extent do you agree or disagree?

It is an undeniable fact that both teachers and parents have immense impact on the tiny minds of children. Thus, for decades, people have been debating as to who amongst them has more impact on the minds of children. It seems that parents win over teachers in some areas and vice versa.

Impact of teachers is high because children's intellectual and academic development takes place in school under the monitoring of their teachers. Next, teachers also take care of linguistic development and basic skills including social and behavioural etiquettes of children. Moreover, children always look up to their teachers as they are answerable to them. Furthermore, children also see their parents offering respect to the teachers and this gives an impression to tiny tots that teachers are more respect worthy and influential. So they tend to follow after them.

On the other hand, influence of parents can never ever be underestimated. Firstly, parents are constant companions, guides and witness to all the joys and sorrows of children in their childhood. Secondly, emotional bonding of children with their parents is extremely high, which also strengthens the influence of parents. Finally, it is also true that teachers keep changing in the academic life of a child but the parents are always there.

Finally, I think both parents and teachers have their share of influence on the little, impressionable minds of children. If I assess deeply, I believe that teachers play an important role in intellectual aspects of child growth and parents have their major share in the emotional and social development of children.

◆ ◆ ◆

97. **It is seen that rate of unemployment is very high in some countries. Because of this, some people say that there is no need to provide education beyond primary level to the pupils of such a country.**

Do you agree or disagree with the statement?

Unemployment is a great concern for many nations in the world. It has plentiful adverse implications. This is the reason an argument is presented by some that such a country should not spend more money for providing education to its school going students. However, this argument seems extremely pessimistic to me.

There are numerous reasons why governments must not stop providing education to their young ones. To begin with, education is the key for employment. Most countries where lack of jobs prevails, it is also observed that the literacy ratio and number of trained skilled workers are low. This implies that unemployment is directly proportionate to deficiency of education.

Moreover, education opens options for people not only in their own country but also in foreign nations. They may go to other countries as immigrants, earn money and can remit the income back home. This revenue often helps in boosting the economy of their home country.

Finally, educated youth is capable of attracting international corporations and industries which invest heavily in the country and can create number of jobs for the local people. All such development is possible only if adequate education is provided till the tertiary level to all the students of the country.

However, some short sighted people say that educating youth is very expensive. The authorities need to allocate extra funds to provide proper academic knowledge, which puts pressure on other basic facilities like transport and healthcare. They also add that less jobs and an educated, unemployed youth is a devastating combination as the youth may turn hostile and indulge in criminal activities.

Conclusively, I firmly believe that no child should be deprived from being educated. It is an investment that will certainly bear fruits in terms of economic developments in forthcoming decades.

◆ ◆ ◆

98. **A country's future depends on its young people. Therefore, it is often argued that governments should invest heavily in its youth.**

   Do you agree or disagree?

It is true that today's children will be young after a decade and they will be taking control of all the systems of the nation in forthcoming decades. In this context, if the forthcoming leaders are not well nurtured, the future of the country is likely to be bleak. Thus, investing in youth should be a compulsion for all the countries.

There are several reasons why the youth must be taken care of by the governments. Firstly, an educated and skilled graduate of today will be a competitive and skilled employee or employer in the future. In addition, they can adapt to and flourish in all facets of life and work. Secondly, such youngsters can enhance economic growth of the country. Consequently, the GDP (Gross Domestic Product) of the country also rises. Thirdly, with a developing economy, social, political, financial and intellectual standards of life rise and the citizens can have an excellent existence to cherish.

Moreover, a healthy, well brought up, educated youth always makes a better and compatible workforce as they can tackle any task at work and are capable of giving their best over a long period of time with consistency. Finally, we can take certain countries like America, who have invested heavily in their youth and these days, USA is one of the most economically developed countries in the world. Such status is largely owing to the skilled workforce they produced since early 1990s. The same is now true for countries like India and China as they are still preparing a generation that is skilled, educated and healthy and ready to uplift the economy of their country.

In conclusion, I must say that investing in youth is to secure the future. These youngsters whom we nurture today will surely reward the society with the fruits of economic, social and intellectual development.

◆ ◆ ◆

99. **Some people assert that sports help to a greater extent to build peace in the world.**

Do you agree or disagree?

There is a general view that sporting activities help to build peace in the world. I wholeheartedly agree with the proposition. Be it at the level of an individual, a society, a country or the world, sports activity is a positive channelling of energy which kills negativity and brings about joy and peace.

At the level of an individual, it helps to build physical fitness in terms of strength, agility and stamina. In addition, there is a sense of competition and a pursuit towards betterment of self. Also, in team sports a person learns the virtues of participation, sharing and management which go a long way in building character. Thus, there is no doubt that such positive individuals are the backbone of a peaceful world.

At the level of a society or a country people take pride in accomplished sportsmen from their region and instead of wasting energies on petty rivalries, sports competitions help them to stay in a healthy contest with each other. For example, the football clubs in Europe have built an identity over and above a country or a region and therefore play an important role in uniting people.

Further, at the international level, sports play a very important role in diplomatic relations and the relations of the populations of different countries. Owing to historical or political reasons, not all countries are at peace with each other. Sports thus can be an ice breaker as competitors from these nations create a common stage for politicians and others to interact. Intense patriotic energies find a release too as is seen in the case of an India Pakistan cricket match.

To conclude, in total agreement with the given proposition I assert that governments should work towards building healthy sporting relationships within the country and with other countries as well.

◆ ◆ ◆

100. Group and team activities are more important than the actives done alone, because they teach us important life skills.

Do agree or disagree?

There is no doubt that group and team activities teach us important life skills. But to say that they are more important than activities done alone is not right according to me. For a fulfilling life a healthy balance of both is required.

Group activities teach us the virtues of sharing, patience, team spirit, public relations and even management skills. Children who do not have siblings or loners who do not interact much with people are seen to develop some negative traits in their persona as they have never had a healthy sharing relationship. On the other hand when we work alone on a task it lets us evolve a keen ability to concentrate, pursue perfection and overreach our abilities. We are not obliged to work according to the wishes of anyone else so we become our own critic and guide and this goes a long way in building an individual personality. Many great scientists, artists and musicians have been known to have worked alone.

Both kinds of activities inculcate a sense of responsibility and belonging. In team work you have a certain role to fulfil and you cannot falter as regards that and in the case you are alone, if you do not work with responsibility, you know you are bound to fail. Performing a role in a team makes us feel that we belong to the group. On the other hand, in working alone when we put forth a unique talent that also helps us find our own place in this world where everyone is defined by what they do.

Therefore, for the healthy growth of an individual both teamwork and individual pursuit are essential. Neither can be considered more important than the other.

◆ ◆ ◆

101. **Some people believe that children should do organized activities in their free time while others believe that children should be free to choose what they want to do in their free time.**

Which of these opinions do you agree with?

Many people are in favour of organized activities for children during free time while some say that children should be left alone to select what they wish to do during these hours. I personally believe that organizing activities for them is a better idea and within that we should give them freedom to follow their own direction.

During childhood, proper guidance is essential for children to develop in a healthy manner. To begin with, parents and teachers should not only guide them in the domain of academics but also plan constructive activities for them to make good use of free time. Secondly, in the present times satellite television, internet and computer games are a big lure for the children. If they are completely let free they are sure to waste most of their time in passive activities. It is not that such activities should be totally denied but fixed hours can be assigned to them so that not all free time is wasted in them.

Thirdly, organized activity is not any kind of binding. Keeping in mind the child's inclinations and interest, guardians should make it possible for children to access facilities that help them to follow what they like. With a system in place, a child is free to follow his or her own path, be it painting, sports, singing, dancing or skating etc.

Thus, I do not believe that children should be completely left alone to opt what they wish to do in their leisure time as this can lead to disastrous results. Parents and teachers should direct activities for them and guide them at every stage to ensure that the kids grow up into responsible adults.

◆ ◆ ◆

102. **Some people think that no one should be allowed to work after the age of 65. Others say that people should be allowed to work for as long as they want to.**

Which of these arguments do you agree or disagree with?

Governments and private institutions all over the world have a prescribed retirement age that is usually around 65 years. There has been a raging debate if this is a good idea or people who are fit and healthy should be allowed to continue beyond this age as well. In my opinion, retirement age should be decided on the basis of the nature of job one is engaged in and also with respect to the proficiency one possesses.

Firstly, in the case of jobs that require intense physical fitness like the field jobs in the army, navy an air force it is essential that there is a fixed retirement age so that the quality of service is not affected. Secondly, jobs that have a very repetitive pattern like those in the clerical departments of government offices should have a strict retirement policy because after a point in time it is impossible for employees to keep up the standard of results required. Thirdly, in the fields such as sports and fashion, even though there is no prescribed retirement age yet individuals know that they have a short shelf life and as their youth passes them by so does their profession come to an end.

On the other hand, for some fields of human endeavour, I feel that employees should be given a choice if they wish to work beyond a certain prescribed retirement age. A committee could be set up to determine their level of proficiency and if it deems the employee fit and the employee too wishes to go on working then there should not be a forced retirement.

Conclusively, I opine that there should be a fixed retirement age for the positions where constant physical and mental efforts are required as I have discussed above. However, for all other jobs, people should be allowed to work if they are capable to fulfil the job requirements.

◆ ◆ ◆

103. **Nowadays, an increasing number of countries are confronted with the disappearance of cooking skills.**

What is the situation like in your country?

Do you agree that the young children should be taught home cooking in school?

There is no doubt that with pressures of modern life more and more young people have little or no cooking skills. The situation in my country is no different. Though, becoming a chef is a rather popular professional choice owing to cookery shows on television, yet day to day home cooking is considered a boring and cumbersome task.

There are plentiful benefits of teaching culinary skills to school going children. The first and foremost benefit of this is that they learn importance of food ingredients that they eat in their meal and the role of each of them in maintaining their health. In addition, during their learning lessons, they also realise that there is joy and warmth and whole-someness to a fresh home cooked meal. Unfortunately, regardless of the amount young professionals earn, they mostly eat out and ruin their health which, according to me is a far more expensive option apart from being unhealthy.

Thirdly, we all learnt in our schools that 'Home is where the hearth is'. If there is no proper running kitchen in a family the adhesive to hold the family members together is missing. Finally, food is not something that we just eat but it also is a cultural tradition that we carry forth. If we stop to cook, a part of our culture would die with us.

To sum up, I feel if children are taught to cook at school and alongside that are made aware of healthy and unhealthy eating habits it would be very nice for a society and a country.

◆ ◆ ◆

104. **Full time university students spend most of their time behind their academic subjects. Some people say that they should engage in other activities also.**

To what extent do you agree or disagree?

University students have a lot of academic work on hand and it is usually seen that they do not engage in any extracurricular activities. Some people think that this is not right and they should involve themselves in fields other than academics as well. I agree that this indeed should be the case.

Youth is the time when we are building a foundation for our entire life. There is no doubt that academics is essential but if we do not explore other fields at this stage then later in life with demanding professional requirements and a family to take care of we shall not get the time to do so. Also, only bookish knowledge cannot help us to achieve success in life more so, in the present times, where being multi-talented is not an advantage-rather, it is a basic requirement. In addition, practical knowledge as well as management and public relation skills are the need of the hour.

Thirdly, at the level of the university, our perceptions are still unformed and raw and exposing them to different kinds of tasks will help us enrich our lives. This is almost essential because, at a later age, the body and mind loose the agility and freshness of youth and it is too late to try different things or enjoy them.

To conclude, I firmly believe that alongside academics, students at university level should engage in multiple kinds of activities like learning and appreciating music, dancing, understanding fine arts, managerial tasks etc. This shall help them to broaden their horizons, live a more meaningful life and become responsible citizens of the world.

◆ ◆ ◆

105. If a person becomes successful or unsuccessful, it is only because of his/her luck.

Do you agree or disagree with the statement?

I disagree with the statement given here. There is no doubt that luck plays a role in the success or failure of an individual but that this is the only determining factor is not true. Hard work and perseverance are two other determinants of the results of his or her actions.

Luck can open a door for us but what we do with that opportunity is completely dependent upon our viewpoint and the efforts we put in thereafter. For example, a person might come to inherit a profitable business by a stroke of luck but if he does not have the ability to run it properly and neither the inclination to work hard, there is no way that he would achieve success.

Secondly, one might put in little effort and yet reap great rewards. For instance, a student who does not study much but happens to cheat during an exam may score well. Yet, this scenario cannot be repeated in all exams and all through one's life. Thus, such success is unsustainable. Thirdly, there are cases where an individual puts in lots of effort but fails in the end because of bad luck. To exemplify, take the case of a brilliant student who because of a roll number mix up gets below average grades. Again, these instances are far and few and many times even reversible.

Finally, I believe that success or failure are a result of our own actions and not a result of luck. Each failure is a lesson for life and we are more intelligent and better prepared after suffering a failure. Similarly, each success teaches us that there are far more milestones to be reached.

◆ ◆ ◆

106. **The spread of multinational companies and globalization is increasing with time. Some people say that it will bring positive effects for everyone.**

Do you agree or disagree?

The world has become a global village as most countries have come to espouse the free market economy model. There are numerous multinational companies with operations and markets for their products spread across the globe. This trend is on the increase and it is largely believed that it shall bring positive effects for everyone. I agree with the proposition here.

With the world as one big stage there is a common ground for everyone to relate to which means the playing field is levelled and nobody has more advantage owing to their place of birth. This creates a larger opportunity for people to pursue economic prosperity. Secondly, weaker economies and poor nations have a role to play as well because manufacturing units come to be located here. In this way their populations can find jobs and uplift themselves from poverty. Thirdly, products can be made available world over and no longer do we pine for 'foreign' made goods as the same can be bought in the local market.

There is no doubt that there are concerns of exploitation of cheap labour in developing economies and the increasing divide between the rich and the poor. But to my mind these are the initial problems of the process of globalization. Once, it reaches its zenith there is no doubt that it shall help us to deal with poverty. The labour shall also get its due rights as it realises that it is an important link in the global chain because globalization not only brings jobs in its wake, it also brings awareness.

In conclusion, considering the benefits and positive effects of globalisation on both the developed and the developing nations, I wish to state that spread of multi-national companies and globalization is a very good development.

2. DISCUSSION (37)

1   **Some people think schools should educate pupils according to their academic ability, and others believe pupils with different abilities should be educated together.**

Discuss both views and give your opinion.

Considering the wide gap in intellectual abilities of children, it is often argued by some that students in schools should be taught according to their learning abilities. However, this argument only looks good on paper.

Selecting pupils according to their academic ability is not advisable due to various reasons. First, such a system of filtering students gives a sense of inferiority to those who are not in the group and a feeling of superiority to those who are selected. This is harmful to both groups of students in the long run. Secondly, it is often seen that students show inconsistency in their academic performance. For example, a student who gets 60-70% marks may develop interest in studies at any stage during his academic life and can uplift his academic scores to 80-90%. If we separate candidates, chances of such transformation in average candidates will be almost zero. Finally, some weaker

The Ultimate Guide To IELTS Writing

students may get inspired by other bright students and may learn to perform well in their studies if they all study together.

The other side of this argument says that if we separate students according to their learning ability, their learning can be enhanced to far better levels than what can be achieved in a mixed class. Moreover, some complex concepts can also be taught to them to make them intellectually sharper and more capable. Furthermore, in a mixed class some intelligent candidates may come under influence of spoilt children and may ruin their academic prospects.

To sum up, if I see this issue in the light of benefit of intelligent candidates, the argument may seem appropriate. However, its overall effect on the student community is likely to be more harmful because it may hurt self-esteem of students and this cannot be permitted under any circumstances.

◆ ◆ ◆

2.   **Some people think that teachers should be responsible for teaching students to judge what is right and what is wrong so that they can behave well. Others think that teachers should only teach academic subjects to students.**

Discuss both views and give your opinion.

A teacher's basic duty is to teach academic subjects and for that they are assigned a syllabus and a term to complete their task. However, ensuring academic success and moulding a child into a better individual are fundamental responsibilities of a teacher. Hence, teaching only academic subjects does not satisfy all the objectives.

A child grasps the happenings in the surroundings and understands them as per his or her perception. If he does not know what is good or bad, he may accept some evils as a part of life and become comfortable with them and indulge in activities like watching TV excessively, talking loudly, using slang, smoking and so on. Indulgence in such activities causes the child to misbehave and distracts him from studies. Therefore, teachers must teach children what is positive and negative for them because a teacher's position comes immediately after the parents in a child's life. It is observed that nowadays both parents work and cannot devote sufficient time to their offspring; in such a situation, a teacher's role becomes even more important.

The understanding of what is acceptable and unacceptable helps in many ways. Firstly, when a child knows it, he is more inclined towards studies and becomes more responsible about life. Secondly, his academic performance and behaviour improve that make him an all-round success. Finally, it also prevents juvenile delinquency as the child stays away from such activities.

However, some people argue that teachers must concentrate only on academia as the child learns other lessons from his family. In addition, they assert that parents are the best teachers when it comes to behaviour.

As per my opinion, it is true that the child learns many things from parents but teachers should also teach positives and negatives of life, as this is the first step towards shaping a better and well-behaved individual which leads to a better society.

◆ ◆ ◆

3.   **Some people think that there are benefits in going to private secondary schools. Others feel that private secondary schools can have negative effects on the society as a whole.**

     Discuss both views and give your opinion?

Importance of education in present era has been the highest ever in the history. It has increased the demand of secondary schools. As a result, many private secondary schools have come into existence. However, it is difficult to state explicitly whether they are a positive or negative development for the society.

Private secondary schools offer many benefits. First, they offer qualitative competence i.e. the quality of teaching in private schools is often superior over government schools because in private schools teachers have to continuously update themselves in order to keep their jobs. This is an unlikely occurrence in government schools where job security comes in the way of the growth of teachers.

Secondly, private establishments can offer numerous facilities like school buses, better infrastructure, computer laboratories and extracurricular activities because they charge higher fees and they do not have to rely on grants from the government. Finally, private schools can cater to a large number of students thereby meeting the demand of more schools in a city. Hence, they help in fulfilling the objective of making education available to as many as possible.

On the other hand, there are some drawbacks also. To start with, owing to the job insecurity, teachers in private schools often incline towards private tuition classes, which results in degradation of teaching quality. Next, privatization brings professionalism i.e. private schools often charge very high fees that most middle class families cannot afford. In addition, they also demand heavy donations at the time of enrolment. In the end, such a scenario creates imbalance in society because to study in such schools is a privilege and parents often resort to unacceptable ways for getting their children into such schools.

All in all, I think private secondary schools are necessary in today's world. However, they have considerable adverse effects on society also. Still, we can get better fruits of private education provided the government takes effective steps to prevent corporatisation of schools.

◆ ◆ ◆

4.   **In some countries, married couples plan to have a baby at a later age due to the demands of their professional career.**

Discuss the advantages and disadvantages of it and give your opinion.

Globalisation has had plenty of side effects on our life and work style. The tendency in married couples to avoid conception is one of them. This attitude seems to have more drawbacks than benefits.

Today's life obliges both partners in a marriage to work and to advance in their careers to meet the increased financial requirements. This is why, they may not get adequate time to conceive and look after a baby. Moreover, childcare is becoming expensive in today's world, which also forces some parents to work for a few years, plan their future financially and then go for a baby. Furthermore, it is observed that practical work experience is helpful for the intellectual growth of working women. Now, if women give birth to a child immediately after marriage, their entire focus shifts to the baby, which further affects their personal and professional growth.

On the other hand, this attitude is harmful in many ways. First, conceiving a child during middle age is harmful to the women as their natural stamina and strength reduce with age. Second, the hormonal changes in women's body also affect the growth of the child in the womb and this may have adverse effects during the time of pregnancy. This is especially more harmful because to avoid pregnancy, married women take lots of oral contraceptives that lead to a hormonal imbalance. Finally, it is also seen in many couples that one of the partners becomes career oriented and does not want a child at all. Such incidences create conflicts between the couple and may result in breaking of the relationship.

In conclusion, although it is important to give attention to the professional career and growth, married people should also consider the troubles that might happen during pregnancy at a later age and take a decision accordingly. Because, I think, such a tendency is dangerous and it is bound to change in the future according to me.

◆ ◆ ◆

5.   **Some people say that fashion affects our lives in a negative way. However, others say that it has more positive effects on our lives.**

      Discuss and give your opinion.

In today's world, it is rare to find a person who is untouched by fashion because its presence is felt in every corner of this world across societies, countries, genders and age groups. Spread of fashion as a whole is not bad for the humans provided it is perceived as a novelty or a creative pursuit.

Fashion is indeed positive for our lives for many reasons. First, it is considered as youthful and creative. This implies, when we follow fashion, we feel younger, energetic and creative. In addition, such positivity fills our life with good vibes and helps us to do better in other aspects as well. Secondly, fashion also gives a good platform for creative people to explore their ideas to enrich the arts of our times. Finally, we must not forget the fact that fashion as an industry also gives employment to millions of people across the globe.

On the other hand, a mindless pursuit of fashion also has a few negative consequences. First, it can harm people if they follow fashion just to show off. Some people waste their money on looking younger even if the expense is out of their reach. The second aspect is ignorance. In the rush of following fashion, sometimes we forget its implications on our health. For example, many girls use different cosmetics without knowing their possible adverse effects on their skin.

In conclusion, I admit that fashion must be followed wisely. If it is followed blindly, it always affects our health and financial condition. However, if it is followed mindfully, it becomes a form of art which helps us to lead a joyous and creative life.

◆ ◆ ◆

6.   **Some people think spending a lot on birthday celebrations and weddings is a waste of money. Others think that it is important to the young people and society.**

     Discuss both views and give your opinion.

The importance of recreational and celebratory activities is mounting amongst young-sters day-by-day. They believe they should spend hefty sum on celebrations and make them memorable. This attitude is acceptable provided it does not create any financial burden on them.

This is an era of globalization, where people do not find enough time and holidays to celebrate festivals and rituals. Moreover, globalization has given affluence and easy access to exclusive and exotic paraphernalia to the youngsters. Once they enjoy all these, they want to make them a part of their celebrations in order to make those events memorable in their life. Furthermore, media is also playing a vital role in inculcating importance of celebrations by repeatedly showing the same on television and in maga-zines. Youngsters find a sense of self-actualization in receiving compliments for an oc-casion they organized and others enjoyed with great pomp.

On the other hand, excessive expenditure is a waste of material wealth and this is harmful in many ways. First, youngsters are easily driven away to show off their wealth. In such situation, they borrow money to throw parties and other celebrations. Second, it is seen that many a times invaluable food, water, electricity etc. are wasted by the people. The same material can be used for poor and needy people and this can generate a genuine sense of self-actualization.

Finally, it is true that there are some concerns of wastage of money and materials in spending big on social events. However, if a person is capable of spending and he wants others to join the same, I think there is nothing wrong in it because it can be important to the person who spends the money.

◆ ◆ ◆

7. **Modern lifestyles are completely different from the way people lived in the past. Some people think the changes have been very positive, while others believe they have been negative.**

   Discuss both these points of view and give your own opinion.

It is undeniable that the average person's lifestyle has changed enormously during the last few decades owing to the huge impact of modern technology and economic development. I think the positive impacts certainly outweigh the negative ones.

Some people believe that modern life is much better than in the past. As evidence of this, they point to improvements in health care and education and the general rise in the standard of living. Moreover, they argue that machines have changed working conditions and reduced the need for hard physical labour. Furthermore, they talk about the large leisure industries that have transformed people's concept of vacation and entertainment.

On the other hand, it can also be argued that some changes have had a negative impact on our lives. For example, there have been adverse effects on both natural and human environments. In addition, stress from all the pressure in today's schools and workplaces may have reduced the quality of life in social terms. Having access to more things and more entertainment cannot compensate for the loss of social relationships. One reason for this loss is that families spend less time together and, as a result, divorce rate and even crime has increased and people do not have any sense of community.

In conclusion, I think there is evidence to suggest that some of the changes we have experienced in the modern world have affected our lives in a negative way, especially in terms of the family and the environment. But overall, it is clear that most of these developments have been good for the majority of people. I feel we need to ensure that these positive changes are sustained and shared more in the future.

◆ ◆ ◆

8   Nowadays many people prefer to shop in supermarkets rather than small shops or local markets?

Is this positive or negative for development?

Discuss and give your opinion.

Owing to innovations in the retail sector and introduction of shopping malls, shopping has become a pleasant experience rather than a boring responsibility in this era of consumerism. This development has directed buyers towards malls and supermarkets from local shops or markets. It seems to be a good development, which is here to stay for a long time.

The trend of buying things from supermarkets or malls is indeed good for most consumers. First, such places offer lots of convenience in terms of easy reach, facilities like parking, air conditioned climate, free home delivery, better support while buying the products and so on. Secondly, products are displayed properly and are available in multiple kinds of packs and in desired quantities in supermarkets. Hence, a customer remains assured about the availability of the products that he wants.

Third, buying from malls and supermarkets is often symbolized as status in the society. People often go to such places just because elite class of society goes there. Lastly, supermarkets often give more discounts and customer loyalty rewards and credit for a certain period which is not possible for local markets to offer.

The Ultimate Guide To IELTS Writing

On the other hand, local markets do offer some benefits to customers. As small shop owners do not spend heavily on infrastructure and interior, their operating cost is lower, which motivates them to offer more discounts to their customers. Secondly, most local markets are traditionally popular and located in close proximity to the city areas'. Therefore, customers can get an easy access to them.

To sum up, buying from shopping malls and supermarkets gives a pleasant experience compared to that of local markets. Thus, I think this trend is indeed positive for the future of retail markets.

◆ ◆ ◆

9.   **Modern shopping malls are highly convenient for people. However, small markets are still popular among consumers.**

      Discuss both views and give your preference.

It is a fact that with every passing day new shopping malls are opening in many cities across the world. Shopping is being perceived as a corporate concept. However, small markets are still popular among consumers because of their particular advantages.

First, shopping malls offer many benefits. To start with, the layout, infrastructure and interior design of such malls are so attractive that people are motivated to visit them. Next, they offer amenities like parking, air conditioning, security, escalators and so on. All such facilities make the malls a preferred choice for many consumers. However, they do have some limitations. To begin with, they are not affordable for small scale and commodity traders. Because of this, many reputed retail shop owners opt to stay in small markets only. In addition, higher investment and input costs oblige the traders the malls to increase their profit margin, which is a disadvantage to consumers.

On the other hand, small markets have their typical benefits. To start with, we can find many shops of a similar range of products at one place. These places offer better visibility of the shops to the customers, which, in turn enhances competition amongst the traders and obliges them to keep prices at an optimum level that benefit the buyers. However, small markets are chaotic places where parking, security and hygiene are always a problem for visitors.

To summarize, both places have their own benefits and drawbacks. In my opinion, malls are suitable for consumer durables and garments whereas small markets are suitable for perishable commodities like vegetables, fruits, groceries and so on. But, looking at the present scenario, I assert that malls are gaining popularity because of the convenience they offer.

◆ ◆ ◆

10. **Many Countries host international sporting events these days. What are the positive and negative impacts of hosting such events?**

Discuss both the sides and give your opinion.

Organizing international sporting events is becoming a frequent phenomenon in all continents of the world. These days, we see many countries are eager to host international sports events. This is indeed a profitable step for the host countries.

The first and foremost benefit of hosting international sports events is that the host country gets huge attention of international media, business and corporate groups, athletes and tourists. Next, the host country gets a boost in foreign revenues in the form of sponsorship and rights of satellite broadcast. Moreover, local athletes come into limelight as representatives of the host. This is extremely useful in spreading awareness of sports activities at the local level. Finally, the country also acquires diplomatic and political consideration among the elite group of developed nations.

On the other hand, hosting international sports events is highly expensive and needs lots of funding from the government. Now, the government may face opposition if a large mass of its population is in dire need of basic necessities. Moreover, if the host fails to manage the event properly, its reputation is affected internationally. For example, India was the host of Common Wealth Games 2010 and we read in the media that the arrangements were not up to standards. In such cases, rather than gaining, the country is losing reputation. Finally, countries have to spend immensely on security of athletes and spectators if there is a high risk of terrorist attacks and other threats.

In conclusion, I firmly believe that hosting international sports events is indeed good for the country for diplomatic and political reasons. Foreign revenues, sports awareness and betterment of their athletes are furthered as well. However, the host should be able to meet the standards of organisation and should be able to fund the entire project without affecting its allocation of budget for the basic needs of its population.

◆ ◆ ◆

11. **Some say that the government should stop supporting the professional sports activities and the cultural performances, and instead begin supporting schools to encourage children to take up sports and arts.**

   Discuss and give us your opinion.

Adequate attention to sports and cultural activities apart from academics is essential for the all round development of children. This is the reason why governments support professional sports and cultural performances. Some sections of the population believe that this should be the responsibility of the schools and not of the government who should support the schools instead of individuals. I agree with the view but only to an extent.

There are some reasons behind this. Firstly, it is difficult for individuals to access governmental support. If the aid comes to the school it is much easier for the students to gain from it. Secondly, it is simpler at the level of the school administration to determine genuine candidates from those who are not serious. But if the aid directly comes from the government there is a greater chance of it falling into wrong hands. Thirdly, schools use the fund to build sports infrastructure which can benefit not one but many aspiring professionals.

On the other hand, government aid becomes essential at the international level of professional sports and cultural events. To begin with, it is difficult for educational institutions to undertake the expenditure involved at this level and thus, support from the government is absolutely essential if we want medals at the Commonwealth, Asian or Olympic Games. Also, cultural groups go to perform in many foreign countries and without institutional support, such trips would be very difficult to make. Finally, governments can gain long term benefit in terms of attracting tourism and thus, they support such activities.

The Ultimate Guide To IELTS Writing

In conclusion, I feel that when it comes to day to day sporting activities then the government should extend support to schools rather than individuals. But at the level where a sport or cultural performer represents a country, governmental support is absolutely essential.

◆ ◆ ◆

12. **Some people believe that personal happiness is directly related to economic success. Others argue that happiness is a kind of personal feeling and has nothing to do with one's financial status.**

Discuss both viewpoints and give your own opinion.

It has been said for centuries that money can buy countless things but it cannot buy happiness. This saying is often challenged by many and has been proved incorrect at times as well. However, it is indeed true that financial success is not the only parameter to measure one's happiness.

There are plentiful reasons why happiness does not directly depend on economic status. First, I would like to quote a survey conducted by the United Nations a few years ago on happiness and according to that, people of Bangladesh were the happiest and people of the USA were somewhere near the bottom of the list. Now, this survey not only challenges, but defies the belief of those who consider money as a parameter for happiness. Moreover, happiness is a feeling that can come as a reaction to the surroundings or some activities or it can be a state of being for some, where it is constant and does not depend on any external situations.

I think true happiness is a state of being and not a momentary, short-lived reaction, which depends on the outer circumstances and economic status. In this context, any reaction that is particular to a situation is bound to cease with time. Consequently, the happy feelings associated with the same will end as well. I would like to share my experience when I bought my first car; I was ecstatic and overjoyed but I stayed in that state of mind only for a few days.

On the other hand, it is also believed that people become happy when their needs, expectations and luxuries are satisfied. To add to it, we come into this world to acquire wealth and as a wealthy man enjoys a privileged life, it is commonly perceived that to gain comfort and luxuries and finally happiness, money is compulsory.

I believe that real happiness can never be attained by money because it is short lived and vanishes soon. True happiness is a state of being, which is beyond monetary gains and wealth.

◆ ◆ ◆

13. **Considering the problems of pollution and traffic jams, some people argue that cars should be banned from centre of big cities.**

    Discuss the advantages and disadvantages of it.

    Also, suggest what actions can be taken to solve this problem.

Downtowns of metropolises are usually historic city centres the roads of which are narrower and the habitation is denser as compared to the new urban development. Thus, vehicular movement here is far more congested. My opinion is that we need to find a middle way as banning cars completely is not very feasible and allowing them at all times can be very difficult also.

Banning cars from entering this area can resolve a lot of problems such as frequent traffic jams, pollution, accidents, the stress of driving in such congested environs etc. Also, there are many historically important sites which are at risk when pollution levels rise or when there is a higher chance of impact from accidents.

Yet, a car is a comfort vehicle which takes one right from the boarding point to the exact destination. To park it somewhere on the way and take another transport or walk to the city centre would be very uncomfortable for most city dwellers. Also, people not being able to drive right to the footstep of a shop or a market might mean that there is reduced customer flow.

Therefore in this case a sheer black and white solution is not possible and we need to take the middle path. One option could be that there are fixed hours every day during which cars can enter the downtown, thereby limiting their presence in there. Secondly, specific arteries could be identified where cars are allowed and adequate parking should be provided in such a way that from these carefully picked nodal points most areas of the downtown are accessible. Thirdly, a possible solution could be that there is a public transport system with very frequent service specifically for the downtown area, at the peripheries of which there are comfortable parking lots. People can park the car, board the transport and thereby much less time and comfort is thus compromised.

◆ ◆ ◆

14. **Some people say that self employment is better than a job in a company or an institution.**

   Discuss both modes of work and give your opinion.

Owing to innovations in industries and education systems, we can see enormous opportunities for the people to pursue. However, there is a debate whether one should opt for a job or believe in self employment. In my opinion, self employment holds the upper hand in this debate.

There are many reasons why self employment is better over a job. First and foremost is the immense growth opportunity it offers. A self employed professional because he is the leader of his business can determine his own growth chart. The second benefit of the same is freedom. In our own business, we get the freedom to explore and to experiment with new ideas in accordance with the trends in the market.

Lastly, our business gives us independence. We are free to make certain changes in the policies of business and can take the liberty of pursuing personal, social or family related responsibilities as we do not depend on the permission of anyone. Also, one is answerable only to self.

On the other hand, jobs do have certain benefits. One of them is security and safety. We get a fixed salary and the income is secured as far as we are employed. This means, we do not have to worry about ups and downs in business and meeting our overheads. Another benefit is less stress. Once we are home, we can be totally relaxed without any burden of work.

All in all, it seems that jobs do offer some safety and reduced stress. However, considering the freedom and opportunities of growth that lie in business, my personal opinion always goes in favour of self employment.

◆ ◆ ◆

15. **Some people think robots can improve human life in future; while others think robots may affect society in a bad way.**

   Discuss both viewpoints and give your opinion.

Robots have been hailed as one of the most fascinating scientific inventions in the history of mankind. These days, we can see robots doing almost everything a human can and the future seems to belong to them. However, as each invention comes with its positive and negative implications, I would like to ponder upon both before giving my verdict on the same.

First, if I consider the benefits we can get out of robots, I must say that they have been indeed a blessing for millions. These days, robots can work in conditions where humans find difficulty in giving their best. For instance, from manufacturing to surgery, there are numerous work conditions that demand consistency, accuracy and precision. It is proven that robots have outperformed humans in most of them. Moreover, robots can certainly reduce manpower expenditure because they do not need allowances, perks, incentives and additional fringe benefits. All they need is proper maintenance and they can work incessantly.

On the other hand, letting robots take over all the work has its own drawbacks. One of them is technical troubles that we may face. It is obvious that robots are machines and any malfunction can cause unimaginable damage and in medical procedures, a fraction of error can be fatal. Second important disadvantage is creation of unemployment. If robots take over all the jobs, skilled labours will be jobless and that may have hazardous social implications.

Finally, I think robots are indeed useful in certain conditions. However, they can be dangerous if they underperform. I believe that robots are and will be needed by humans and they can be fruitful to us provided they are maintained properly.

◆ ◆ ◆

16. **Some people say that parents have the most significant influence in a child's development. However, others say that things like television or friends have the most important influence on them.**

    Discuss both views and give your opinion.

It is said that parents are the first teachers of a child in life and so they seem to have the maximum influence on their children's life. However, some argue that these days, children are under higher influence of friends and television. It seems to me that parents' influence outweighs other factors in the development of the offspring.

There are many reasons why parents' impact is very high on children. To initiate, parents are the first human contact for any child. Henceforth, their words, emotions, behaviour, culture and lifestyle shape the personality traits of the kid. This happens so because the child's mind is like a plain canvas. Whatever is printed or painted on it stays there for a life time. Moreover, the child's first words, first steps, first tears and first smile happen in front of his parents. He or she learns how to see the world with the help of his parents and so their influence is bound to be the highest.

On the other hand, some people say factors like friends and television have stronger influence on children's minds. They say that after a certain age, children pay more attention to their friends and spend more time watching television and playing with friends. They also say that friends and television are able to influence anyone's mind, and so, a child's tender mind is bound to be affected to a greater extent.

Conclusively, it is true that the impact of TV and friends can be more at times in some cases. However, I firmly believe that parents' influence is the strongest on any child's mind compared to any other person or media.

◆ ◆ ◆

17. **It is said by some that museums are meant for entertainment. On the other hand, some people say that they are only meant for education.**

    Discuss both views and give your opinion.

The Ultimate Guide To IELTS Writing

Some people perceive a museum as a place where ancient, historical and rare articles are preserved. However, to me, museum is a place that connects the present to the past. Hence, in this context, the predominant purpose of any museum is education and not entertainment.

There are numerous reasons to support this notion. Firstly, museums are the only place where antique and historical articles are preserved. Thus, if anyone wants to gain access to our past, he or she has to only visit a museum. This information is not available anywhere else. Secondly, when we visit any museum, we get instantly connected to the culture or the lifestyle of the past. This not only makes us aware but also educates us about the past.

Finally, all articles preserved in the museum do contain all available information on them for the visitors. This feature facilitates lots of students. For example, when I was a child, I had a hard time in understanding some historical events. However, I then visited a museum where I gained all the knowledge which I had not been able to acquire from my history teachers.

On the other hand, some people say that many people feel entertained when they visit museums. They add that museums should offer more and more facilities that can entertain visitors as they are the places which contain things that are no longer useful in the present.

All in all, even though some find museums a place to amuse and refresh people, I firmly believe that museums hold the link between today and the yester times and hence, museums ought to be used for education only.

♦ ♦ ♦

18. **Do children behave better when they are rewarded or when they are punished?**

   Discuss both views given and offer your own opinion.

Issues like ways of bringing up children are always open for a debate as people keep putting forth their differing views all the time regarding such topics. Some say that children become more disciplined if they have the fear of punitive actions. However others say children behave better if they are positively rewarded. It is true that you reap what you sow.

There are several reasons why children should not be punished. First, science has now proved that almost all actions taken by humans in this world are based on some expectations. It is also seen that when children do not get the desired attention, they are inspired to do something that forces others to notice them. In order to inculcate traits of better behaviour in their tender minds, we must stop punishing them and start rewarding. Second, when any action of children is rewarded positively, they start understanding the importance of good behaviour. It is one type of psychological conditioning where they comprehend the significance of strength of character. Finally, better rewards always satisfy their needs of love, which, in turn, gives immense confidence, courage, maturity and responsibility. All these traits are essential in moulding better citizens of the world.

On the other hand, some people often say that punishment is the best way to prepare children for better behaviour. They add that punishment is highly effective in training young minds because the fear will certainly not let them behave in a bad manner. Moreover, certain children are highly notorious; they can be trained properly only if they are under some threat.

All in all, I firmly believe that punishment is like taming and reward is like grooming. Its grooming that differentiates a human from an animal. It has to be understood that we are here to be groomed and not to be trained or tamed.

◆ ◆ ◆

19. **Some people think that national news is very important and they stay up-to-date with national news. However, some say international news is more important and we should stay updated with that.**

    Discuss both points and give your view.

News is indeed an important aspect of our everyday life. Its importance cannot be described or valued on any scale because it is a type of knowledge and all knowledge is invaluable power. In this regard, some people prefer international news over national. I think both have their importance but one should always be concerned more about what is happening in one's own country.

There are many reasons why I think domestic news is more relevant than international happenings. Firstly, all of us are largely affected by the events that happen around us. These events can be political, climatic, civil administration related, or of business and economy. All these events affect us to some extent depending upon our type of work or business. Secondly, we can take our everyday decisions based on the news updates. For example, if the weather forecast predicts heavy snowfall or rainfall, we can change our route or modify timings of our work or leisure trips. Finally, it is observed that events that happen around us contribute in shaping our lifestyle and our socioeconomic status as well.

However, in certain cases, some people do need to pay more attention to international news. To begin with, people who work in or have a business that is highly sensitive towards international events i.e. foreign exchange dealings, stock markets or news channels etc. have to be informed about the same. Even people like me who work as visa consultants are affected by changes that various countries introduce in their immigration or student visa policy, have to stay up to date regarding overseas news as.

All in all, although, some peoples' work expects them to keep a close eye on international news, it is necessary for all of us to stay in touch with local news.

◆ ◆ ◆

20. **Some parents think computer games are better for children and they should be allowed to play more of them. Whereas some parents argue that they are harmful to children.**

Discuss both views and give your opinion.

Today's children are bombarded by countless versions of video games, be it on the mobile, tablet PC, a computer or a laptop. This development has generated two schools of thought: one in support of the technologically powered games and one in opposition. However, my inclination is towards those who oppose.

The Ultimate Guide To IELTS Writing

Computer games are indeed harmful to children in numerous ways. To begin with, computer games compel children to sit at one place and play for hours. This can have adverse results in the long run as sitting postures of almost all children are not healthy and accurate. Moreover, incessant exposure to a computer screen is harmful to their tender and young eyes and we all know the possible consequences if one's eyesight gets affected at a very young age.

Furthermore, computer games also oblige children to stay alone and prevent them from interacting with their peers or others. This is egregious as children miss out on important lessons of socializing. Finally, most children either stay hungry for a long time or overeat while playing games as they do not really pay attention to this aspect of their being. Such unhealthy food intake can lead to multiple health problems for them.

However, some parents support the idea of their children playing computer games. They say that computer games help children to get tech savvy at an early age. Next, they add that it helps children to develop their psychological strength and general intelligence. Finally, they assert that such digital entertainment is safe as children do not have to step out of their homes.

Conclusively, I opine that computer games are an evil that can certainly harm young children and can physically and mentally weaken the youth of the future. So, according to me, children should never be motivated to play computer games.

◆ ◆ ◆

21. **Some believe elderly people should live in nursing homes, others think they should live with the family members.**

   Discuss both views and give your opinion.

We live in a world that is constantly transforming and in turn we are modifying our lifestyle, culture, customs, traditions and family systems. It is also true that not all the changes are good and some of them are indeed very unwelcome. The notion of some short sighted people that aims at keeping the elderly in nursing homes is nothing but a result of a self-centred and negative mindset.

There are enormous benefits of elderly people living with the younger family members. To begin with, they have wealth of knowledge, experience and skills. As a result, they can be extremely helpful to the youth of the family when any trouble arises. Next, they can shower the warmth of their love and emotions on the youngsters. In today's stressful and highly competitive life, such love is a boon for a young life burdened with daily strife.

Thirdly, elders can work as a guardian angel for the working youth and the children in their family. Elders not only take care of the children but also help them in learning the lessons of morals and ethics in their early age. Finally, older people also help the society by offering their voluntary help to their family and community. By doing so, they keep themselves engaged with some activity, that yields them respect and satisfaction.

On the other hand, some people argue that confining the elderly to nursing homes may be a better idea. They assert that many families have conflicts because of the generation gap and that problem can be eliminated easily. Next, youngsters can concentrate and dedicate their earnings to themselves as they do not have any old person in the house to look after. However, this system sends a wrong message to the community that elderly people are a burden and so they should be caged to such places.

Finally, after assessing both the sides, I opine that the idea of keeping the elderly in nursing home is abominable. I see more benefits of them living with their family rather than spending lonely, depressing hours in aged care homes.

♦ ♦ ♦

22. **Technological and scientific advances are changing the food people eat. Some believe that these changes can be harmful to the health of people. Others challenge this.**

   Discuss both views and give your opinion.

As we all are living in the most advanced technological era, all the aspects of our day to day life are influenced by science and technology. Hence, the food we eat has been transformed to a great extent with the help of new technology. In the coming paragraphs, I am going to discuss drawbacks and benefits of impact of technology and science on food with respect to the health of consumers.

Enhancement of technology has always helped in deepening the understanding of the food that we eat. We can explore the nutritive value, medicinal applications, mutual compatibility and shelf life of raw or finished food products with the help of technology. Moreover, we can plan and prepare better, resulting in healthier and tastier recipes that can be customized to the needs of the target consumers. Furthermore, particularly healthy food options can be searched and made available to the people who are in medical need of the same.

On the other hand, it is often argued that technology can make the food tastier but not healthier. This is not wrong in many cases across the world. For example, consumption of hamburgers, potato chips and popcorns is rising. However, it was found in the USA that the synthetic chemical used in popcorns to enhance its taste can be a potential carcinogen*. This can be extremely dangerous for the health of people who consume such products. In addition, introduction of science and technology has prompted food businesses to focus on the taste buds of consumers to enhance the sale and for the same, they add excessive amounts of salt, sugar and other synthetic chemicals that are not good for our health.

All in all, advancements in technology have always had noble intentions. However, it is the profit oriented use of technology which motivates some people in modifying food. Hence, I opine that judicious and noble applications of technology must always be entertained as they are for the good of the people.

* Carcinogen = a substance that can cause cancer

◆ ◆ ◆

23. **In many countries, a prison sentence is considered as the best way to decrease crime. However, education is often argued as a more effective way.**

    Discuss both views and give your opinion.

___

OR

In most countries, imposing a prison sentence is the most common solution when people commit a crime. However, if they were to receive better education, it could prevent them from becoming criminals.

Discuss and give your opinion on the same.

Education has been presented as an alternative to imprisonment by many for the last few decades. The debate has become intense with time. However, looking at the current scenario, imprisonment is still more effective in reducing crime.

There are ample reasons for this. One of them is, imprisonment allows the criminal to stay alone and with himself, and this is a great opportunity for anyone to introspect and change himself. Secondly, such penalty is a strong message to those who may be thinking of committing a crime. I think fear of being caught and confined in a jail is the most effective tool in controlling such tendencies. Finally, putting the convict behind bars is also a way of justifying the pain, hardship and troubles faced by the victim. Otherwise, if the convict is simply educated and counselled to not to commit crime, the victim may lose faith in the judicial system of the country.

On the other hand, education is backed by some as an option for criminals. First, education inculcates the correct morals and importance and benefits of a crime free society in the minds of the criminal. Secondly, it is also seen that most criminals are illiterate and unemployed. Therefore, offering education and certain skills will surely help them in leading a life with self respect. However, it is also seen that a major chunk of criminals these days are well educated. Thus, it is evident In conclusion, I firmly believe that education is not as effective a way of reducing crime as imprisonment is. Had it been at all the case, the governments would have already converted all prisons into schools.

◆ ◆ ◆

24. **Zoos should be merely meant for entertainment or should there be some other purpose also?**

    Discuss and give your opinion.

The Ultimate Guide To IELTS Writing

In the past zoos served the facility of bringing the wildlife to the cities for the entertainment of people who could not go to the forest to see them. With time zoos are being equipped with newer roles to play not only for the animals but for the society as well.

There are three important purposes that the zoos can serve other than entertainment. First, they should serve as an education centre for the children. By visiting zoos children can understand the wildlife. They can be taught the importance of animals as the role of each in the ecosystem is brought to light.

A second purpose that can be fulfilled at the zoos is the setting up of a facility of research and development. Nowadays many zoos are being used to breed endangered species to prevent them from becoming extinct. In addition, the zoos can be used to cross breed animals to produce a genetically stronger offspring that can survive longer. On the top of it, new medicines and vaccines can also be prepared to protect them from various diseases, which is a great contribution to the veterinary science.

Finally, zoos offer safety to the animals. Animals are protected in the zoos from various natural threats such as natural calamities like fire, droughts, floods and their predators etc.

All in all, according to me zoos have great potential to transform their role from place for entertainment to a place for education, research and development and a safe home for animals. I think governments should come forward to transform the zoos to improve their perception and importance in the society for the benefit of animals and the nature.

◆ ◆ ◆

25. **In many countries the proportion of older people is increasing. Does this trend have more positive or negative effects on the society?**

Discuss and give your opinion.

The proportion of older people is rising in many countries because of numerous revolutionary inventions in the field of medicine and technology. We have made health care effective, in reach and more efficient. This has contributed in increasing the lifespan of people.

Rising numbers of old people can have many adverse effects. Such effects can be divided into three main categories in my view. First is expenditure. As the age progresses, the human body becomes more vulnerable and prone to diseases. This leads to higher expenditure on health care. Moreover, the monetary rebates and perks given to them are also high like pension, discount in public transport, relaxed tax norms and so on. Governments have to increase the tax burden on society to compensate the expenditure they incur for taking care of the old.

Second is employment. Higher density of old workers prevents young workers in getting jobs and promotions. Because of this, the rotation of vacancies stops. This increases unemployment in young people and therefore has hazardous consequences. Third is crime. It is observed that old people save money for the last stages of their life thereby becoming soft targets of criminals as many of them stay alone. In many countries, we can see that incidents of old people being attacked and sometimes even killed for money are increasing these days. Police departments have to invest considerable energy and money in solving such cases.

However, an older population can be useful to the society also. Firstly, they are helpful at home in routine work and bringing up children. Secondly, they also offer voluntary help to the society in many administrative aspects. Finally, by sharing their experience they prevent the society from many harmful things.

To sum up, I think there are more disadvantages of rising density of old people. However, by utilizing their abilities in creative and constructive ways, societies can compensate the expenditure incurred and also help them to lead a better life.

◆ ◆ ◆

26. **Zoos are sometimes necessary but are a poor alternative to the natural environment.**

Discuss arguments for and against keeping animals in zoos.

Owing to spread of industries worldwide and accompanying deforestation, climate patterns in the world have been changing drastically. This has made zoos an essential option for the survival of animals. It is an inevitable change and we as a society have to take necessary actions favouring animals.

Keeping animals in zoos offers numerous benefits. First is safety. Animals are protected against all natural calamities like fire, floods and droughts. In addition, they are also safeguarded against their killer spices. What is more, they live under the supervision of veterinary doctors who take care of their health, give regular checkups, medicines and vaccines to protect them against diseases and disorders. Next, they also get better quality food in zoos because governments take the responsibility of zoos and provide necessary funding also. Finally, zoos prevent many animals from going extinct, as they breed successfully in a controlled environment.

However, there are also some drawbacks. First, animals live in an artificial environment. They lose their freedom and hence they also lose their natural abilities like hunting, reproduction, tree climbing and so on. Here, the saying, 'A hut of independence is far better than the golden cage' is applicable to them. Secondly, human interference also disturbs them a lot.

To sum up, it is true that animals lose their freedom when they are kept in zoos. However, I strongly believe that they get better protection in zoos where they can live longer; otherwise, they are vulnerable and would succumb to climatic changes without human assistance.

◆ ◆ ◆

27. **Some people say that children should learn all the subjects equally. Whereas others think that they should only learn what they are interested in.**

Discuss both views and give your opinion.

It is evident that students do not have equal interest in learning all the subjects they study. Some people say that they should study all the subjects equally. However, others argue that children should only study the subjects of their interest.

Those who say that students should study all the subjects in same proportion support their view with two main arguments. First, equal study of subjects gives thorough knowledge of all disciplines to the students. It is significant because now we have faculties that require acquaintance of a combination of subjects. For example in bio-informatics, student must be good at biology, mathematics and electronics. Finally, globalization obliges many economies to change and new fields are emerging. New fields often offer extremely rewarding remuneration scales. What is more, they are more adventurous and exciting. If students have studied all the subjects, they can promptly switchover to novel fields and can have a lucrative and productive professional life.

On the other hand, some people argue that children should study only the subjects of their liking. They say that when a student studies subjects of his interest, his understanding and grip over that discipline is often miraculous. They add that only these students can become great scientists or researchers and can reach the top. They also assert that people on top never need to change their vocation because they are the most successful and satisfied professionals in the world.

In the summary, I believe that both study of all subjects equally and study of only subjects of interest are not good notions individually because neither all students learn all disciplines equally nor all students can become top professionals. Hence, I assert that at the early stages we should teach all subjects to develop competence and at a tertiary level, they should be offered a choice to specialize in fields of interest.

◆   ◆   ◆

28. **Some children have to live at different places during their childhood because of transferrable jobs of their parents.**

Discuss the advantages and disadvantages of living in different places in childhood and give your opinion on whether it is good or bad to stay at different areas for children.

Living life in different places during ones growing years is always full of a variety of influences. Such exposure is very important at a tender age because childhood lays the foundation of the entire lifespan of a person and if it is open to such varied experiences, one's life is bound to be enriched.

Spending childhood at various venues offers many benefits. First, children in such a situation always experience a multicultural neighbourhood, which makes them expressive and extrovert in nature. In addition, interacting with different people enhances their communication skills, confidence and understanding of different cultures, races and languages.

Second, children evolve an adaptive body. They learn to easily adjust to differing environments and hence their body evolves higher immunity for varying climates and seasons. Finally, such children, when become adults, can take up any job that requires extensive travelling like marketing or a position in the media. Their smart communication skills can open avenues of call centres or public relations jobs for them and thus they can avail the advantage of their multi-regional, multi-cultural and multi-lingual exposure.

However, it has some drawbacks also. First, such children remain self-centred, as they generally do not have a close friend circle owing to the frequent changes of locale. Second, their exposure to various cultures at times confuses them, resulting in the loss of their indigenous culture. Finally, their study is the worst hit because they have to change schools frequently, which requires a lot of effort from them to adapt and yet perform better at different schools.

To summarize, living in different places does enhance the personality of a child. However, at times, rapid and frequent changes in accommodation may have some adverse effects on children. Hence, I assert that changes in the area of residence should be admitted only in unavoidable circumstances.

◆ ◆ ◆

29. **Should young children be encouraged to follow a strict set of rules based on culture and tradition or should they be allowed to behave freely?**

   Discuss both views and give your opinion.

Since ages, there are divided opinions in different cultures regarding the ways to bring up children. Some always back the strict and religious set of rules whereas others always defend freedom from such rules and advocate giving a free reign to children. It seems that the time has now come that we should step out of traditional boundaries.

Strict sets of rules often kill creativity and inhibit individual development. We all are different and we come in this world with different abilities. Now, if similar cultural or religious rules apply to all, it is discouraging indeed. In addition, such compulsion often forces people to rebel against the set up. Those who rebel may reach great heights in their lives like Jesus Christ, Gautam Buddha, Swami Vivekanand, Salman Rushdie, Freidrich Nietzsche and so on. Vice versa, those who cannot break free against the confinements of stringent set of religious and cultural protocols of behaviour often get repressed and live a doomed life.

On the other hand, freedom gives birth to creativity. It also promotes faster individual growth and, contrary to most who believe that freedom makes people irresponsible, I think liberty can inculcate virtues of responsibility at a faster pace in our minds. However, a minute proportion of people may misuse the freedom for negative purposes but they cannot be used as example to limit opportunities for a whole lot of other people.

Finally, I agree that freedom gives more opportunities to grow in life. Provided children are prevented from hurting anyone, they should be given as much freedom as possible.

◆ ◆ ◆

30. **Some people feel that the design of newly constructed buildings in big cities should be controlled by governments. Others think those who spend for the construction should be given freedom to design the building as they wish.**

Discuss both viewpoints and give your opinion.

The field of construction has seen dramatic transformations in the last few decades. We have seen skyscrapers in almost all the countries, along with that, a breed of people have come into existence who want complete control over the design of the building. Both sides of this demand are discussed in the following paragraphs.

Governments ought to regulate the construction and design of all the buildings that are under construction to ensure a coherent urban environment. Also this seems to take care that certain essential safety measures are observed and followed by the constructors. And, it's the government's duty to ensure that standards of Floor Space Index (FSI), space for parking, elevators, arrangement of fire safety system, water supply, availability of basic facilities, sanitation and so on are met.

Apart from such regulations, I think the owner should be allowed to design the building as per his or her needs. It may be possible that some people have specific needs related to the purpose of the building and such intentions must be respected by the authorities. Imagine, if such freedom was not given in the past, a building like the Opera House of Sydney might not have been constructed. Finally, it is fortunate that these days, owing to such freedom, we can see buildings like Burj Khalifa in Dubai.

All in all, I assert that if the safety and regulatory measures are respected, governments must provide freedom of design to those who fund the cost of construction of any building. I think such independence is a fundamental right of every citizen.

◆ ◆ ◆

31. **The world of work is changing rapidly. Employees would not be able to depend on the same job or same working condition for a long time in the near future.**

    Discuss the cases of rapid change in world of work and how people can be prepared for the future.

It is a fact that our work and working conditions have changed a lot and they will be changing at an even greater pace in the future. There are few competitive people who shall be able to adapt to these changes. However, others do need specific training to survive in these circumstances.

Because of globalization, companies want fast growth. This has forced the world of work to transform to a great extent. First, the types of jobs and qualifications required have changed. Now, we should have higher qualifications and should be prepared to work longer hours to survive in today's working conditions. Second, to attain fast growth, companies implement various strategies that require a lot of skills in employees. Third, implementation of technology has made significant changes in the way people work.

Today, we can see a person sitting in India and working for a company located in USA. In addition to this, mobility in the job is also higher as present day employees travel widely during their job.

It is also true that only a competitive person survives in the changed world of work. However, there are many ways by which we can increase the pool of skilled and competent workers. To start with, they must be taught English, as it serves as the basis of new learning and becoming competent. Moreover, management skills like time management, interpersonal and communication skills, marketing and customer care skills etc should be imparted to ensure a better output from the employee. Finally, employees must be made tech savvy. The knowledge of computers and its applications including the Internet must be imparted.

In conclusion, according to me, there are enormous changes in today's work environment. However, by inculcating efficient training programs, we can prepare today's employees for the future growth and create a progressive work culture.

◆ ◆ ◆

32   Some people believe that those moving abroad should try to adapt themselves to the new cultures. While some think that there is no need to do so.

Discuss and give your opinion.

It is indeed an important social issue being debated on an international level that whether migrants should adapt to local cultures or not. It appears that to merge into the host culture and to adapt to the local climate proves to be more fruitful.

Adapting to the local cultures is beneficial in many ways. First, migrants understand the host culture and religion, which enhances their intellectual growth and tolerance. Second, they can develop better social and professional contacts which are of immense assistance in getting a good job or support in other necessary requirements of surviving and growing in a new setting.

Finally, migrants who have merged with the host cultures can have an overall satisfaction of living in a foreign country. This is extremely important in developing a global community of skilled people.

On the other hand, some people argue that we should never forget our ethnicity and never leave our culture as it is the original identity of any individual. Moreover, in most countries, skilled people work very hard and thus cannot spare enough time to interact socially with many people. It might affect or distract them from their work too.

All in all, I believe in a popular saying, "In Rome, do as Romans do." I do not insist that we should simply leave our culture behind, but, if we want to settle in a foreign country, we must adapt to the local cultures in such a way that we face no hassle in settling there. At the same time we should be able to nurture our ethnicity and continue to take pride in our traditions.

◆ ◆ ◆

33. **Some people believe that immigrants should adopt the local culture when immigrating to a new country. An alternative view is that they can adapt to a new environment by establishing a minority community.**

   Discuss these two views and give your opinion.

Immigration has always been one of the important aspects of the human life on this earth. These days, we see lots of people immigrating to different countries for varied reasons. This has caused a huge debate on whether immigrants should adopt the culture of the host country or not. It seems to me that one has to be flexible enough to survive and grow in a foreign country and at the same time one has the responsibility to preserve one's traditions and pass it on to the next generation.

It is said, 'In Rome, do as the Romans do'. There is no doubt that when immigrants adopt local culture, their life becomes easier as they go with the flow of their surroundings and show no resistance to embracing change. This helps immigrants to get a warm response from the host country which, in turn, helps them to establish businesses and settle down, eventually rising into prosperity. Also, it is not only about financial growth but warmth and friendship are essential for a happy life in a foreign location.

However, an individual is always known by his culture and if he loses it, he loses his identity as well. Therefore adjusting to a foreign culture should not mean that one breaks all ties with ones past. This can have negative psychological implications and even the coming generations shall not inherit a history that immigrants brought with them. Also, the ties of one's culture are that which bring about the feeling of community within immigrants, therefore giving a sense of security in a foreign setting.

Thus said, according to me, it is of prime importance to accept the culture of a foreign country in order to settle down there. However, one should also be careful of the possible consequences of extremity in this regard and therefore maintain a healthy equilibrium of both cultures in life to stay psychologically and socially happy.

◆ ◆ ◆

34. **In some countries students who misbehave have to leave the school and are not allowed to continue their education. In other countries they can return to their studies after a suspension period.**

    Discuss both options and give your opinion.

Unacceptable behaviour of some students is a problem that schools all over the world deal with. In some cases the punishment is really harsh where the student is made to leave school and not allowed to continue his or her education any further. At other places students are suspended for a while and then accepted back in the school. I believe in the second method, that is, students should only be suspended as a punishment and not disallowed all together.

Suspension is a punishment period where firstly the child learns the difference between right and wrong. Secondly, he or she repents the actions and sees the pain it causes to the self and to family members. Thirdly, once they are accepted after suspension they feel confident that they have a second chance to prove themselves.

In the case where the student has to leave school and is not allowed to study any further there is a great risk of ruining his life and academic career. The child may have committed a mistake, but, to not give him another opportunity would be a very strict punishment. There are some extreme cases where some children are repeat offenders and do not learn from successive punishments. In this case they need psychiatric help and counselling and may be even special institutions to train them. Thus, the mainstream school system may not accept them but there are other options for them to learn and become better individuals.

Therefore, I believe that just because a very small percentage of student offenders need special care, it does not mean that we harshly punish all those who make mistakes. Suspension for a period is a much better option if exercised with responsible guidance.

♦ ♦ ♦

35. **Some people think that politicians have the greatest influence on the world. Others, however, believe that scientists have the greatest influence.**

    Discuss both views and give your opinion.

Each class of human beings be it doctors, engineers, scientists or politicians have an influence on the society they live in and upon the whole world as well. In my opinion it is not possible to decide whether scientists have more influence or politicians do. We can discuss the role of both and compare and contrast their contributions but we cannot state one better than the other.

Scientists work to improve the human relationship with reality. It could be physics, biology or chemistry, in each field they constantly discover, invent and construct to make human life richer and evolved. Simple things that we take for granted like the burner in our kitchen, the washing machine or the car are a result of scientific endeavour over centuries. Very simple things like a torch or a cloth or a toothpick require industrial manufacturing processes that are based on scientific know how. Without science human beings would be as good as animals, so scientists have an immense influence on human life. Yet, there are drawbacks too. All weapons are a scientific contribution as well and the worst of all are the atomic bomb and chemical weapons that can cause mass destruction.

Politicians on the other hand decide the trajectory of nations or even regions. They decide over financial, territorial and infrastructural issues which are the support frame of any society. Running a city administration or a country's government is a job that boasts of immense power. Thus, the influence of politicians is great even though they are at times corrupt, illiterate and hard-hearted.

Thus, in my opinion both politicians and scientists have great influence on a society or a country. The progress and evolution of humans will stop if any of these roles ceases to exist.

◆　◆　◆

36.　**Some people think that it is better for a child to grow up in the country-side than in the city, others disagree.**

Discuss both views, and give your own opinion.

For a long time now migration to cities from the rural areas is a consistent phenomenon. There has been a raging debate about raising children in the countryside or in an urban environment, as a result of this. I personally feel that in the present times we should raise our children in the cities.

There are many reasons where the urban area offers more benefits. First, cities have more earning opportunities, better infrastructure and well-developed education and health facilities. Second, it is possible here to raise a child well and give him or her every possible support to enable his or her development into an intelligent and responsible human being. Third, cities are nodes of connectivity to other countries of the world. Therefore, if one grows up in an urban environment there is a good chance of being exposed to other cultures and many academic and professional opportunities may open up. As a result, the child also becomes more tolerant and accepting.

On the other hand, cities now are very polluted and overcrowded while the countryside offers a relatively peaceful and pure atmosphere. So a child shall not be exposed to the harmful aspects of urban environment here and can grow up in a secure setting. In addition, since the beginning of the school days, an urban child lives life of competition. This, at times, makes the child more self-centred and inconsiderate towards others.

　　　　　　　　　　　The Ultimate Guide To IELTS Writing

To conclude, I opine that even though the villages are more peaceful and pollution free, we should bring up our children only in cities if we wish to give them a good opportunity to have a fulfilling life.

◆ ◆ ◆

37. **Many countries are experiencing population growth and a need for more homes. Should these new homes be constructed in the existing cities or should new towns be built for this purpose?**

Discuss and give your opinion.

Population growth is forcing many countries to build homes for the teeming millions. People want to live as close as possible to business hubs and therefore new constructions occur in suburbs of these cities. Looking at the resultant massive pressure on the city there are suggestions that new towns should be built to accommodate more people rather than constructing in existing cities. I believe that a city administration cannot follow, strictly, one path out of these two and a balanced approach has to be undertaken.

Expansion of an existing city is a good idea because it already has a functioning infrastructure and a good network of services In place. If more man-power were to join the same, the city could grow further and facilitate more variety of tasks which are not possible to accomplish in a smaller establishment. At the same time, care needs to be taken that the city is not over-burdened to an extent that it begins to break apart. Also, the government cannot only build houses but it also has to see that there is proper provision of all kinds of facilities and their regular maintenance as well.

On the other hand, building new towns is a great idea if implemented in the right manner. Each small community of people has an operative economy and some supporting infrastructure of services. If the government were to look into the industrial and or agricultural development of a place, a new township could take birth and create more jobs for people and therefore places to live in as well. Chandigarh in Punjab and Gandhinagar in Gujarat are the best examples of the same in my country.

Thus, in my opinion, both processes, that of expansion of existing cities and of building new townships goes hand in hand in the progress of a nation as it tries to make place for its increasing population.

◆ ◆ ◆

3. COMPARE AND CONTRAST (17)

1.   **Now a days, people throw away old things and adopt new things.**

   Do the disadvantages of throwaway society outweigh any possible economic advantages?

It is general human nature that we always seek novelty. Sometimes it is genuine, however, many times it is a temptation only. Those who always adopt new things come under a rapidly growing category, called throwaway society. I think, disadvantages certainly outweigh its perceived and hypothetical advantages.

Today's throwaway society has generated many problems. Firstly, many a times we adopt new things to satisfy our never ending craze to be better and different, which leads to a loss of money. This craze also inspires us to work hard and earn more. As a result, victims of this mentality become more materialistic. In addition to this, they have to earn more to buy more, therefore, they may move away from ethics and moral values, which is a big loss in today's world.

Thirdly, throwaway society also generates a collection of waste. To manage this dump is a headache for today's governments. The dump leads to a rise in pollution. Many thrown away articles are non-biodegradable, which may affect our ecosystem. For example, many countries have been dumping such tonnage in the sea, which has had adverse effects on the marine life.

On the other hand, some economists support its perceived advantages. Firstly, they say that throwaway society helps in the growth of manufacturing, technology and research related industries. Secondly, there is a rise in employment opportunities and a growth curve is seen in the global economy. Thirdly, adoption of new things always helps us in improving our standard of life.

All in all, I believe the concept of throwaway society is certainly harmful to the world in so many ways. It has adverse effects on the social set up, ecosystem and environment. Hence, disadvantages of throwaway society outscore its perceived economic advantages.

On the other side

It is a human nature that we always want new things. Many times it is genuine. However, at times it is a temptation only. Those who adopt new things are labelled as belonging to a throwaway society. However, the merits of throwaway society are certainly higher than its demerits.

Throwaway society offers enormous economic advantages. Firstly, when we need new things, the related manufacturing industries develop with the demand. This leads to a growth in research and development. Ultimately, there is a creation of more employment opportunities that contributes to general prosperity.

Secondly, technological innovations are speeding up the invention of new products in almost all segments of the markets. We can improve our standard of living, if we are ready to switch over to new things. Finally, thrown away things can either be recycled; this makes the availability of raw materials at a cheaper rate and it also preserves the natural resources; or they can be sold at an affordable rate to the people who cannot buy new things. It helps the availability of all products across the social strata.

On the other hand, the throwaway society raises some concerns also. First, this society contributes to a collection of waste and to manage this dump is a headache for today's governments. Second, it also creates pollution. Many thrown away articles are non-biodegradable, which may affect our ecosystem. For example, many countries have been dumping such tonnage in the sea, which has had adverse effects on the marine life.

All in all, our nature to adopt new things has made our life so much convenient. I am sure that the trend towards an even better life will continue. Hence, I think, the economic advantages of the throwaway society outweigh its disadvantages.

◆ ◆ ◆

2.   **In some countries, young people do not take care of their elderly relatives. Instead, they appoint trained professionals who take care of the elderly.**

   Is it a positive or a negative tend according to you?

Owing to rapid changes in lifestyle, work patterns and social set up, young family members these days do not pay attention to the problems of the older members of their family. It is also seen that they often hire competent professionals to look after the elderly in the family. This development is not very positive and may create social and cultural complications.

There are numerous reasons why I think this is a negative development. Firstly, it is a moral responsibility of young ones to take care of their older relatives in the family. If they turn deaf ears to old people, children in the same family also grow up with similar understanding and they will do the same when they become young. Secondly, such practice is very harmful to the social and family set up as old people worked hard and nurtured their children and now when they need support, the children turn their back on them at the time of reciprocation. The institution called family thus breaks down.

Thirdly, elderly people often feel lonely and rejected when they see that their own offspring does not have time for them. Such a situation may lead older people into depression and related health problems. Finally, trained professionals are not family members and hence they cannot show love and warmth to the seniors.

On the other hand, qualified professionals do offer some benefits. To begin with, they can be with the elders all times in the house and can provide the right treatment in case of emergency, which can be life saving at times. Next, many youngsters may have to travel or work in other cities for a long period, and here, hiring trained professionals is the only option left.

All in all, it seems that trained health professionals may give competent services and can offer an alternative. However, I firmly believe that youngsters in the family must look after their elders as it is one of their fundamental duties.

On the other side

Owing to rapid changes in lifestyle, work patterns and social set up, young family members these days cannot pay attention to the older members of their family. It is also seen that they often hire competent professionals to look after them. This development is the need of the day and is beneficial to all.

Hiring qualified professionals helps in many ways. Firstly, since youngsters cannot spend too much time in caring for the elders because of increased working hours and stress in life, hired professionals can spend time with elders and can make them feel wanted. Secondly, trained people can offer competitive services and they are a boon in emergencies because it's their knowledge that can save life of older people.

Thirdly, professionals are also trained to socialize and provide emotional support to the elders, which motivate them to stay socially active. Finally, it is also seen that conflicts occur within the two generations in the family and that may create troubles for all. In such a situation, the presence of a professionally trained person with the elder is of great help and support.

However, taking care of elders is one of the fundamental duties of youngsters and they cannot escape from it. Next, old timers often seek love and warmth from their own blood and if they do not get it, they may become victims of frustration and may develop related illnesses. Lastly, such a trend gives a wrong message to the children of the family as they grow in an environment where they do not develop any tolerance towards older people of the family.

All in all, it is morally correct that youngsters ought to look after the elderly in the family. However, I do not see anything wrong in hiring qualified professionals for this job as they can offer more benefits to both, according to me.

◆ ◆ ◆

3. **For some people, shopping is not just about buying what is necessary, but is a form of entertainment.**

    Do you think it is a positive or negative development?

Perception of shopping has been transformed from just being a routine task into an interesting and enjoyable experience. A major chunk of shoppers these days go for shopping just to be entertained. However, this development is not encouraging for the society.

There are many reasons why shopping meant for entertainment is not good. First, shoppers often waste too much time in visiting various outlets. Consequently, they lose their focus and are diverted away from other essential responsibilities of their life and relationships. Secondly, owing to excess exposure to shopping, people become spendthrifts and often shop beyond their financial reach. This is extremely harmful to them as well as their families because financial burden emerging from excess spending leads to bitterness in their bonding. Finally, those who cannot spend enough often feel inferior and in extreme cases, they may take up illegal activities to earn money. Youngsters are more prone to such risks because they are more vulnerable.

On the other hand, increased interest of all classes of people in shopping has made it a throbbing industry worldwide. It is indeed a welcome step for those who seek careers in retail segment because more jobs are now available in retail industry than ever.

As per my opinion, those who use shopping as a tool for entertainment are under a risk of social, financial and psychological imbalance. Thus, even though shopping gives benefits to those who are employed in the sector, I think, perceiving shopping as a source of entertainment is indeed harmful.

◆ ◆ ◆

4. **Increased world demand of oil and gases cause the taking up of search operations of fuel in remote or even untouched natural places.**

   Do the advantages of this outweigh the disadvantage of damaging those places?

It is an undeniable fact that oil and gas explorations are going on at a frenzied pace owing to an outrageous usage of fossil fuels across the world. This has compelled us to explore isolated or even uninhabited places to meet the surging demand for oil and gas. However, this search might lead to hazardous consequences.

If we look at the advantages, they are obvious and evident. We need more fuel and this never ending thirst can be quenched by more sources of crude and gas. Moreover, these days, habited places and locations create huge problems for the explorers to conduct the drilling work. In addition to the discomfort, it is risky as well because any drilling needs to be done with intense precautions and a small mistake in the same can cause the loss of many lives and can damage public property.

Now, if we turn our head towards disadvantages, they can be both predictable and unpredictable. First, isolated and untouched natural places do contribute to our eco-system. They have a certain role to play and if their flora and fauna is disturbed, the consequences of the same can be felt globally. Secondly, some places, like the north and south poles can get affected if too much of drilling work happens there as it can cause polar ice caps to melt faster and can result in increased sea levels. Finally, remote and untouched places are homes of some natural species. Now, drilling for fossil fuels can certainly endanger all those species, which may have its own consequences in future.

All in all, even though the craving for oil and gas seems rampant and encourages drilling at different places, I strongly assert that we must avoid such exploration because, it can create severe adverse effects that will have disastrous consequences for us and our future generations as well.

◆ ◆ ◆

5.   **Many children these days have their own mobile phones.**

What are the advantages and disadvantages of it?

It is indeed true that mobile phones are reaching the pockets of everybody in this world and children are also not exempted from this widespread phenomenon. It seems to be beneficial for children but, in reality, it has more drawbacks.

There are several reasons why children should avoid mobiles as much as possible. The first factor is risk. Children are vulnerable and are a soft and easy target of thieves who can quickly overpower or cheat children and snatch the phone off their hands. This situation can be extremely dangerous in some cases. Secondly, kids can be distracted by overuse of cell phones. Most of them use mobile phones for entertainment and trivial activities like chatting or surfing the internet. In addition, some school goers also indulge in indecent uses of the internet, which can be very harmful for their tender minds.

Thirdly, it is scientifically proven that mobile waves harm our body. It is also proven that they can harm children's body in higher intensities because their bodies are more vulnerable than adults'. Finally, some children also use mobiles to flaunt their affluent financial status. This phenomena is very harmful to all those who use mobiles.

On the other hand, some people state that children can be benefited by keeping cell phones with them. They say that mobiles are a boon in emergency and they can call their parents or relatives when they are under any threat or in trouble. Moreover, children learn using electronic gadgets at a young age; hence, they become techno savvy right from their childhood.

Conclusively, it is true that mobiles may help kids in case of emergencies, however, after studying an array of drawbacks of using cell phones, I assert that mobiles do more harm than good for children.

◆ ◆ ◆

6   Many countries import food materials from other countries.

Do you think the advantages of imported food materials from other countries outweigh its disadvantages?

Owing to globalization, it is indeed easy for all the countries to import goods from other nations. Hence, importing food from other countries is a very popular and common trade practice. It seems that, as a whole, imported foods may have higher drawbacks than benefits.

First, let us have a look at the benefits. Imported food can certainly offer a great range of variety in the receiving country. It is true that many varieties, for example those of spices or dry fruits or grains, do not grow in all countries. However, they are a common ingredient in most exotic food recipes. Thus, in such cases, the food has to be brought from another country. Moreover, some healthy and economic food variants can certainly help the denizens a lot. Also, nutritious and healthy food options actually fall in the essential category and have to be imported.

Now, let us assess the other side. Importing foods has certain disadvantages as well. To begin with, such trade always puts pressure on the economy of the country as valuable foreign revenues go to the supplying country. Next, such trade also makes the people from the importing country to be dependent on the food. This can be harmful because when commodity prices rise, they have to shell out more money from their pockets to have their favourite food dish. Furthermore, the people of the receiving country may develop detachment to their traditional and cultural food items and this can be an egregious social consequence of importing food.

Finally, looking at the advantages and disadvantages of importing foods, I believe that excepting essential food ingredients, countries should avoid importing food because it seems to have more cons than pros.

◆ ◆ ◆

7. **International tourism has enormous benefits, at the same time; it has some concerns for local inhabitants and the environment.**

Do the advantages of international tourism outweigh disadvantages?

It is an undeniable fact that leisure, hospitality, tourism and aviation industries have seen tremendous growth in the last few decades. It is estimated that international tourism will continue to grow at a good pace. Excepting some issues, international tourism has a number of benefits to offer.

The first and foremost benefit offered by international tourism is revenue generation. The places of attraction are visited by international visitors. They stay and spend their money over there thus bringing prosperity for the host country with them. Second, such places also attract huge foreign and domestic investment from hospitality and tourism and other concerned industries. This leads to a growth in the infrastructure of the area. Next, it also provides handsome employment opportunities to local people and helps them to upgrade the standard of their lives.

The Ultimate Guide To IELTS Writing

Third, foreign visitors are attracted towards local arts and traditions. Such exposure is always advantageous to particular cultures as they become popular around the world. What is more, the revenue generated from international visitors can also be used in the betterment of indigenous people and the environment.

On the other hand, international tourism raises some issues. Firstly, as many people visit the place, the maintenance of the place becomes very difficult for the government. For example, people throw away rubbish like plastic bags, empty food packets and cans that are dangerous to the local environment. Secondly, as the places develop in infrastructure, they swell in size also. This development obliges indigenous people to move away from the area.

Finally, as per my opinion, international tourism offers a vast number of benefits. However, it raises some concerns, which can be taken care of by the government if they impose strict rules.

◆ ◆ ◆

8   **Some people like to work for a few months in a year and for the rest of the time they do what they like.**

     Do advantages of this job pattern outweigh its disadvantages?

In today's world we can see a phenomenon unfolding in niche contexts where people work only for a few months during one year and in the remaining time, they do whatever they feel like. This is indeed a brave initiative and needs courage, faith and adequate resources. The effects of this tendency are discussed in the paragraphs to come.

Such a routine helps people in many ways. First, people can enjoy and pursue their hobbies and can engage in different assignments and projects which are important in their life. Second, it is often observed that those who work in such a pattern have a better performance to show because they do not suffer from monotony.

Third, those who live and explore life on their own often bring new and innovative ideas in their work and many a times their ideas do click. This is because as they stay out of the work environment, they can think out of the box and can see things objectively and creatively. Finally, such work pattern also keeps them away from stress and boredom and helps them live a happy, contended and satisfied life.

On the other hand, such tendency can be harmful to some people. If they do not work round the year, they may not get a secure job, which leads to instability in their career ahead. Secondly, most occupations need constant updates, which is possible only for those who work regularly. Lastly, such work pattern cannot bring in high profile jobs to people and thus, their financial growth can be limited.

In summary, such a work pattern is good for those who give priority to their hobbies and likings and have enough resources to meet the needs of life. However, they may not have a steadily growing career and hence, I think, one has to garner financial security before adopting such a life-pattern.

♦ ♦ ♦

9. **Grandparents take care of the children when their parents are out at work.**

What are the advantages and possible disadvantages of this?

In today's highly developing and fast growing world, it is almost essential for both the parents to work so that they can meet the financial requirements of their family. In this case, grandparents take care of their children and this is very beneficial for the children.

There are three major advantages of this. First, as grandparents usually stay at home fulltime, because of this, children never feel lonely and they get all that love and warmth they expect from a family and this is a boon for them. Second, grandparents also assist grandchildren in their studies. In addition, they also can go to school to drop them and pick them up. What is more, they also impart the knowledge of their culture, ethics and moral values to the children and make the latter familiar with religion and rituals.

Finally, children are safe in the presence of grandparents. As they monitor the activities of their children with their experienced eyes, they protect them from many excesses like watching TV for a long time, moving into wrong company, or developing bad habits and so on. This also gives a sense of security to the parents who are at work. They can better concentrate on their work and can strengthen their financial position.

On the other hand, there are some possible limitations of grandparents. Firstly, because of the generation gap, some old people cannot develop understanding with their children and this can have some adverse consequences. Secondly, physical limitations of grandparents deprive them from being of company to their grandchildren. However, this happens in a negligible number of cases.

To conclude, though there are some limitations, I think, grandparents are the best people in this world to take care of the children at home and kids who have this opportunity are very fortunate according to me.

♦ ♦ ♦

10. **More and more measures to improve the security levels in large urban areas have been introduced in many countries because of the increased crime.**

Do the benefits of these security measures outweigh the drawbacks?

It is a fact that, today, people live under constant surveillance in large urban areas because these areas are more developed and richer. So, crime rate is higher as the biggest motive behind most crimes is money and it is available in many forms and in ample quantities in these areas. This confirms the compulsion of security measures.

Large urban areas are economic proliferations and hence are the centre of all commercial activities. We can find there rich people, latest technological equipments and many precious items in homes, offices and showrooms. As wealth is available all around, criminals are attracted to it. Here, protection is very vital and there is a non debatable need to introduce more measures of security.

These means help the governments a lot. Firstly, it is easier for any criminal to hide in the crowd or in any structure because city areas are denser but latest security cameras help in detecting the culprit. Secondly, the identification process is very sophisticated and accurate with the use of scanners and sensors that do not give any criminal an opportunity to commit a crime and get away with it. Finally, when a criminal is aware of such systems, he is reluctant to commit a crime. This reluctance helps a lot in preventing crime in the urban society.

On the other hand, it is often argued that higher security makes life mechanical and degrades humans into a commodity. Next, there is no privacy in such areas as everyone feels that he/she is being monitored constantly and this thought makes them uncomfortable and vulnerable. Lastly it can be said that we have become dependent on machines every day and there is a sense of panic when they fail to work.

Finally, though there are few drawbacks of means of security regarding breach of privacy, I think the benefits of protection are much higher for the urban society.

◆ ◆ ◆

11.   **There are social, medical and technical problems associated with the use of mobile phones.**

   What forms do they take?

   Do you agree that the problems outweigh the benefits of mobile phones?

The Cell phone is one of the best inventions in the field of communication. Every day, technological advancements are making possible newer and better models of the same. It has some social, medical and technical concerns. However, its advantages outweigh the disadvantages.

Social problems are of the form of loss of manners and misuse. To start with, we can see people talking loudly on their mobile phones at colleges, hospitals, at a meeting or even while driving. Such manner deficient behaviour creates difficulty for others and for the users also. Moreover, people take pictures or record others' movements without their consent. This leads to the misuse of those photographs and can lead to crime.

Next, there are medical issues also. Mobiles generate strong electro-magnetic fields and a constant exposure is dangerous to our body. It can lead to brain tumours, heart troubles or even impotence in males.

Furthermore, it has some technical concerns also. Many people do not know how to

---

The Ultimate Guide To IELTS Writing

operate a mobile and because of lack of knowledge, they are cheated at times for minor technical applications. In addition, some people mishandle the parts of the instrument. For example, mobiles run on lithium battery that can explode in the direct sunlight and in water, which can be life threatening.

Thus, mobiles do have social, medical and technical issues. However, I think with proper handling, counselling and stricter legislation, all the issues can be taken care of. What is more, it is a boon for communication, data-storage, Internet accessibility and so on. Thus, they are gaining in their usage and popularity.

Summing up, considering all the aspects, I assert that the difficult issues related to the mobile phones are far less than the benefits associated with their usage.

◆ ◆ ◆

12. **More people will work from home and more students will study at home if computer technology becomes cheap and accessible.**

   What will be the advantages and disadvantages if this happens?

Computers are transforming our world into a global village. Moreover, this technology is getting cheaper and easily accessible to everyone. This development is going to enhance online working and distance learning in the world. There will be fruitful results of this occurrence.

The benefits offered by cyber space are astonishing. First, tele-workers have flexibility of working hours so that they can fulfill personal, family and social obligations more easily. In addition, such work always promotes skills over seniority. Hence, the employment problem among youth can be easily solved. Second, elderly people can also work from their home and can earn their living, which can be a big contribution to the global economy. Third, students can get qualifications from overseas universities at home. What is more, they can study with better concentration at home. Finally, this development reduces travel as people stay at home. This is a boon for the environment because it helps in reducing pollution.

However, it has some drawbacks also. To begin with, being social animals, humans like to interact with each other. In conditions where they always work from home, people will feel isolated and lonely. This may lead to psychological problems in extreme cases. Next, industries like marketing, insurance, repair and maintenance, transport etc. will have to face a hard time because their customers no longer come to the market but are happy in their residences. Therefore, people who work with above-mentioned industries will have to travel extensively to reach out to their consumers.

Finally, computer technology is surely going to revolutionize in the way people work and study. It will have a great impact on human life. According to me if this development materializes, it will be more advantageous for the world.

♦ ♦ ♦

13. **E-mails have had a huge impact on professional and social communication. However, their effects have been positive as well as negative.**

Do the advantages of using e-mail outweigh its disadvantages?

It is certainly true that the use of e-mail has greatly changed the way we communicate with each other at work as well as socially. However, it is also true that not all the effects of this innovation have been positive, although advantages outnumber disadvantages.

A common criticism of e-mail in the workplace is that it causes extra work and stress. This is because most employees receive more messages than they can answer every day and since e-mail writers expect a quick response, this further increases pressure on employees. Other objections to e-mail for both social and professional users include the way it encourages people to spend even longer hours at their computers. Further, there is also the danger of incoming messages allowing viruses into our computer system.

In spite of these negative effects, however, e-mail has brought important benefits as well. One such advantage of using e-mail is that it is a fast and easy way to communicate with family, friends and work colleagues wherever they are in the world. It not only allows people to stay in touch with each other, but it also allows them to send digital files like pictures, music, diagrams, text etc. very quickly, cheaply and with very good quality of reproduction. This is a huge advance on the earlier communication systems, and the low cost of e-mail implies that it is used by almost everyone.

To sum up, while there are some obvious drawbacks to using e-mail, this fast and user-friendly technology has greatly improved our ability to communicate both professionally and socially. Therefore, I think e-mail has brought us many more benefits than disadvantages.

♦ ♦ ♦

14. **Nowadays, in some countries, single young adults prefer to live away from their parents. They usually do so to study or work in different places.**

   Do you think this trend has more advantages than disadvantages?

It is indeed true that the number of young people working or studying away from home is higher than ever. This trend has emerged out of some factors typical to an interconnected world where each node offers different services from the other.

There are several benefits of this situation. To begin with, certain academic courses are not available everywhere. Thus, students have to go to other cities where they can acquire education in the field of their choice. In addition, certain cities have developed a reputation of quality education providers. This also attracts students to those universities from across the world. Secondly, if we assess professionals, certain industries are well developed in some parts of their country. For example if we talk about information technology in India, it is highly developed in the Southern parts of India. Thus, to get a competitive work environment and a handsome salary package, a computer engineer ought to settle in that region. So, this arrangement is almost essential for students and professionals who seek vertical growth in their careers.

On the other hand, there are certain drawbacks of staying away from home. Firstly, both, students and employees who are away from their home often feel lonely. They lack the emotional support, love, warmth and care given by their parents and in certain cases, loneliness may lead to severe psychotic issues. Secondly, youngsters have to be more responsible compared to their years, in all aspects of life, as there is no one who can guide them. Finally, their lifestyle gets disturbed as they have to eat outside and sometimes, the food is neither hygienic, nor healthy.

To conclude, I assert that the system of working or studying away from home has offered excellent growth opportunities. Therefore, I believe that this setup has more advantages as compared to disadvantages.

♦ ♦ ♦

15. **Some people argue that public transportation should be made completely free of charge.**

Are there more advantages over disadvantages of this decision?

Public transportation is like a lifeline in big cities across the world. Governments spend billions of dollars every year in developing and maintaining public transportation systems. Since it has a wider reach, some argue that it should be made free for all. The idea seems good but not feasible for any government in this world.

There are several reasons why public transportation should not be made free for all. First, maintaining and developing public transport vehicles and routes is extremely expensive. These mammoth expenditures are met with the revenue received from passengers. Now, if the transportation is free, funds allocated from the government's budget will be so high that it can affect the economic growth of the entire nation.

Secondly, it is always observed that free things have no value. When the public finds it free, they may not respect it and sometimes such facilities are likely to be misused by people and in such cases, the spending by the government will rise unexpectedly. Finally, free transportation vehicles often get overloaded with commuters, which further creates problems in traffic management. In addition, vehicles used for transportation will also have to face higher wear and tear.

On the other hand, keeping public transport usage free of cost does offer some benefits. One of them is, countless people of the country will be benefited by that system. It will help increase mobility of commuters and help the cities to expand properly. Next, the increasing problem of traffic jams, rising noise and air pollution can certainly be controlled to a great extent.

Finally, making public transport free might help in controlling pollution and traffic related issues. However, I firmly believe that it will create more problems for the governments across the world and thus it can never be made free for all.

◆ ◆ ◆

16   In some countries, it is possible for the people to have access to a variety of food that has been transported from all over the world.

Do the benefits of imported food outweigh its drawbacks?

Owing to globalization, the food people used to eat has also moved with them across continents. These days we can get cuisines of different countries almost everywhere in the world. This is a welcome trend according to me.

Food from foreign countries can be beneficial in numerous ways. First, the newcomers who bring their food with them do not feel that they are totally away from their homeland. This is essential for them to survive and grow in a new country because eating is directly related to health and happiness and consequently, to their work efficiency. Secondly, they share their food variants with local people and make them aware of it. This is useful in developing tolerance, harmony and balance among people of different cultures who live in the same region.

Lastly, imported food helps local people to adopt and create a richer fusion to their benefit. For example, the proportion of vegetarian people is very high in India. Hence, restaurants like McDonalds and KFC have introduced pure vegetarian meals which are appreciated by Indian people. Such blend of food patterns brings about a sense of abundance across cultures in the world.

On the other hand, some people argue that imported food is harmful to local cultures. They say that food reflects culture and it is often prepared by considering the health and climatic requirements of that region. Now if we bring food from another region, it may not be suitable to the local people and may affect their health. They also assert that if youngsters like the foreign food, they will forget their traditional food habits and may develop detachment from their indigenous culture.

All in all, even though there are concerns of the health of local people and cultural diversification, I think imported food is indeed a welcome idea. If we want cultural equality and balance in our world, we must not prevent food from travelling across continents.

♦   ♦   ♦

17. **In some countries, schools remain open for more hours so that children can be looked after because their parents are working.**

     Do the advantages outweigh disadvantages of this?

Life in the present makes it essential for both parents to work and therefore it is not possible for them to watch over their children. Thus, schools in many countries offer to look after these children beyond school hours so that the parents can come to take them after office.

There are many advantages to this. Firstly, children are at a secure place where they face no kind of danger from the outside world. Secondly, the school staff is responsible and trained and takes proper care of them every day and even during an emergency like a child getting hurt or sick. Thirdly, in an academic environment, children are engaged in constructive activities apart from studies or even extended help for their homework and projects. Thus, they are in a setting that keeps them occupied and prevents them from falling into the trap of bad activities in the absence of their parents.

Compared to the advantages, the disadvantages are not too many. To begin with, in the case where the school administration is not responsible enough to employ trained staff for this after-school activity there is a possibility that children are not given due attention and care. Also, in the event of a child given hostile treatment in school from a teacher or fellow students, his or her torture can extend if the parents choose to let the child remain in the premises after study.

Finally, even though there are there are exceptional incidents where children are mistreated at the school, I think it is rather advantageous that a child is taken care of by the school authorities for extra hours when the parents are at office.

♦   ♦   ♦

---

4. CAUSE AND EFFECTS (3)

1 **Today, many parents force their children to study all kinds of courses in their early age.**

   What are the reasons behind this?

   What effects do you think this practice would bring to the children?

Today's era of cut-throat competition has made life rather difficult for children. We can see most parents pushing their children not only to study more but to attend and excel in extra-curricular activities as well to make their resumes attractive in the future. This trend will definitely make children more intelligent but at the expense of their childhood.

There are two main reasons behind such a development. First, most people want their children to be highly competitive and capable of executing multiple skills. This is because when they grow up, they will not have to face any problems in getting a job or conducting business and can thereby have financial security. Secondly, out of jealousy and comparison, most parents observe what others' children are doing. Now, just to keep their own children ahead in the race, parents oblige them to learn different skills and to join courses for the same.

This tendency has both positive as well as negative effects on children. If we talk about the positive effects, children do learn different skills and become well adapted to life. Next, they evolve a better understanding of the world and are well prepared to take up challenges. Consequently, this attitude enables them to face any situation in life.

On the other hand, kids lose their innocence, fantasies and joys of being a child. They do not get enough opportunity to pursue what they like to do. This inhibits their growth and can turn them negative about life.

Finally, I must admit that motivating children to learn new skills to make them better individuals is a welcome thought. However, if it comes at the cost of their childhood, I do not go with it. Children must be given enough space to grow and blossom with freedom and calmness.

◆ ◆ ◆

2. **It is seen that older adults are not given enough respect and facilities in many countries.**

    What could be the reasons for this?

    What are the effects of this?

It is true that some societies do not offer due respect to the older people. This is not a wise approach as a whole because it creates many difficulties for both elderly people and governments.

The prime factor is that older people are weak physically and cannot do a full-time job. Hence, their contribution to the economy of their country is often negligible. What is more, because of reduced income, they expect tax-rebates, pension, discount on public transport and so forth. Next, with the increasing age, they require higher and intensive health care facilities. All these issues contribute negatively to the economy of the country. Therefore, some countries show reluctance in offering support and respect to old people.

On the other hand, there are egregious consequences of lack of support from governments to the old age population. Neglect of elders leads to dissatisfaction in their minds for the system and the country. They become frustrated and turn pessimistic about life. Furthermore, lack of health care support from governments creates financial burden on their family members, which creates problems among them. Consequently, such development leads to imbalance in the society and people perceive old age as a curse.

Finally, deficiency in respect and support towards elderly people can be disastrous for many countries. According to me, such countries must change their approach towards older people and try to use their skills in constructive and useful ways to achieve and maintain positive growth in all age groups of the country.

◆ ◆ ◆

3. **Nowadays, children play computer games for long hours. They do not play old traditional games.**

    What do you think are the reasons for this?

Do you think it influences children in a good or a bad way?

Technology is influencing all the areas of life and entertainment is not an exception. Today's children are always found busy playing games on computers, which is not a very positive development.

There are certain factors that prompt children to play these games. First, computer games are rich in graphics and have excellent background music. Thus, they are visually more appealing and more entertaining as well. Secondly, the lifelike graphical presentation on screen helps children in having a real life feeling when they play games. Finally, most parents these days are working and thus, they avoid sending their children to playgrounds because they think children are not safe if they spend too much time away from home. Therefore, parents keep motivating their children to engage in some gaming activities at home.

This development affects the physical and mental health of children. Let us consider the health problems first. Children spend too much time sitting at the gaming console. This can create potential problems in their back muscles and eyes. In addition, most children also eat junk food while playing games. Their eating patterns become erratic and they often become victims of indigestion. This can lead to problems of obesity and overweight.

Now, let us analyze mental implications. Playing computer games over a long period of time hinders psychological development of children. Some games may contain explicit or violent content which can cause psychotic disorders in their tender minds. Finally, playing a game alone also inhibits social interaction, which can result in lack of relevant skills in them.

Conclusively, even though, conditions often oblige parents to permit their children to play games on screen. I firmly believe that excessive exposure to computer games is indeed harmful for children.

◆ ◆ ◆

5. PROBLEM AND SOLUTIONS (17)

1. **Children from age 7-11 now spend more time watching television and/or playing video games than before.**

    What are the effects of this on children, families and society?

    What are the possible solutions to this problem?

It is indeed true that urbanization is obliging children to spend more time inside their homes rather than playing outdoors. Simultaneous to this has been the communication revolution. Consequently, children have taken to activities like watching television and playing video games in a big way. However, such habits if taken to the extreme can be very harmful for them.

Watching television and playing video games are passive activities and they have certain negative effects. First, children sit on one place for hours and keep watching TV or playing video games. This makes them lazy as there is absence of any physical activity. Second, during such activities, children eat lots of junk food like chips, popcorn, pizza and so on. As a result, they become obese and lose their efficiency when it comes to studying and playing sports. Thirdly, such passive activities if done for longer hours do not really refresh them. Rather, children feel mentally fatigued after watching TV or playing video games and they become short tempered. Finally, such negative effects on children create an imbalance in society as they do not grow up into responsible and grounded individuals.

To address this problem, actions at all levels are important. First, schools should take adequate measures in counselling children on drawbacks of such passive activities and motivate them to stay away from them. Second, parents and teachers should collectively work in the direction of making lives of children more active and creativity oriented. Finally, governments, if possible should limit number of television programs available for children in order to prevent them from being couch potatoes.

To conclude, I believe, with the above mentioned steps we can be successful in inculcating creative, active and healthy habits in children.

◆ ◆ ◆

2. **Many people complain about stress at work.**

How can employers reduce stress at work and what can employees do on their own to solve this problem?

Stress seems to have become a companion of employees in the present day era. It is one of the most discussed and debated issues across the corporate world. It is also seen as a threat to the humanity. However, it can certainly be reduced if employers and employees both take sincere steps.

Employers should take care of certain important aspects that help in reducing stress at work. Firstly, every employee needs a clarity in the tasks allotted to him or her and adequate resources to perform the same. Hence, employers should be precise in communicating with their employees and provide them with proper assistance. Secondly, employers should offer justifiable remuneration to their workers else, they will be under stress and underperform. Finally, healthy working conditions with respect to physical and mental human capabilities are very essential to reduce stress at work.

On the other hand, employees should also take some actions to eliminate stress at work. To begin with, they must be honest, punctual and dedicated to their work. Some workers have a tendency to play office politics that disturbs the work culture and environment. Secondly, proper time management and regular skill enhancement are virtues that every employee ought to develop in order to remain stress free. Finally, ethical, cooperative, considerate and committed behaviour is the key to stay away from any conflict or mind games that give rise to a lot of stress.

In conclusion, adequate facilities, working conditions, good salary and clarity in work should be provided by employers and honesty, dedication, work ethics and other corporate soft skills should be developed and followed by the employees in order to curb stress according to me.

◆　◆　◆

3. **Natural resources such as fresh water, oil and forests are fast disappearing from the Earth.**

Why is this happening? Is that dangerous?

Suggest a solution for this problem.

For the last few decades, the earth has been witnessing an incessant reduction in its natural resources. This scenario can be attributed to excessive population, widespread industrialisation, globalisation and urbanisation. All these are largely responsible for rampant usage of natural resources like water, fossils fuels and rain forests. It is indeed an alarming situation and it must be addressed immediately.

There can be devastating consequences of such a development. Lack of availability of water and oil will create a huge imbalance in the economies of all the countries, which will pressurize the economic growth and other essential services like health care, education, transportation and so on because scarcity of these two resources is directly proportionate to inflation. In addition, lack of rain forests will create disturbances in weather cycles. Consequently, there can be more natural calamities. Further, irregular and unpredictable weather always affects farming. As a result, due to reduced agricultural yield, the vicious cycle of inflation shall be set into motion.

There are plenty of ways in which this problem can be solved. First of them is reducing air and water pollution. This will help in proper water and air consumption and will put brakes on deforestation. Secondly, excessive usage of oil and electricity must be curbed in order to have a green and healthy climate. Finally, better alternatives in transportation and construction must be introduced to reduce fossil fuel consumption and to check the need of more land.

Finally, as per my opinion, it is certainly true that lack of natural resources like oil, water and rain forests can put the survival of the earth at a risk. However, with proper care and management, this situation can be handled and the life span of our dear earth can be increased.

◆ ◆ ◆

4. **City dwellers do not tend to develop close relationships with their neighbours.**

Why is this so and what can be done to improve contacts between neighbours within cities?

It is indeed true that urban people are not so keen on having close relationships with their neighbours. This is emerging as a serious social concern across the world. However, I think very little can be done to address this.

There are many reasons why this situation has emerged. Firstly, changes in work hours and lifestyle have prompted people to stay in their homes and communicate less with their neighbours. Secondly, there are ample entertainment and leisure options available for today's urban families. Hence, they opt for watching TV, playing games on computer or even surfing the internet at home. Thirdly, affluent city people often prefer to go for luxurious options like recreation clubs and movies. Finally, it is also seen that professionals are frequently transferred to different cities by their companies, and so, such employees do not form close bonds with their neighbours because they know that such closeness will not last long.

However, there are a few steps that can be taken at an individual level to address this situation. We, at a society or community level should increase interaction among neighbourhoods. We can also co-operatively plan activities that include interaction, participation and involvement of all who live nearby. For example, a sports contest, social gathering for leisure or for welfare will help people to know their neighbours better.

Conclusively, I think it's a trend that is occurring at a socio-cultural level and so, not too much can be done to address this problem. Unless there will be a dramatic change in our lifestyles, this situation will not be completely eliminated though it can be checked to some extent.

◆ ◆ ◆

5. **People prefer to use their own transport these days.**

   Why is this so?

   What can be done to encourage people to use public transport?

Private vehicles are becoming more and more popular and are being utilized higher than ever in this world. For some environmentalists, it is a concern that needs to be addressed. Reasons and possible solutions to this situation are discussed in the following paragraphs.

If I look at the factors behind a surge in private vehicles, the first reason that I see is convenience. You can start or stop your vehicle at will and plan your route according to the requirements. For example, you can stop your car at a supermarket while going back to your home from office. Secondly, it offers privacy and safety. You are safe from any pranksters and you can do your own work, listen to music or even talk to your clients regarding important business deals while moving in your own vehicle. Finally, a private vehicle accords a certain status to the user, which is an important point to consider given that man is a social animal.

There are some solutions possible to increase use of public transport. To start with, I think awareness of using public transport and its benefits should be highlighted more among the people. Secondly, regular public transport users should be given some perks like concession passes for their tickets. Thirdly, some extra luxurious features should be offered like first class travelling facilities, tight security and privacy in sections of all public transport vehicles and routes. Finally, government could hike some taxes for private vehicle owners or introduce toll taxes to discourage them from overusing their vehicles.

In conclusion, it is true that people prefer to use their own vehicles to commute. However, considering the concerns for the climate, we should take active steps to inspire people to use public transport more.

◆ ◆ ◆

6. **Some people spend a lot of money on things that are unnecessary, while, so many people in this world do not even get anything to eat.**

   Why do you think people do it?

   What can be done to stop them from doing so?

Globalisation and rising affluence in certain countries have given us the luxury to become spendthrifts. This phenomenon is on the rise in all countries across the world. The reasons and probable suggestions are discussed in the paragraphs below.

If we throw light on the factors behind the overspending tendency of people, the first and foremost evident reason is the obsession to shop. Some people in big cities are always lured by fancy marketing techniques and displays of large stores and when they visit such places, they cannot stop themselves and go and shop for things they do not actually need. Also, shopping gives a momentary sense of power to them. Secondly, some people have grown up in such a culture where they have seen their parents going shopping without any valid reason or cause and they carry this 'legacy' of being spendthrifts. Lastly, consumers also buy things just for show off. Many families in this world are always enthusiastic to display their financial superiority and for the same, they keep exhibiting their purchasing power to their friends or peers.

However, there are some steps that we should undertake in order to change this situation. To begin with, proper education and understanding of the economics of spending should be imparted to the young. This helps them in comprehending the value of money and will prevent them from overspending. Moreover, they can also be shown the plight of people who are not lucky enough to get a day's meal. The benefits of social work and offering support to less privileged mankind are obvious and need to be brought to the attention of such consumers. Finally, some fine or penalty should be levied on people who waste things. For example, there is a fine in Germany if you waste too much food in a restaurant.

Conclusively, I think that stopping overspending is a highly subjective matter and hence, no direct or widespread actions can be taken to address the issue. However, certain steps like spreading awareness and inculcating good values in the youth can help in controlling this attitude.

♦ ♦ ♦

7.   **Recent figures show that there is an increase in number of crimes among the young generation in big cities throughout the world.**

What are the possible reasons for this?

Give suggestions to solve this problem.

Juvenile delinquency is one of the biggest problems of today's world. Prisons in the big cities of most countries are teeming with young criminals. This shows that youngsters are indulging in criminal activities at an increasingly alarming rate.

There are many reasons behind this. Firstly, youngsters are more vulnerable and their basic nature is adventurous. Crime requires daring and most youngsters commit their first crime to get the thrill. Later, unfortunately, they cannot come out of that swamp. In addition, movies also portray criminals as heroes that inspire the youth to imitate them. Secondly, globalization has created huge disparities in the world. Moreover it has ignited a thirst in people to earn more and do so really fast. Consequently, it leads more youngsters to adopt criminal activities because they think it to be the shortcut to riches.

Thirdly, the whole world is divided into many factions because of regional, racial, religious and intellectual reasons. Everywhere, the powerful person tries to dominate the weaker being. Such a scenario has given birth to a revolutionary tendency and even terrorism and it is the youth which is at the forefront of these unfortunate developments.

To solve this problem, we should impart quality education that can make youngsters more aware, sensitive and less vulnerable. Next, we should show them films or documentaries of miserable ends that criminals meet. This can instill fear in young minds and stop them from entering the world of crime. Finally, we as individuals should change ourselves and try to be more responsible about life, society and the world.

To sum up, I believe only giving suggestions and preaching may not provide the desired solution. However, if, each one as a person changes himself into a better individual then, I think, we can make this world a better place to live in and leave behind a rich heritage for future generations.

◆ ◆ ◆

8. **Some young people are watching television for long periods of the day.**

    Why do they do this?

    Give reasons and suggest what should be done to encourage them to live more active lifestyle.

Couch Potatoes, a term coined by Oxford University for those who watch television for long hours, connotes a serious problem for the society at present. There are many reasons which lead to this situation. However, few timely steps can prevent the adverse effects.

Young people watch television for longer hours because of several factors. First is the stress at studies and/or work. As youngsters strive to compete and work hard at the end of the day, they are exhausted. Here, a need for relaxation emerges and they opt for watching television. Unfortunately, it is a passive activity but it is being perceived nowadays as a means of relaxation. Second, higher competition amongst satellite channels has resulted in innovative programs that attract all types of people. Finally, young people are fond of movies, music, sports, adventure and fashion. Exclusive television channels are available these days for all such activities to woo them and keep them glued to the screen.

There are few suggestions put forth here to resolve this problem. Firstly, going for a walk every night after dinner gives good exercise and fresh air that really recharges the body. Secondly, one should try to develop a new hobby like reading books, learning a musical instrument, or something in the field of sports, arts or crafts. This brings out the creativity of a person. Finally, one can join any social or cultural group where they can indulge in creative activities.

To conclude, it is true that day-by-day, couch potatoes are increasing in number, which is a negative sign for social development. I assert that by implementing the above mentioned suggestions, young people can change their lifestyle from passive to active and can lead a satisfied and successful life.

◆ ◆ ◆

The Ultimate Guide To IELTS Writing

9. **Too little actions have been taken to prevent species of plants and animals from dying out and becoming extinct. The world knows this problem for many years.**

   Why has the world taken little actions to prevent these?

   What actions should be taken to stop it?

It is a fact that the many plant and animal species have gone extinct due to rampant exploitation by humans and this activity has not been stopped. However, now awareness to protect the world from the adverse effects of such activities is fast spreading.

History reveals that the ignorance and the lack of awareness among the people are prime reasons behind the carrying out of such activities. We have always targeted short-term benefits without bothering about the long-term consequences. In addition, for centuries, countries around the world have always been rushing behind the economic and industrial growth. Hence, authorities have misguided the people and diverted their focus on such areas only. However, few political parties like the Green Party in the UK tried to raise the awareness but majority of the politicians exploited this issue only to earn publicity.

On the other hand, there are few steps possible to stop this. First, strict and uniform legislation must be imposed across the world. Moreover, to set an example, severe punishment must be given to those who break these laws. Second, the importance of such issues must be spread throughout the world. Subjects pertaining to the environment must be added in the school and college curriculum. Next, industries should be encouraged to produce environment friendly products that do not exploit nature in any way. In addition, they should be given benefits like 'carbon credits' to maintain their green temperament.

Finally, it is true that we have been ignoring our environment to our own peril. I think by implementing laws and spreading awareness, we still can make this world a better place to live in. We all must remember, 'Nature is not our property, it is a heritage that we must preserve for the next generation.'

◆ ◆ ◆

10. In many countries more and more young people are leaving school but
     are unable to find jobs.

     What problems do you think youth unemployment causes for individual
     and for the society?

     What measures should be taken to reduce the level of unemployment
     among youngsters?

It is a tradition in many societies that after finishing high school, youngsters find a job to fund
their further studies. This experience makes them independent, mature and sincere. Nowadays,
many school leavers are not getting a job and this is a rather worse development of our times.

Many difficulties can occur for an individual and a society when school leavers are unemployed.
Firstly, unemployed youngsters are unable to gather the required funds for their tertiary education. This deprives them from universities and they are literate but not qualified or competent.
Hence, they have to do a blue-collar job to survive. Secondly, such a scenario frustrates them
and makes them rebel against the system. This frustration can lead to increase in crime. Thirdly,
less number of graduates are able to fill the posts for the qualified people. This creates an
imbalance in society and inhibits the economic, industrial and intellectual growth of the society.
Finally, such imbalance stops the progress of education as a segment because universities
cannot earn out of less students. This is dangerous for many research-oriented activities as
universities become unable to finance them.

There are few suggestions to meet the solution of this problem. First, governments should
enforce employers to reserve a proportion of their workforce for the school leavers. Second,
many a times a school fresher cannot do a technical job. Therefore, some technical and practical employment oriented courses should be added in the school curriculum. Last, universities
must award scholarships and offer flexible payment options to the students to motivate them to
acquire tertiary education.

Finally, according to me, there are bad consequences if the school leavers remain unemployed.
However, better legislation, better subjects offered at school and flexibility at the level of tertiary
education can solve majority of the difficulties.

♦ ♦ ♦

The Ultimate Guide To IELTS Writing

11. **A lot of old people are suffering from loneliness these days. They also lack physical fitness.**

   What do you think are the reasons for these problems?

   Can you think of possible solutions?

It is indeed true that number of old people is increasing rapidly in today's world. Thus, it is obvious that problems related to old age will also mount. I think, proper care and measures will enable us to deal with this situation.

There are several reasons why they feel lonely. To begin with, the concept of nuclear families is increasing speedily these days. Most joint families are breaking down into small units, which, in turn, oblige elderly people in the family to stay alone. Next, migration of young members of family for better career and academic options is very common now. This also creates loneliness for the seniors in the family.

Multiple factors are responsible for the ill health of the older people. To start with, many elders of today lived a stressful life when they were young. Such stress leaves its bad effects on the body, which surface faster when the body gets old. Secondly, pollution is increasing everywhere these days. It surely shows its harmful effects on the vulnerable bodies of old people.

On the other hand, I think there are some possible solutions to these problems. One of them is, governments across the world should give more medical support to elderly people so that they can live a healthier life. Moreover, they should be assisted with proper training about living more active lifestyle so that they do not feel lonely and they stay fit. Finally, arranging certain skill based trainings for them will surely help them to find some creative activities that keep them occupied.

All in all, even though problems of old people are increasing, I firmly believe that this can be controlled with the help of effective measures and joint efforts of the government and individuals.

◆ ◆ ◆

---

12. **The movement of people from agricultural areas to big cities has caused many problems at both places.**

   What are the reasons of this problem and how can it be solved?

It is a fact that every day, thousands of people across the world move to big cities of their country. They do so for various reasons but this situation needs to be addressed if we want to bring balance in society, economy and in our culture.

There are numerous reasons why people migrate to big cities from rural areas. First is the tremendous amount of employment and business opportunities available in the urban areas. Cities are densely populated and also have presence of most companies. This generally creates more vacancies and more options for entrepreneurs. Second, cities offer better infrastructure, better health and education services and transportation facilities. Finally, cities also have latest recreational facilities available. All these aspects lure people from nearby agrarian communities to migrate to cities and inspire them to settle down there for their entire life.

The problems that are thereby caused at the urban end are overcrowding of cities and disastrous overuse of resources while the rural context loses its economy and cultural depth. To begin with, we can find a solution to these in aiding the development of rural and agricultural areas. In addition, governments must improve the infrastructure of the countryside so that dwellers in those areas also enjoy better standards of living and good health and education facilities. Moreover, adequate employment opportunities should be created in rural areas so that people of such areas find it worth living in their own village and continue its traditions. Finally, urban infrastructure needs to keep pace with time as well and more civic responsibility should be inculcated in the people.

With the above mentioned steps a balance can be achieved in time so that a very high migration rate can be checked and overall development can be witnessed across all the areas of the country.

◆ ◆ ◆

13. Most of the people aspire to have a successful career and a happy family life.

What problems are involved in combining a successful career and happy family life?

How to overcome such problems?

Life can be complete only if we have both- a successful career and a happy family life. This is a difficult balance to achieve for a number of reasons but there are certain solutions by way of which we can overcome these problems.

A successful career usually implies that people spend much longer hours at their desk than the stipulated office time. This means that one is not able to give sufficient time to one's family. Also, owing to deadlines and peer pressure there is accumulation of stress which expresses itself as misplaced anger in the presence of family. Thirdly, as people do not spend quality time with their loved ones there is alienation and as a result many families break or the children go astray and fall prey to bad habits. On the other hand if one tries to fulfil all demands of the family then it is not possible to deal with the responsibilities at work.

However, there are certain actions possible to address this problem. The first step in this regard is good time management. Much of our time goes waste because we do not have the ability and perseverance to complete tasks in the given hours. What is more, we need to organize, prioritize tasks and make 'to do' lists which have to be diligently followed. Many times it is observed that it is because of the sheer chaos in life that one is failing on both fronts of the office and home. Finally, one should invest energy in relationships to build strong bonds of trust that can take the pressure of one's absence or excess of work.

All in all, with these simple steps, I am sure that we can fulfil our dream of having both- a successful career and a happy home life.

◆ ◆ ◆

14. **It is generally seen that most working people do not do enough physical exercise.**

   What are the reasons behind this?

   How can this problem be solved?

A very commonly seen phenomenon in the modern world is that everyone knows the importance of exercise in life yet very few people find the time to actually follow a daily routine of the same. As a result, most people do not get any exercise which is detrimental to their health in the long run.

The basic reasons behind this development are as follows: firstly, greater competition at the work place means that one has to put in long working hours. When employees do not even get enough sleep, it is rather impossible for them to make time for exercise. Secondly, a lot of machines aid our daily life right from the water pipeline that brings water to our taps to the washing machine, to the dishwasher and to cars etc. Thus, the opportunities of unconscious exercise are minimised as the energy spent on daily chores is considerably reduced with modern comforts. Thirdly, all modes of entertainment are sedentary; even children do not play outdoors now but prefer computer games and play stations. In addition, to refresh a tired mind, people would rather watch a film than go for a walk. So though their mind is rejuvenated, the body suffers.

The first solution to the problem is that we have to resolve to spend some time every day in conscious exercise. Next, a work-life balance has to be achieved so that we can pay adequate attention to our body. Finally, there is an ardent need to involve self in outdoor activities in the evening or the weekends so that the body does not suffer the consequences of passive entertainment.

To sum up, I believe that with the help of simple steps discussed above, we can certainly lead to a healthier life and a happier society.

◆ ◆ ◆

15. **Nowadays people show more anti-social behaviour and lack of respect to others.**

    What are the causes?

    How could we improve the situation?

Modernity, in its wake, has also brought with it a very strict definition of individuality which makes people very self-centred. We see all around us that there is a general lack of respect for others and a lot of anti-social behaviour as well. The basic cause of this to my mind is careless parenting.

If children are not brought up in an atmosphere that teaches a sense of responsibility, there is no doubt that they will grow up into selfish and small minded adults. In an attempt to break free from the strict rule-bound parenting of the past, we have now gone to the opposite extreme of a freedom which has dissolved the boundaries between right and wrong. The parents, in their youth, feel that they have the right to follow their wishes and in turn inculcate the same in children. Thus, there is seen a rise in anti-social behaviour and disrespect. Further, the cinema and media are mirrors of this trend and since youth is highly influenced by them, they all add fuel to the fire.

The situation can only be improved if individuals understand that it is first of all their moral responsibility to live a constructive life and secondly it is required that they impart these values to the younger generation as well. Finally, young people must be taught in schools and colleges to check their sense of independence and realize their responsibility towards the society they live in.

Finally, I believe that improper parenting in certain cultures has created the problem of anti social behaviour. However, with proper education of values and morals, this issue can certainly be addressed.

◆ ◆ ◆

16. **In many countries, young people become richer, healthier and live longer, but they are less happy.**

    What are the reasons for this?

    What can be done about it?

It is a commonly observed phenomenon that the young generation in many countries is earning a lot, is healthier and even lives longer but most of them are unhappy. The reasons for that and the possible solutions to address the same are discussed in the paragraphs below.

There are many reasons which lead to this state of unhappiness despite being successful and rich. First of all, in the modern age, individuality is given a high degree of importance and most people prefer to live in relative isolation so that they can work as they will and do not have to adjust to any other human being. Such isolation leads to loneliness and depression. Secondly, free market economies attract the consumer in all of us and in a rush to buy all we can, we become very materialistic and competitive. This development motivates us to earn more than others and this gives rise to negative emotions of jealousy and vengeance which lead to unhappiness. Thirdly, the unit of a family is slowly dissolving away. People not only remain distant from colleagues but also do not wish to adjust to family members that are the older generation or even children. Consequently, divorce rates and childlessness have been increasing in all such countries.

However, the situation is still not out of hand. If we strike a good work-life balance we can be successful as well as happy. Moreover, effort has to be made to reach out to others in the family, in the friend circle and at the work place. Furthermore, we should try to grow spiritually to understand that more material wealth does not mean more happiness. Finally, we should make time for exercising, meditation and social interaction. These help us to get a stronger foothold in life and be happy.

To sum up, in my opinion, with proper care and maintenance of work and life equilibrium, we can certainly make a happier, content and healthier society.

◆ ◆ ◆

17. **It is observed that some ex-prisoners commit crimes after being released from the prison.**

    What do you think is the cause?

    How can it be solved?

It is common observation that many criminals turn out to be repeat offenders. This is a huge problem for governments of most countries and it is essential to look into the causes and solutions of the same.

Firstly, committing of a crime is a result of a certain kind of psychological attitude which, if not treated, can lead to a repeating of the past offences even after suffering punishment. Secondly, a person who has been to jail is subject to social alienation as he loses respect in the community he comes from. As a result, when he or she returns, there is a feeling of loss of belonging which can lead to frustration and criminal tendencies. Thirdly, sometimes social causes like weak governance, civil war or economic strife lead to crime and even after the jail term of a person is over, these causes may still be present and returning to the same context may force a person to take to crime repeatedly.

The first solution to this problem that comes to my mind is that jails should not only be confinement cells but also reformatories. Prisoners have to be extended help in the form of psychological and spiritual counselling so that the violent and anti-social tendencies in them can be removed and they walk out as better human beings. Moreover, friends and family have to make a sincere effort to watch and guide the activities of such people. Furthermore, if a social or political cause is responsible for the crime then there has to be an attempt on part of the government or social reformists to improve the situation at hand.

Finally, I believe that this problem can certainly be solved to a great extent with the help of proper care at governmental and social level.

◆ ◆ ◆

6. MISCELLANEAOUS (24)

1. **University lecturers are now able to put their lectures on the internet for students to read and so the importance of attending face-to-face lectures has been reduced.**

   Do you believe that the use of the internet in formal education is a good idea?

What future effects will the internet have on academic study?

Internet has become inevitable in accessing information and communication in today's world. It is applied in almost all the aspects of life hence education is not an exception. University lecturers have started uploading lectures on World Wide Web. According to me, it is a welcome step however; it does not seem to serve the genuine purpose of classroom education.

Usage of Internet cannot be advantageous for a majority of students in many ways. Firstly, Internet is a one-way communication. Thus, it creates a passive type of learning atmosphere and science has already proved that passive learning cannot yield fruitful results. Secondly, studying lectures on the Internet cannot give the charm of a classroom environment where a lecturer can solve the difficulties of students and increase their level of understanding. Thirdly, Internet requires computer and electricity that can be expensive for many students.

In addition to this, the system itself offers some drawbacks i.e. sitting against the computer screen for longer hours is not good for our eyes and back. Next, it is only a visual media that ends up making the study mechanical and stereotypical. Consequently, it reduces the student's interest in the study.

On the other hand, learning lectures on Internet offers some advantages. Firstly, they can be attended and viewed by so many people who cannot come physically to the classroom for example: disabled students, working professionals and foreign students. Secondly, it provides convenience; they can study at their ease and can use navigational tools on the computer to browse through the whole document. Finally it also saves time of going to the university.

To conclude, I believe that internet is useful in many ways. It may be used extensively in future. However, it is certainly not the best way of imparting education as it has more drawbacks than benefits.

One more answer

Over the past few years, computer technology has started to change many aspects of our lives. One of these is our approach to teaching and learning. Many people believe that the internet will greatly enhance students' lives but in my opinion, the costs will outweigh the benefits.

One future effect of the internet on academic study is that the level of the lecturer/student contact that we are used to may be reduced. This might happen simply because students do not need to spend so much time on the university campus. The same may be true of lecturers. If they are able to put their lectures on the World Wide Web, they may choose to do this from their home and so they are less available for consultation and thus, interaction with their students will be affected to a great extent. In my view this would be a great disadvantage. In my home country, tutors usually stress the importance of regular, informal meetings and student's work could suffer if efforts are not made to maintain these.

Apart from the negative impact that the Internet may have on student/lecturer relationships, I think we also have to consider the disadvantages to students' health. Studying is by nature a very sedentary activity involving long hours of reading books and writing assignments. In addition, these activities are usually done alone.

Furthermore, going to campus offers students a change of scenery, a bit of exercise, and an opportunity to meet and socialize with other students. If it is no longer necessary to leave home because lectures are available on the Internet, then students may suffer physically and mentally because of this change.

To sum up, I appreciate that the Internet will add value in imparting education, I do not agree that it is the best means of transmitting educational information and I think we have to put up effective guards against developing an unhealthy dependence on it.

◆ ◆ ◆

2.   **In most countries, the number of plant and animal species is declining. What is causing this?**

     What can we do to change the situation?

It is indeed a disheartening piece of information for the entire world that we are losing variety and numbers in both animal and plant species. There are some man-made factors responsible for this situation. However, appropriate measures can certainly help in solving this problem.

According to me there are three main reasons behind the loss of variety in both plants and animals. First of them is deforestation. In an urge to develop infrastructure, governments pay a lot of attention to urbanisation, special economic zones, industrial estates and power plants. Thousands of trees and plants are cut to construct them. As a result, a variety of plants die. Consequently, animals that rely and live on such plants also die as their prime source of food and shelter is lost. Secondly, globalisation has promoted immense industrial and economic growth, which, in turn has given rise to a new phenomenon called "Global Warming", which is responsible for disturbance in weather cycles and causes species of plants and animals to go extinct. Finally, increasing population across the world is also accountable for the loss of plants and animals because most fertile land is used to grow edible and cash crops and thus the land for other plants and their dependant animals is snatched away.

However, this situation can be improved by taking some steps like creating sanctuaries for plants and animals, breeding endangered species in controlled environments, implementing strict legislation favouring the protection of such species and so on. But, on top of it, if we, the humans do not understand the importance of our companions, the situation may not improve any time soon.

Finally, I must admit that the most intelligent creation of the nature is the most dangerous enemy of species that coexist with him and unless he awakens, enlightens, it is indeed difficult to envisage a brighter future of this earth.

♦ ♦ ♦

3. **We have often thought of creating an ideal society, but most of the times we have failed in making this happen.**

   What is your opinion about an ideal society?

   How can we create an ideal society?

The term 'ideal society' seems to be very vague because everyone perceives ideal

The Ultimate Guide To IELTS Writing

things on his/her own mental, social and cultural conditioning. I firmly believe that this is the main reason why we have not been able to create an ideal society because what is ideal according to me may not be ideal according to someone else living in the same city. Consequently, deficiency of a common direction and common goals shall never let happen the creation of an ideal society.

My understanding of an ideal society is fairly simple and easily comprehensible. First, I believe that here everyone should have the right to basic necessities like food, shelter, education, health services and an easy access to most services offered by the government including a public transportation system. Secondly, an ideal society is free from criminal and immoral activities and all individuals live in harmony and peace. Lastly, the goal of every individual is to attain spiritual salvation through the path or religion he/she feels comfortable with and there should be tolerance to allow the coexistence of all.

To create such a society, we need to open more and more meditation centres rather than restaurants or hotels. I believe that easy access to spiritual resources would lead most to attain high levels of consciousness. Moreover, we can also modify our education system and base it on spirituality and self realization, which will teach children to stay out of all types of fear and anger.

Finally, the efforts of making an ideal society have been taking place since our origin and I believe we are doing better with time because in today's world, we see our life styles are getting similar. This is a pivotal step in bringing uniformity because it will bring homogeneity in the efforts of creating an ideal society.

◆ ◆ ◆

4. **Some organisations and companies require their employees to wear a uniform.**

   What kinds of jobs require uniforms?

   What are the disadvantages of wearing uniforms at work?

Creating an identity is one of the most essential requirements for many companies and institutions. Asking employees to wear a uniform is one of these techniques. However, it is not essential for all types of jobs and one has to apply the dictum judiciously.

I think almost all public sector jobs need uniforms because this helps people in identifying them and approaching them instantly. Jobs like that of the police, public transportation, hospitals, government offices and many more need uniforms. This smoothens administration also, for example, when a police cop is present in his uniform, a criminal would be afraid to commit a crime in his presence. Furthermore, in crowded places like government hospitals, patients and even staff members can easily point out concerned persons with the help of the uniform they wear. The same is true for some other jobs as well. Employees in hospitality, aviation or any other establishment where interaction with people is very high should wear a uniform to offer better services and generate reputation for the organisation in the minds of customers.

However, there are certain disadvantages of the uniform as well. One of them is, similar clothing creates monotony in the work environment, which may affect performance of workers. Next, employees can never hide their identity and that can be a risk in some situations where the customers decide to rebel.

Conclusively, making uniform compulsory is not bad provided the organisation has well justified needs of uniforms for their employees. However, I assert that compulsion should be judicious and well justified toward all who are concerned.

◆ ◆ ◆

5.   Some people think that paying regular tax is enough to contribute to the society. Others argue that being a citizen, there are more responsibilities, as well, to fulfil.

    What is your opinion?

It is true that paying regular taxes is one of the fundamental duties of a responsible citizen. However, the duties are certainly not limited to that; a responsible citizen does far more than that for his country.

Paying regular and accurate tax is the most accepted and well respected way of serving the nation by most denizens. They think their government has adequate administrative staff to carry out all the functions of public interest. In this process all a government needs is money and that is paid by the civilians in forms of taxes. I also support that it is one of the best and the most effective ways of serving the nation.

However, I think a good citizen's responsibilities are not only confined to tax payment. They should offer their services in other areas to their authorities as well. Firstly, every good citizen must abide by the laws of his country to help the administration in carrying out its duties and with this they can set a good example. Secondly, one should always take good care of the public property and use the resources judiciously in order to prevent unnecessary maintenance expenses and to help in preserving natural resources, respectively.

Next, citizens must take active part in elections and choose the right person to rule the nation. This is immensely important because the right leader can enhance the progress of the state. Finally, all civilians should also prevent others from breaking the law and inform the police if someone is found to be doing so.

In conclusion, I admit that paying tax is an important duty that every person must fulfil, however, there are other important and essential responsibilities that all civilians must follow in order to make their countries grow in all dimensions.

◆ ◆ ◆

6. **Nowadays people are forgetting national celebrations and enjoying more on their own on the days that are personally important to them.**

    What are the reasons behind this and is it a good or a bad trend?

It is a commonly observed phenomena that in each country celebrations of national importance such as independence day, birthdays of national leaders or even national festivals are losing importance in the lives of people. People prefer to celebrate their own anniversaries and weddings rather than spend time and energy on national occasions. According to me this is not a good trend.

National festivals bind a whole population together as one. Also they carry within them our shared history and traditions. For example the independence day of India is a day to remember our freedom struggle and all those who laid down their lives for our freedom. Festivals like Diwali and Holi are commemorations of events in our mythology and these stories belong to the history of our civilization and not us alone.

If the whole country celebrates an occasion there is a widespread festive spirit and a jovial atmosphere all around. We feel a part of a larger family as compared to events that we celebrate at home be it our birthdays or anniversaries. In any case with the advent of advanced communication technology our lives have become less social and loneliness, stress and frustration are very commonly seen in people. Occasions of national importance now offer us that rare opportunity to feel that we belong.

There is no doubt that each one has the right to celebrate personal and family events with as much pomp and show as they want. Family functions are important for our psychological well being and general happiness.

In conclusion, I feel that human beings cannot entirely give up the pleasure of personal celebrations. But if they do not pay attention to national events and treat them only as public holidays it would be injustice to our duties as a citizen and an emotional and psychological setback for our personality.

◆ ◆ ◆

7. **Write an essay on the effects of pollution and daily waste created by humans.**

Explain in detail how it is affecting us.

What measures should we take to make things better in this regard?

All kinds of pollution and discarded garbage constitute one of the most serious problems of today. If they are not addressed soon, they can create a hell on earth for all of us. First, let's look at the harmful effects created by the waste and pollution. The air we breathe, water we consume and land that we farm on are all negatively affected by these. When natural endowments get contaminated and contain harmful impurities in them, they can cause life threatening diseases and disabilities in humans. In addition, animals, plants and other vegetation on the planet are also victims of it. As a result, the food we eat is losing its nutritious value. Finally, countless animals and birds succumb to such polluted climate and this is a big blow to the ecosystem of the earth.

There are certain measures we must take in order to reduce the harmful effects of pollution and waste. To begin with, we ought to use as much recyclable material as possible. This helps us in controlling the waste generated on the earth and will also help the resources on the earth from getting used up. Next, more emphasis should be given to the invention of biodegradable material so that we can live a more environment friendly life. Moreover, proper management of industrial waste is the call of the hour. Maximum damage to the land and the water is done by improperly managed industrial garbage. Furthermore, more usage of energy efficient vehicles is also a need of the day. With the help of them, we can control air pollution.

Finally, we must understand that we do not own the earth. It is a legacy, a heritage that we have to maintain for our future generations. Hence, we ought to take actions that lead us to a cleaner, greener and healthier earth to live and flourish on.

♦ ♦ ♦

8.   **Some people believe that young people today know more of what is happening in the world compared to the youth of the past.**

What is the position in your country?

Give your opinion on how important it is for the young people to know aboutthe happenings in the world.

Owing to the phenomenal revolution in the field of communication in the last few decades, youngsters today can easily update themselves about the events happening in the world. Apart from conventional media like newspaper or magazines, today's youngsters use communication devices like smart phones, tablet PCs and laptops. In my opinion, it is indeed a welcome development for the youth and for the society as a whole.

The youth are more aware of current happenings in different aspects of social life, economy and politics. In India, with the mobile and internet connectivity available in small towns and villages, now youth of these areas are well informed of the latest developments in their immediate context and those at the national and international level. As an Indian I feel really happy to have witnessed this transition.

This knowledge plays a vital role in the economic, social and intellectual growth of the youth. Staying in touch with the latest developments in the fields of education, employment and all other areas of their interest motivates them to spend their time in a more diligent and creative manner. This is the reason why people from the countryside are suddenly coming into the limelight as with the help of the latest gadgets, they get far more opportunities to showcase their talent to the world as compared to times gone by.

Finally, I must say that the apt saying "knowledge is power" is being realised at its best in today's era. According to me, knowledge is the only tool which can bring equality and harmony in the world and therefore it is of prime importance for our youth to be well informed.

◆ ◆ ◆

9.   **Happiness is considered very important in life.**

      Why is it so difficult to define?

      What factors are important in achieving happiness?

Happiness is the positive response of a person in a given situation to his surroundings and/or happenings. It is a personal and a subjective feeling because it comes from being in tune with reality. It is a very important aspect of life because everyone tries to be happy all times follows different ways to achieve this goal.

For every individual, happiness means different things and hence people perceive happiness in their own way, which is based on their psychological conditioning. It is not surprising that in a given condition, at a given time, two different individuals may react in opposite ways. This shows that it is next to impossible to give a universal definition of happiness.

There are many factors in achieving happiness. According to some, material wealth is the best way to achieve happiness. They try to acquire all the material possessions to be happy. Next, some people go for health. They think that only a healthy body can ultimately lead to happiness.

Furthermore, some opt for socializing to achieve happiness. They try to be happy by getting respect and enjoying the company of others. However, all these ways have their limitations and such happiness withers quickly.

Finally, some follow the spiritual path to be happy. Spiritual path teaches us to go beyond the limitations of emotions and psychological conditioning of the mind. By doing so, we can get eternal happiness, which is not affected by any feelings and we are always happy or in other words 'enlightened'.

All in all, there are many ways to achieve happiness. However, according to me, only an objective, spiritual and beyond-the-mind insight can make a person eternally happy, which is the first step towards salvation.

◆   ◆   ◆

10. **It is a general assumption that education is vital for individual development and well being of the societies.**

What should education consist of, in order to achieve/complete these functions?

Discuss and give your opinion.

It is certainly true that education does not mean technical knowledge. It has a much wider meaning that covers individual development and betterment of societies. Education cannot be 'given' but it can be imparted. Hence, to fulfil these requirements, it should have comprehensive content and efficient methods of imparting the same need to be employed.

Education plays a vital role in conditioning the minds of students. If the content is deficient, it leaves the students' minds blank, which will be then conditioned in unimaginable ways. To avoid this, apart from technical subjects, education must include subjects that help them in understanding practical life. For example: communication skills, management skills, social and religious responsibilities, and awareness about the good and bad

---

aspects of life need to be taught. Moreover, it should help them in dealing with social and real life problems by inculcating the habit of reading books and knowing about works of social workers and leaders.

In addition to this, the way of imparting education is also important because good content cannot satisfy the objectives if not imparted properly. Hence, classroom training is not sufficient. Here, we can use technology to facilitate the learning by way of movies or documentaries; arrange lectures of spiritual orators; train the teachers to improve their skills and make the learning interactive by various innovative methods. We have to show the truth of the world to the students and by employing efficient practical training programs, we can plant the seeds of a better individual and thereby a better society.

Finally, according to me, education serves as the basic mould for any individual. It has to have all required aspects that can shape the student into a responsible individual, which, ultimately can lead to a progressive world.

◆ ◆ ◆

11. **Many Kinds of animals have a danger of dying out.**

   Do you think of it as a case?

   Give your view on how government and individuals can prevent some animals from becoming extinct.

Animals are creation of nature. If any species of animals are dying, I think it is a case and has to be given enough attention. There are many reasons of our doing that are causes of it. However, such a situation can be taken care of by being responsible in some ways so that animal species can survive on this earth.

The government can play a vital role in this case by identifying the endangered species and reasons behind their reduction. After that, they can set out to take necessary actions. Firstly, they should develop sanctuaries for example, in India; the government has developed a sanctuary in Gujarat for lions. The number of lions has increased rapidly as a result. Secondly, they can identify people responsible for the extinction and punish them severely to set an example for other unidentified culprits. Thirdly, government can also fund zoos and research centres to breed endangered species thereby increasing them in number. Finally, governments can also start public awareness programs so that a wave of sympathy and support can be generated to make the job of preservation easier.

At an individual level, we can do so many things. First, we can help government and other organizations by voluntarily participating in awareness programs and draw attention of other people towards the issue. Next, we can also inform the government about some people or activities that are harmful to animals. Moreover, we can donate generously to organizations that support in programs like research, breeding and awareness of and about endangered species.

Finally, I strongly assert that we have to consider endangered species as a case and not a minor problem because we live in an interconnected world- the loss of one affects all others, even us.

◆ ◆ ◆

12. **Most people spend a majority of their adult life in their workplace and hence, job satisfaction is an important part of an individual's well-being.**

   What factors contribute to the job satisfaction?

   How realistic is the expectation of job satisfaction on part of the workers?

It is indeed true that almost all of us spend a major proportion of our adult life at our workplace. In this case, to attain satisfaction from the work that we are doing is extremely important.

Certain aspects are considered vital in achieving job satisfaction. First of them is money. All of us work to get money and it is extremely important for all workers to get paid properly. Many a times, workers are dissatisfied with the improper payment standards of their employers. Second, everyone aspires for respect and status. Most workers expect good acceptance from the society for the job they do. It is observed that in some cases, status and respect often are even over salary. The last is individual inclination towards a specific vocation. Some people have an innate liking towards some field of work and if they are kept away from it, they often underperform.

However, it is often noticed that, at times, expectations of workers are not justifiable. Often, they simply compare perks and facilities that employees get in other organisations rather than evaluating what they are giving to their own company. Consequently, they develop pseudo-dissatisfaction which ultimately affects their work life and their performance.

In conclusion, I admit that satisfaction at work is indeed an essential aspect of most of us. Thus, it should be addressed properly by employers in terms of being fair with everyone and by employees in terms of having justified expectations. If this balance is attained, the organisation will grow at an unprecedented speed.

◆ ◆ ◆

13. Lifestyle and culture of different countries have become more similar.

Why is it so?

Is it a positive or negative development?

It is a fact that lifestyles and culture of various countries have become identical. There are many reasons behind it. Such turnout seems good on the first glimpse. However, it has negative impacts on the long-term progress.

There are many factors for such similarities. First, globalization has encouraged many people to travel and migrate to other countries. Second, Multinational companies have long started to market and manufacture their products across the globe. This has brought many similarities in the way we live and use the products. Finally, satellite television channels inspire people to adopt the lifestyle and culture of developed countries by promoting it to earn more revenue. However, such development looks good only superficially.

There are many negative implications of such adoption of lifestyle and cultures on the people of developing countries. Once they become used to living such a lifestyle, they prefer to migrate to developed countries where the standard of living is higher and those who cannot do so may lead dissatisfied lives. This can also motivate them to adopt illegal ways. Every culture and lifestyle has negative aspects as well. When we adopt them they also bring those negative traits to our life. In many developing countries people have forgotten their original religious festivals and started celebrating Christmas and other festivals of western countries. It is not wrong as such but ignorance of their historic festivals is a warning bell for their vernacular cultures and languages.

On the other hand, it has some positive effects also but they are limited to the developed countries. They can market their lifestyle and related products and sell those things aggressively. This brings profits only to those companies and nations who are selling and not to those who are spending.

To sum up, we cannot deny the fact that day by day our lifestyle and culture are integrating into each other. However, according to me, this development is negative in long run and in the future we may see a trend reversal.

◆ ◇ ◆

14. **Figures show that in some countries the proportion of population of age 15 or younger is increasing.**

    What could be the current and future effects of this development on those countries?

In many countries, it is seen that birth rate and the newborn survival rate have increased because of better medical facilities. This has shot up the proportion of people of 15 or less in the population of those countries. It has some stiff present impacts; however, the pains can be compensated for in the future.

Presently, this situation leaves many negative impacts on those countries. First, higher number of young people require more schools. Governments have to invest a lot in setting up educational institutes. Second, these people are more prone to diseases and they require better and intensive health care that includes vaccines and medicines. Finally, without contributing to the economy, these youngsters consume bigger resources available in the country. As a result of all these, governments have to allocate a sizable proportion of their income to nurture them. Consequently, they have to increase taxes to invest in the future of their juveniles.

If the youngsters are nurtured well, they can help their country grow in the future because they will be educated and equipped with higher physical, mental and technical skills that can drive the economic growth of the nation. This growth can place their nation in privileged class of developed countries.

However, there can be dangerous outcomes if youngsters are not nurtured well. They become dissatisfied with the country. As a result, either they migrate to a better country or may be even go on to indulge in crime. For example, in Afghanistan, so many young and illiterate people are becoming terrorists and are a danger for the world.

Finally, looking at the scenario, I assert that the countries that have a higher juvenile population must invest heavily in them because this investment will bear fruits of economic development in the future for them as well as for the world.

◆ ◆ ◆

15. **Some businesses observe that people who just finished college have a hard time interacting with colleagues and working as a team.**

What are your suggestions to address this problem?

Youngsters have daring dreams and ambitions when they enter the corporate world right after college. In some organizations, they face difficulty in relating to the ground reality and contribute as a team member with their co-workers. This problem can be solved with some effective steps that should be taken at both the educational and the organizational level.

At the college level, there are some actions possible to make the young graduate a competitive employee. First, subjects like marketing, communication skills and organizational behaviour should be included in the course curriculum in all disciplines. These courses enhance students' skills to interact with people, improve their perception of a company and sharpen their abilities to cooperate with teammates. Next, in every specialization, there has to be a corporate project that enables students to work in a company as an apprentice and this shall improve candidates' exposure to the practical working pattern. This phase helps a lot in dissolving the ambiguity in students' minds, between theory and practice.

At an organizational level also there are some steps possible. First, every employee must be given intensive in-house training where he must be explained about the structure, strategies, and working pattern of the company and the expectations from him. After this, the employee can work as a trainee in the company under supervision of a management team made up of equal proportion of senior and junior skilled workers of the organization. This enables the trainee to feel comfortable and to interact freely with them. Finally, everyday there should be a precise schedule given to trainees to leave no room for confusion.

All in all, I assert that with the help of proper training at both college and company level, we can certainly eradicate these difficulties and make the corporate world a better and comfortable place to work for our fresh graduates.

◆ ◆ ◆

16. **People in the past lived a long and healthy life.**

   Give some reasons why they lived longer.

   What should the society do to use the ability of elderly people in a positive way?

There are no doubts that people in the past lived a longer and more importantly a healthier life. They did so because of many factors. This essay contains a discussion of both - the reasons for their better life and suggestions to involve old people.

In the past, lifestyle was a major factor that helped people to live a peaceful, stable and tension free life. For instance, working hours in the past were limited and people followed a disciplined approach in their routine chores including sleeping and meal times. Such an approach prevented them from anxiety, blood pressure, indigestion and other numerous psychosomatic disorders. Moreover, they lived in small towns where everything was available at short distances so modes of transport were limited. Thus, there was far less pollution that also guarded them against many ophthalmic, respiratory and skin diseases and helped them in living a longer and healthier life.

Finally, their eating habits were healthier and their diet included fruits, vegetables and other traditional and seasonal preparations, compared to today's life where the diet largely comprises of junk food, colas, chocolates, ice-creams and so on. This difference is accountable for the higher intake of nutrients like vitamins and minerals by the earlier generations compared to the present humans and helped them to live healthy and free of diseases.

Now, the higher number of older people in today's society is becoming a burning issue for many countries because they are thought of as dependant population. In my opinion this is a pessimistic view. The older population can contribute to the society by taking up consulting and counselling jobs. They can also be a help at social service centres. Finally within a household they can take care of their grandchildren and impart knowledge and their experience to the youngsters.

Thus, I firmly believe that we should learn healthy eating habits from the generations of the past and make our life more fulfilling. Also, we should respect our elders and give them a creative role in the present day social setup.

◆   ◆   ◆

17. **What would you prefer? A job, which is highly rewarded with monetary gains or a job that focuses more on social service?**

     Give your opinion with reasons and examples.

It cannot be denied that man is a social animal. We are responsible for ourselves, our family and our society. Hence, it is very important for us to do a job that helps us in fulfilling all responsibilities. I think, a job with monetary gains is more helpful in attaining all the objectives.

When we earn more, we can cater to social concerns more effectively. Firstly, to do a job with higher income requires a lot of hard work for the organization and the industry. This leads to a contribution to the economic development of our country. In addition, we also pay higher taxes to the government. Such money is used by the government in the development of various facilities for our countrymen. By doing so, we are fulfilling our social responsibilities.

Secondly, we can use a proportion of our money for the well being of our society. We can donate the money to various institutions like, charitable trusts and hospitals, temples, NGOs, orphanages and so on. In addition, at times we can directly help people with the money, for example, paying fees for poor students and patients, building houses, setting up employment opportunities etc. Such activities can give us satisfaction as we fulfil our social responsibility and they can be done well by money.

On the other hand, there are so many issues where money is of no use at all. Many jobs include social concern and not high in monetary gains like; the army, police, NGOs, or even independent social workers. In such jobs we can put physical efforts to help people, society and the country. Such jobs involve a risk to life also but they too bring in respect and happiness and a real sense of achievement and fulfilment.

Finally, I prefer jobs with higher income because I want to use a big chunk of it to help people in upgrading their life and thereby contribute to the economy of my country.

◆ ◆ ◆

18. **Even though there is a lot of advancement in the field of science and technology, we greatly value artists that are musicians, painters and writers.**

What can arts give us about life that science and technology cannot?

Since his existence, man has been searching for ways of entertainment, long lasting happiness, fulfilment and salvation. To attain this, he has developed so many vocations. Materialistic pleasure and comfort through science and technology is one of the ways that gives us subjective, short-lived happiness. However, arts can help us in attaining fulfilment in our life.

There are ample things that science and technology are unable to give us about life. Firstly, art is an expression of imagination of its creator. As it comes from the heart, it is a pure form and always believed to be close to nature. Art is a valuable asset we have received from our ancestors.

What is more, art can provide us entertainment, relaxation and it reenergizes us to work hard and lead a better life. That's why we can see so many professionals who work for more than 12-14 hours a day, spend some time to pursue art because by doing so they can express their emotions in a creative way.

Moreover, when we pursue arts, our creation, contribution or appreciation gives us satisfaction and fulfilment. Even today we appreciate artists like Pablo Picasso, Leonardo Da Vinci and so on. Contrarily, will we really remember the first computer and mobile phones in the future? In addition, we all know that arts existed centuries before whereas science and technology did not.

Finally, it is a fact that arts carry the heritage of our culture and traditions and that's why they are very close to our life as compared to science and technology that can give only comforts. I think it is possible to imagine life without science and technology (even today, so many tribes are living such a life) however; it is absolutely impossible to imagine a life without arts.

◆ ◆ ◆

19. **These days, scientists can tell whether a child will become criminal or not by examining the child at an age of three.**

    Do you agree that crime is a product of human nature?

    Do you think we can stop children from becoming criminals?

It is indeed a fact that today's brain mapping and psychometric techniques are extremely effective in judging someone's nature and their possible future as well. Such techniques are also raising lot of questions in the minds of people regarding the origin of crime and the possibility of preventing child from being a criminal.

However, I largely disagree with the notion that crime is a product of human nature. There are countless examples in this world where a person commits a crime under the influence of circumstances. For example, if one's existence is jeopardised he commits a crime just to defend himself. In addition, it is also observed that there are very few people who like to commit crime. Generally, most criminals also avoid crime and try to get their work done by creating fear in others' minds. On the other hand, it is also true that a minute proportion of criminals are abnormal and sadists who like to give pain to others and so they commit a crime.

I think there are certain ways that can help us in preventing children from becoming criminals. Firstly, children should be educated and groomed properly. This goes a long way in preventing them from breaking the law when they become adults. Secondly, inculcation of morals and values is essential for transforming a criminally inclined child to a sober and responsible citizen. However, as we have discussed earlier, certain crimes are done under abnormal situations and such crimes are extremely difficult to eliminate.

Finally, I personally do not agree that crime is a product of mind. However, I do agree that proper training and conditioning of children in their childhood will certainly help us in reducing the number of criminals on this earth.

◆ ◆ ◆

20. **While visiting foreign countries, visitors should take full advantage of learning the culture and traditions of that country.**

How can they learn about the culture and traditions of the host country?

Why do some visitors strive to learn the same and others are not interested at all?

Visiting a foreign country is probably easiest now compared to anytime in the past. This has also generated interest in some people to study the culture and traditions of different countries they visit. In this essay, ways to learn the local culture and mindsets of people regarding the same are discussed.

There are several ways through which the host country's customs and culture can be learnt. Firstly, visitors can interact more and more with local people, visit cultural and historical places where the local way of living and belief systems are easily accessible. Secondly, visitors may go to local libraries where they can read books and other printed material related to the culture. Thirdly, they should also go to museums, attend cultural events like folk dance, opera, drama etc. and also see vernacular architecture.

On the other hand, there are certain reasons why some people do not show any keen-ness in learning about local culture. To begin with, learning and understanding about the way of living of people of other countries is completely subjective. Some people do not have any interest in it. Moreover, some people go abroad for business or studies or some go to participate in an event like a sports meet. Now, for such people it is next to impossible to spare time for any other aspect as it may hinder their actual purpose of visit.

Finally, several ways are there whereby we can study foreign culture while we are on a visit to a particular country. However, some cannot do so because of their own limita-tions and/or likings.

♦ ♦ ♦

21. **Violent films and TV programs are among the most popular forms of en-tertainment today.**

   Why do you think these programs are so popular?

   Propose possible reasons to explain the large number of their viewers.

It is indeed unfortunate that people these days watch programs that are full of violence. As they are gaining popularity, commercial film and TV producers are trying to introduce such content even more.

There are several reasons why such programs are gaining their viewership. Firstly, life in today's world has become stressful, hectic and competitive. In addition, we have de-veloped a wonderful virtue of comparison. All these factors force us to work harder and better all the time. In this rush, most of us have to suppress our anger and other emo-tions on regular basis. As we suppress anger so much, such mindset motivates us to watch action packed programs more and more. By doing so, most of us can vent out our suppressed anger and psychologically, it is safe for the human mind as well.

In addition, in real world, bad often wins over good but in films and TV programs, fortu-nately, good wins over bad and if that victory is violent, it is bound to grab more eyeballs. Finally, owing to strict legislation and surveillance, violence is almost eliminated from real life in most countries. Thus, watching such action on a screen of a cinema or a TV is the only option left for anyone who wants to see it.

In conclusion, it is indeed true that the numbers of people who view violence on screen are increasing worldwide. I think the reasons behind this rise are evident and hence, I personally do not think that it is a bad trend.

◆ ◆ ◆

22. It was revealed in a recent survey that happiness levels in developing countries are higher than those of developed countries.

Why is this so?

According to all the Holy Scriptures, ancient epics and religious books and testaments, it is happiness that the entire human race is after. Thus, variety of debates, surveys and speculations take place about happiness. I am not surprised by the poll that says people in the second world are happier than the people of the first world.

I think we all commit a fundamental mistake of linking happiness with money. Money can never give long lasting happiness. Hence, this can be a reason that explains the result of the survey.

People in developed countries live a lavish lifestyle where they do not indulge in much physical activities which can help them in burning calories. In addition, cut throat competition at intellectual level and vigour to outperform always give stress and related diseases like hypertension, diabetes and so on. Such style of living does not permit the people of developed countries to enjoy their economic status. I think these are the reasons why people in developed countries may live longer but they fall sick more.

On the other hand, people of a developing country often have higher satisfaction levels and lesser demands from life. Moreover, the intensity of social interaction is also very high, which motivates them to share their happiness and joy with each other.

Finally, it is rightly said that what you share with others often comes back to you in multiplied form. First world people share competitiveness and stress with others whereas

---

second world people share happiness with the people of their community. Therefore, I completely agree with the result of the survey.

◆ ◆ ◆

23.   It is observed that shopping on the internet is increasing in its popularity.

Why is it so?

Is it a good or bad development?

With the spread of the worldwide web, online shopping is gaining in popularity in leaps and bounds. In the paragraphs to come, we shall look into the reasons of this development and also discuss if it is positive or negative for the society.

The reasons of increasing popularity of online shopping are that people like to stay in the comfort of their house and order and buy things they wish for. Secondly, going to one shop gives them only a few options but the internet opens up multiple avenues to explore. Thirdly, a lot of sites now offer the 'cash-on-delivery' option so that people are not even worried about giving credit card details online.

According to me, it is a good development. First of all it brings larger choice and comparative prices for the consumer. Moreover, one can order from anywhere and is not geographically limited to access only the shops near to ones house. Furthermore, there is a chance that this reduces congestion on urban roads and the overcrowding in malls.

However, some people say that in shopping from the internet there is a greater risk of being fooled as regards the quality of the product. Also they say that with so much choice, one can become a shopping maniac. Finally, they argue that using internet for longer hours has its own drawbacks on the users.

In conclusion, the increasing popularity of shopping on the internet is a good development according to me and in tune with the nature of modern life.

◆ ◆ ◆

24. **Many people these days travel far for work or spend more hours working.**

   Does this trend have more advantages or disadvantages?

   What do you think about work-life balance?

Increasing competition in all human disciplines has led to much longer working hours for most employees. Also, job openings are rarely found close to one's place of stay. People have to either travel long distances or even stay away from their families on outstation postings. This trend has both advantages and disadvantages and it is not possible to speak in favour of one opinion.

Economic centres of cities and towns are usually few nodes of high activity in the region. There is not enough space for everyone who works there to stay as well in the same area. Therefore people travel from far to reach these nodes. The advantages of this trend are that firstly it opens up more opportunities for professional growth for everyone. Secondly, working in such an environment keeps one in touch with all recent developments in the field which would not be possible in a simpler setting. Thirdly, a healthy work-culture is built over time which is beneficial for the society and the country.

The disadvantages of this trend are that people have to spend many minutes or even hours to travel to and from work and this cuts down on the quality time that they spend with their family and children. Also, they are not able to devote time for activities like daily exercise, socialising etc. Thirdly, spending too much time at the workplace may also have psychological implications for them.

In my opinion, it is essential to have a good life-work balance for a happy and content existence. While we cannot say no to great job opportunities even if they are far from home, at the same time we should try to see that we can make time for other important aspects of life as well.

◆ ◆ ◆

Section 4

This section contains:

- **List of linking words or connectors or cohesive devices**

- **List of useful books for IELTS preparation for candidates**

- **IELTS Writing Band Descriptors**

List of linking words or connectors or cohesive devices

Sequence	Consequence or showing results	Addition	Referring or example
First or firstly	Hence	Also	For example
To initiate with	Thus	And	Particularly
First of all	Therefore	In addition	For instance
In the first place	So	To add	Namely
To begin with	As a result	Moreover	To illustrate
The first (reason/factor) is	On this/that account	What is more	A (good) case in point
Initially	It follows that	Furthermore	In particular
Next	Eventually	Likewise	Such as
Afterwards	Consequently	Similarly	To exemplify
Then	As a consequence	As well as	Just as
After this/that	Thereby	And then	That is to say
Earlier/later	In that case	Too	
Following this/that	Admittedly	Not only... but	
Finally/lastly		Besides this/that	

Showing similarity or equating	Contrast	Contrast	Showing certainty
In the same way	However	Nonetheless	Of course
Accordingly	On the other hand	Alternatively	Obvious
Likewise	Rather	In contrast	Undoubtedly
Equally important	On the contrary	Whereas	Plainly
Similarly	But	Yet	Certainly
	Otherwise	Conversely	Unquestionably
	In spite of	Nevertheless	Assuredly
	Despite	While	Without question
	Though	Whilst	Beyond question
	Although	Even if	Indisputably
	Even though		Irrefutably

Condition	Reason	Summary	Expressing time	Definition
If	Due to	To conclude	When	Means
Unless	Owing to	In conclusion	Whenever	Consists of
Whether	The reason why	To sum up	Since	Contains
So that	Cause	In summary	Before	That is
Provided that	Leads to	To summarise	After	Refers to
For	As	Finally	Ago	Is
Depending on	So	In a nutshell	Until	
	Since	In short	Meanwhile	
	In other words	To recapitulate	While	
	Due to	All in all	As soon as	
		In closing	No sooner than	
		Lastly	Just as	

♦ ♦ ♦

Writing paragraphs in an accurate manner it absolutely essential.

The correct method is that you should either leave a space when the paragraph begins (it is known as British style of writing) or you should leave a line before the new paragraph begins (it is known as American style of writing.) However some students do both, they leave   space before the new paragraph and they also leave a line when the new paragraph begins. Both, the correct and incorrect methods are shown below.

Incorrect method :-

Xxxxxxxxxxxxxxxxxxxxxxxxx

xxxxxxxxxxxxxxxxxxxxxxxxxxxxxxx

xxxxxxxxxxxxxxxxxxxxxxxxxxxxxxx

xxxxxxxxxxx.

Xxxxxxxxxxxxxxxxxxxxxxxx

xxxxxxxxxxxxxxxxxxxxxxxxxxxxxxx

xxxxxxxxxxxxxxxxxxxxxxxxxxxxxxx

xxxxxxxxxxxxxxxxxxxxxxxxxxxxxxx

xxxxxxxx.

Xxxxxxxxxxxxxxxxxxxxxxxx

xxxxxxxxxxxxxxxxxxxxxxxxxxxxxxx

xxxxxxxxxxxxxxxxxxxxxxxxxxxxxxx

xxxxxxx.

Correct methods of using paragraphs in writing. :-

Method 1 (American)		Method 2 (British)
Xxxxxxxxxxxxxxxxxxxxxxxxxxxxxxxxxx		Xxxxxxxxxxxxxxxxxxxxxxxxxxxxx
xxxxxxxxxxxxxxxxxxxxxxxxxxxxxxxxxx		xxxxxxxxxxxxxxxxxxxxxxxxxxxxxxxxx
xxxxxxxxxxxxxxxxxxxxxxxxxxxxx.		xxxxxxxxxxxxxx.
		Xxxxxxxxxxxxxxxxxxxxxxxxxxxxx
Xxxxxxxxxxxxxxxxxxxxxxxxxxxxxxxxxx		xxxxxxxxxxxxxxxxxxxxxxxxxxxxxxxxx
xxxxxxxxxxxxxxxxxxxxxxxxxxxxxxxxxx		xxxxxxx.
xxxxxxxxxxxxxxxxxxxxx.		Xxxxxxxxxxxxxxxxxxxxxxxxxxxxx
		xxxxxxxxxxxxxxxxxxxxxxxxxxxxxxxxx
Xxxxxxxxxxxxxxxxxxxxxxxxxxxxxxxxxx		xxxxxxxxxxxxxxxxxxxxxxxxxxxxxxxxx
xxxxxxxxxxxxxxxxxxxxxxxxxxxxxxxxxx		xxxxxxxxxxxxxx.
xxxxxxxxxxxx.		Xxxxxxxxxxxxxxxxxxxxxxxxxxxxx
		xxxxxxxxxxxxxxxxxxxxxxxxxxxxxxxxx
		xxxxxxxxxxxxxxx.

♦ ♦ ♦

List of useful books for IELTS Preparation :-

For IELTS Speaking Test Practice :
The Ultimate Guide to IELTS Speaking (with free video DVD) By Parthesh Thakkar
For complete practice tests:
Cambridge IELTS 1-9
101 Helpful Hints for IELTS (Academic and General Training)
404 Helpful Hints for IELTS (Academic and General Training)
IELTS On Track (Academic and General Training)
IELTS Practice Tests Plus 1,2 and 3
A book for IELTS
IELTS Testbuilder 1 and 2
IELTS Master Class BY MACMILLAN
For Grammar :
Essential English grammar for beginner level students By Cambridge University Press
Intermediate English grammar for intermediate and upper intermediate level students By Cambridge University Press
Practical English Grammar By Oxford University Press
For beginner level students :
Barron's IELTS
On course for IELTS by Oxford University Press
For development of skills for all modules of IELTS :
Preparation and practice series:
> Reading and Writing Academic and General Training Modules By Oxford University Press
> Practice Tests Book By Oxford University Press

Study English By Insearch Language Centre
For Development of Various Skills :
Reading :
Speed Reading Book By Tony Buzan
Cambridge series for fluency in reading 1-4 By Cambridge University Press
Study Reading By Cambridge University Press
Effective Reading By Cambridge University Press
Listening :
Cambridge skills for fluency in listening 1-4 By Cambridge University Press
Study Listening By Cambridge University Press
Vocabulary :
English Vocabulary in Use By Cambridge University Press:
> Pre-intermediate to intermediate
> Upper Intermediate
> Advanced

Elementary Vocabulary and Intermediate Vocabulary By Longman

IELTS Task 2 Writing band descriptors (public version)

Band	Task Response	Coherence and Cohesion	Lexical Resource	Grammatical Range and Accuracy
9	• fully addresses all parts of the task • presents a fully developed position in answer to the question with relevant, fully extended and well supported ideas	• uses cohesion in such a way that it attracts no attention • skilfully manages paragraphing	• uses a wide range of vocabulary with very natural and sophisticated control of lexical features; rare minor errors occur only as 'slips'	• uses a wide range of structures with full flexibility and accuracy; rare minor errors occur only as 'slips'
8	• sufficiently addresses all parts of the task • presents a well-developed response to the question with relevant, extended and supported ideas	• sequences information and ideas logically • manages all aspects of cohesion well • uses paragraphing sufficiently and appropriately	• uses a wide range of vocabulary fluently and flexibly to convey precise meanings • skilfully uses uncommon lexical items but there may be occasional inaccuracies in word choice and collocation • produces rare errors in spelling and/or word formation	• uses a wide range of structures • the majority of sentences are error-free • makes only very occasional errors or inappropriacies
7	• addresses all parts of the task • presents a clear position throughout the response • presents, extends and supports main ideas, but there may be a tendency to over-generalise and/or supporting ideas may lack focus	• logically organises information and ideas; there is clear progression throughout • uses a range of cohesive devices appropriately although there may be some under-/over-use • presents a clear central topic within each paragraph	• uses a sufficient range of vocabulary to allow some flexibility and precision • uses less common lexical items with some awareness of style and collocation • may produce occasional errors in word choice, spelling and/or word formation	• uses a variety of complex structures • produces frequent error-free sentences • has good control of grammar and punctuation but may make a few errors
6	• addresses all parts of the task although some parts may be more fully covered than others • presents a relevant position although the conclusions may become unclear or repetitive • presents relevant main ideas but some may be inadequately developed/unclear	• arranges information and ideas coherently and there is a clear overall progression • uses cohesive devices effectively, but cohesion within and/or between sentences may be faulty or mechanical • may not always use referencing clearly or appropriately • uses paragraphing, but not always logically	• uses an adequate range of vocabulary for the task • attempts to use less common vocabulary but with some inaccuracy • makes some errors in spelling and/or word formation, but they do not impede communication	• uses a mix of simple and complex sentence forms • makes some errors in grammar and punctuation but they rarely reduce communication
5	• addresses the task only partially; the format may be inappropriate in places • expresses a position but the development is not always clear and there may be no conclusions drawn • presents some main ideas but these are limited and not sufficiently developed; there may be irrelevant detail	• presents information with some organisation but there may be a lack of overall progression • makes inadequate, inaccurate or over-use of cohesive devices • may be repetitive because of lack of referencing and substitution • may not write in paragraphs, or paragraphing may be inadequate	• uses a limited range of vocabulary, but this is minimally adequate for the task • may make noticeable errors in spelling and/or word formation that may cause some difficulty for the reader	• uses only a limited range of structures • attempts complex sentences but these tend to be less accurate than simple sentences • may make frequent grammatical errors and punctuation may be faulty; errors can cause some difficulty for the reader
4	• responds to the task only in a minimal way or the answer is tangential; the format may be inappropriate • presents a position but this is unclear • presents some main ideas but these are difficult to identify and may be repetitive, irrelevant or not well supported	• presents information and ideas but these are not arranged coherently and there is no clear progression in the response • uses some basic cohesive devices but these may be inaccurate or repetitive • may not write in paragraphs or their use may be confusing	• uses only basic vocabulary which may be used repetitively or which may be inappropriate for the task • has limited control of word formation and/or spelling; errors may cause strain for the reader	• uses only a very limited range of structures with only rare use of subordinate clauses • some structures are accurate but errors predominate, and punctuation is often faulty
3	• does not adequately address any part of the task • does not express a clear position • presents few ideas, which are largely undeveloped or irrelevant	• does not organise ideas logically • may use a very limited range of cohesive devices, and those used may not indicate a logical relationship between ideas	• uses only a very limited range of words and expressions with very limited control of word formation and/or spelling • errors may severely distort the message	• attempts sentence forms but errors in grammar and punctuation predominate and distort the meaning
2	• barely responds to the task • does not express a position • may attempt to present one or two ideas but there is no development	• has very little control of organisational features	• uses an extremely limited range of vocabulary; essentially no control of word formation and/or spelling	• cannot use sentence forms except in memorised phrases
1	• answer is completely unrelated to the task	• fails to communicate any message	• can only use a few isolated words	• cannot use sentence forms at all
0	• does not attend • does not attempt the task in any way • writes a totally memorised response			

The Ultimate Guide To IELTS Writing

IELTS Task 1 Writing band descriptors (public version)

Band	Task Achievement	Coherence and Cohesion	Lexical Resource	Grammatical Range and Accuracy
9	• fully satisfies all the requirements of the task • clearly presents a fully developed response	• uses cohesion in such a way that it attracts no attention • skilfully manages paragraphing	• uses a wide range of vocabulary with very natural and sophisticated control of lexical features; rare minor errors occur only as 'slips'	• uses a wide range of structures with full flexibility and accuracy; rare minor errors occur only as 'slips'
8	• covers all requirements of the task sufficiently • presents, highlights and illustrates key features / bullet points clearly and appropriately	• sequences information and ideas logically • manages all aspects of cohesion well • uses paragraphing sufficiently and appropriately	• uses a wide range of vocabulary fluently and flexibly to convey precise meanings • skilfully uses uncommon lexical items but there may be occasional inaccuracies in word choice and collocation • produces rare errors in spelling and/or word formation	• uses a wide range of structures • the majority of sentences are error-free • makes only very occasional errors or inappropriacies
7	• covers the requirements of the task • (Academic) presents a clear overview of main trends, differences or stages • (General Training) presents a clear purpose, with the tone consistent and appropriate • clearly presents and highlights key features / bullet points but could be more fully extended	• logically organises information and ideas; there is clear progression throughout • uses a range of cohesive devices appropriately although there may be some under-/over-use	• uses a sufficient range of vocabulary to allow some flexibility and precision • uses less common lexical items with some awareness of style and collocation • may produce occasional errors in word choice, spelling and/or word formation	• uses a variety of complex structures • produces frequent error-free sentences • has good control of grammar and punctuation but may make a few errors
6	• addresses the requirements of the task • (Academic) presents an overview with information appropriately selected • (General Training) presents a purpose that is generally clear; there may be inconsistencies in tone • presents and adequately highlights key features / bullet points but details may be irrelevant, inappropriate or inaccurate	• arranges information and ideas coherently and there is a clear overall progression • uses cohesive devices effectively, but cohesion within and/or between sentences may be faulty or mechanical • may not always use referencing clearly or appropriately	• uses an adequate range of vocabulary for the task • attempts to use less common vocabulary but with some inaccuracy • makes some errors in spelling and/or word formation, but they do not impede communication	• uses a mix of simple and complex sentence forms • makes some errors in grammar and punctuation but they rarely reduce communication
5	• generally addresses the task; the format may be inappropriate in places • (Academic) recounts detail mechanically with no clear overview; there may be no data to support the description • (General Training) may present a purpose for the letter that is unclear at times; the tone may be variable and sometimes inappropriate • presents, but inadequately covers, key features / bullet points; there may be a tendency to focus on details	• presents information with some organisation but there may be a lack of overall progression • makes inadequate, inaccurate or over-use of cohesive devices • may be repetitive because of lack of referencing and substitution	• uses a limited range of vocabulary, but this is minimally adequate for the task • may make noticeable errors in spelling and/or word formation that may cause some difficulty for the reader	• uses only a limited range of structures • attempts complex sentences but these tend to be less accurate than simple sentences • may make frequent grammatical errors and punctuation may be faulty; errors can cause some difficulty for the reader
4	• attempts to address the task but does not cover all key features / bullet points; the format may be inappropriate • (General Training) fails to clearly explain the purpose of the letter; the tone may be inappropriate • may confuse key features / bullet points with detail; parts may be unclear, irrelevant, repetitive or inaccurate	• presents information and ideas but these are not arranged coherently and there is no clear progression in the response • uses some basic cohesive devices but these may be inaccurate or repetitive	• uses only basic vocabulary which may be used repetitively or which may be inappropriate for the task • has limited control of word formation and/or spelling; • errors may cause strain for the reader	• uses only a very limited range of structures with only rare use of subordinate clauses • some structures are accurate but errors predominate, and punctuation is often faulty
3	• fails to address the task, which may have been completely misunderstood • presents limited ideas which may be largely irrelevant/repetitive	• does not organise ideas logically • may use a very limited range of cohesive devices, and those used may not indicate a logical relationship between ideas	• uses only a very limited range of words and expressions with very limited control of word formation and/or spelling • errors may severely distort the message	• attempts sentence forms but errors in grammar and punctuation predominate and distort the meaning
2	• answer is barely related to the task.	• has very little control of organisational features	• uses an extremely limited range of vocabulary; essentially no control of word formation and/or spelling	• cannot use sentence forms except in memorised phrases
1	• answer is completely unrelated to the task	• fails to communicate any message	• can only use a few isolated words	• cannot use sentence forms at all
0	• does not attend • does not attempt the task in any way • writes a totally memorised response

366

FEEDBACK PAGE

I will be privileged to have your valuable feedback about this book.

How has this book helped you?

What do you like about this book?

Do you have any suggestions for this book?

Sender's name   :

Address   :

Contact no.   :

Email id   :

Please fill this form and mail it to the following address

Mr. Parthesh Thakkar
B/1, First Floor, Arjun Tower,
Shivranjani Cross Roads, Satellite,
Ahmedabad, Gujarat, India
Pin 380015
Phone No. +91-79-26754675, +91-79-30177464

Or you can email your feedback on **parthesh_thakkar@yahoo.com**

IELTS BOOKSELLERS

AHMEDABAD		**KOTTAYAM**	
Atul Book Stall	25356178	D. C. Books	2560599
Book Plaza	26440763	Learner's Books	2567438
Crossword	26424907	H & C Stores	2304351
New Zaveri Book	25357232	Pai & Company	2562391
Reading Tree	64501308	VPublishers Book Stall	2567470
Sagar Books	25354250	Book Centre	2566992
AMRITSAR		**KOLKATA**	
Sunder Book Depot	2544491	Prism Books	24297957/59
ANAND		**LUCKNOW**	
Ajay Book Stall	238237	Books & Books	2281417
Rupal Book Stall	237171	Universal Book Sellers	2225894
BENGALURU		**LUDHIANA**	
Prism Books	26714108/3979	Amit Book Depot	5022930
Gangaram Book House	25581618	**MUMBAI**	
Sapna Book House	22266088	Student's Agencies	40496161
Crossword	25582411	Union Book Stall	24223069
Higginbothams	25325422	Sterling Book House	22612521
Educational Suppliers	26761289	Universal Book Corp.	22078096
Book Paradise	26637466	**NADIAD**	
BARODA		Student Book Stall	2520447
Book World	2361012	**NAVSARI**	
Bindoo Agency	2438602	College Store	258642
Crossword	2333338	**NEWDELHI**	
Bansal Books Stall	2326109	GBD Books	23260022
BHOPAL		Jain Book Agency	23416390/91
Lyall Book Depot	2543624	Om Book Shop	24653792
CALICUT		General Book Depot	23263695
Prism Books	9447884564	Jain Book Depot	23416101
Edumart	2372817	**PALAKKAD**	
TBS Publishers Dist.	2720085	H & C Stores	2526317
H & C Stores	2720620	**PATIALA**	
CHANDIGARH		Goel Sons	2213643
Shivalik Book Centre	2704768	Pepsu Book Depot	2302851
Universal Book Store	2702558	Readers Paradise	2215170
Capital Book Store	2702594/2260	**PUNE**	
Variety Book Store	2702241	Manneys Book sellers	26131683
Book Club Enterprise	9815315447	Goel Book Agencies	24452176
CHENNAI		The Word Book Shop	26133118
Prism Books	42867509	Vikas Books	24468737
Higginbothams	28513519	**RAJKOT**	
COIMBATORE		Old & New Book Shop	2466195
TBHPublishers & Dist.	2520491/6	**SURAT**	
Cheran Book House	2396623	Popular Book Centre	23474165
ERNAKULAM(KOCHI)		Lucky Book Store	22476530
Prism Book Pv1. Ltd.	4000945/2206011	Book Point	2744231
Higginbhothams	2368834	**THRISSUR**	
Pai & Company	2361020/025	Cosmo Books	2335292
Educational Publishers	2372817	Green Books	2361038/14600
D. C. Books	2391295	H & C Stores	2421462
Orient Book House	2370431	D. C. Books	2444322
H & C Stores	2375649/5563	**THIRUVANTHAPURAM**	
Surya Books	2365149	Prism Books	2365063
Current Books	2351590	Higginbothams	2331622
HISSAR		Modern Book Centre	2331826
Krishna Book Depot	235678	D. C. Books	2453379
HYDERABAD		Prabhus Books	2478397
Universal Book Showroom	24757206	Academic Book House	2331878
Prism Books	23261828	TBS Publishers Dist	2720085/6
The Book Syndicate	23445622	Pai & Co.,	2453179
INDORE		Continental Books	2461426
Readers Paradise	4075789	**VALSAD**	
SriIndore Book Depot	2432479	Bulsar Book Depot	222377
JALANDHAR		**COLOMBO (SRILANKA)**	
Kiran Book Shop	2214170	C G Associates	4921546/4816726
Subhas Book Depot	2225081	Sarasavi Book Shop	2821454
Paramvir Enterprises	2236248	Vijitha Yapa Book Shop	2816510
Cheap Book Store	2213183	Jeya Book Centre	2438227
Literature House	2281055	Expographic Books	2787140/41
City Book Shop	2211800	**MALAYSIA**	
KOLAM		Crescent Books (K.L.)	61842448
H & C Stores	2765421	Everbest Media Sdn. Bhd (K.L)	61842003
KOZHIKODE		**NEPAL(Kathmandu)**	
Cosmo Books	2703487	Ekta Books Distributors	4245787
H & C Stores	2720620/1791	National Book Centre	4221269
		SAUDIARABIA	
		Jarir Book Store (Riyadh)	4626000